Please remember that this is a library book,
and that it belongs only temporarily to each
person who uses it. Be considerate. Do
not write in this, or any, library book.

AFTER COLUMBUS

AFTER COLUMBUS

*Essays in the Ethnohistory
of Colonial North America*

JAMES AXTELL

OXFORD UNIVERSITY PRESS
New York   Oxford

Oxford University Press

Oxford   New York   Toronto
Delhi   Bombay   Calcutta   Madras   Karachi
Petaling Jaya   Singapore   Hong Kong   Tokyo
Nairobi   Dar es Salaam   Cape Town
Melbourne   Auckland

and associated companies in
Berlin   Ibadan

First published in 1988 by Oxford University Press, Inc.,
200 Madison Avenue, New York, New York 10016

First issued as an Oxford University Press paperback, 1989

Oxford is a registered trademark of Oxford University Press

Library of Congress Cataloging-in-Publication Data
Axtell, James.
After Columbus: essays in the ethnohistory of
colonial North America / James Axtell.
p.   cm.   Bibliography: p.   Includes index.
ISBN 0-19-505375-3
ISBN 0-19-505376-1 (pbk)
1. Indians of North America—Government relations—To 1789.
2. Indians of North America—History—Colonial period, ca.
1600-1775.   I. Title.
E.93.A954   1988
973'.0497—dc 19   87-34886 CIP

4 6 8 10 9 7 5 3
Printed in the United States of America

For Susan, Than, and Jamie
My ineffable three

Preface

I DID NOT PLAN TO WRITE THIS BOOK; IT JUST GROWED, LIKE Topsy. I was happily launched on the writing of *American Encounter,* the second volume in a proposed trilogy on "The Cultural Origins of North America," when it occurred to me to jot down the papers and articles I had written since the appearance in 1981 of *The European and the Indian,* my first collection of essays.[1] I was surprised to discover at least a dozen items, which sorted themselves into three coherent themes. With a certain amount of rewriting and expansion, they might, I felt, constitute a second casebook in the promise and procedures of ethnohistory. Fortunately, my editor, Sheldon Meyer, and Oxford University Press agreed.

Ethnohistory has come a long way since its effective birth in the 1940s. Many traditional historians now use the term interchangeably with "Indian history," which may be somewhat chauvinistic but in context is perfectly understandable. Yet many of those who bandy the term about do not have a clear understanding of what ethnohistory really is, in theory or in practice. They know only that it has something to do with Indians, whom they know to be in historical fashion, if not exactly why.

In *The European and the Indian* I defined ethnohistory as "the use of historical and ethnological methods and materials to gain knowledge of the nature and causes of change in a culture defined by ethnological concepts and categories." In America, until fairly recently, ethnohistory was virtually synonymous with the study of Indian societies largely through the documentary records produced by Euro-Americans. The ethnohistorical method and perspective are most useful in studies of frontiers, the zones of contact between at least two societies and cultures. Ideally, both sides of the frontier or contact situation receive equal attention. But, in theory, there is no reason why the ethnohistorical spotlight may not fall on the non-native side, using native cultural standards and perspectives to illuminate their opposites.

This collection, then, is a reader in ethnohistory, written by an historian rather than an anthropologist. It not only seeks to look at both sides of various frontiers, but it tries to maintain "A North American Perspective" on the interactions of the colonial Spanish, French, and English with the Indians over the eastern half of the continent.[2] Most of these essays grew out of the research for the trilogy, the first volume of which was published in 1985.[3] Since those volumes concentrate largely on the French, English, and Indians, these essays also tend to focus on the greater Northeast, triangulated between South Carolina, the Great Lakes, and the Canadian Maritime provinces. Two chapters, however, range farther afield, which is more consistent with my classroom behavior and prescriptive philosophy and with the historical legacy left by the "Admiral of the Ocean Sea."

Williamsburg   J.A.
July 1987

Acknowledgments

At bottom, scholarship is a lonely enterprise. Most research and virtually all writing is done in solitude, in the confines of one's own imagination and study. But it is made possible and brought to fruition by institutional and individual support well beyond the thanks of mere mention. While their generosity can never be fully repaid, except in spirit to those who follow, I am nonetheless grateful to the American Council of Learned Societies, the National Endowment for the Humanities, the John Simon Guggenheim Memorial Foundation, the College of William and Mary, and the William R. Kenan, Jr., Charitable Trust for free time, wherewithal, and timely encouragement to pursue the research for and writing of this book. I am particularly grateful to Mel Schiavelli and William and Mary for giving me a comfortable and honorable chair in which to work, and to Ed Crapol and John Selby for making the History Department a congenial home for scholarship as well as teaching.

Many of the essays herein were given baptisms-by-fire at monthly colloquia of the Institute of Early American History and Culture; my thanks to director Thad Tate and the participants for edifying changes and exchanges. The staff of the Earl G. Swem Library invariably answered reference questions and filled interlibrary loan orders with cheerful aplomb. Shirley Folkes's quiet competence has always mattered more than her flawless typing.

As has been true for more years than either would probably care to admit, Jim Ronda and Bill Eccles have done me the great service of reading everything I wrote and the great pleasure of being frank and faithful friends. Their reviews matter most.

Along with that of my ideal reader and wife, Susan. In the midst of "Backwards Day" and other preschool charivaris, she has never allowed me to forget that history that cannot be read with pleasure should not be written at all. With boundless love and grace, she has given me two reminders that while the past is father to the present, so is the historian. I hope that in dedicating this small piece of the past to them (and her), I can flatter them into reading it.

J.A.

Contents

AFTER COLUMBUS

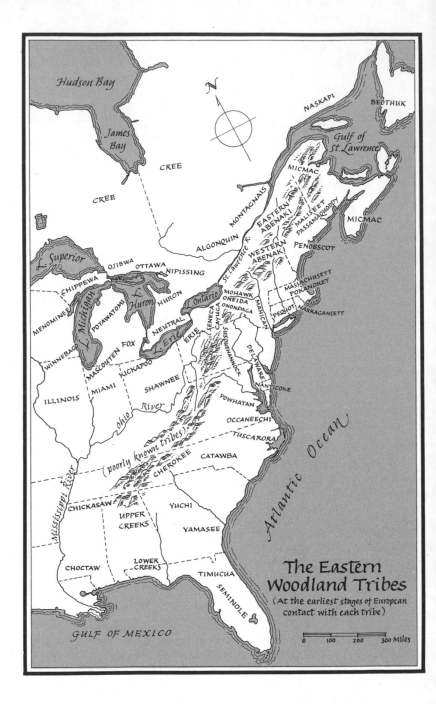

Hudson Bay

James Bay

CREE

CREE

NASKAPI

BEOTHUK

Gulf of St. Lawrence

MONTAGNAIS

MICMAC

ALGONQUIN

EASTERN ABENAKI

MALISEET
PASSAMAQUODDY

MICMAC

WESTERN ABENAKI

PENOBSCOT

L. Superior

OJIBWA   OTTAWA   NIPISSING

CHIPPEWA

MENOMINEE

L. Michigan   POTAWATOMI

L. Huron   HURON

MOHAWK
ONEIDA
ONONDAGA

MASSACHUSETT
POKANOKET

MAHICAN

PEQUOT NARRAGANSETT

NEUTRAL

L. Erie   ERIE

SENECA
CAYUGA

WINNEBAGO   FOX

MASCOUTEN   KICKAPOO

MIAMI   SHAWNEE

SUSQUEHANNOCK

DELAWARE

ILLINOIS

Ohio   River

POWHATAN

NANTICOKE

OCCANEECHI

TUSCARORA

(poorly known tribes)

CHEROKEE   CATAWBA

Mississippi River

CHICKASAW   UPPER CREEKS   YUCHI

YAMASEE

CHOCTAW   LOWER CREEKS

TIMUCUA

SEMINOLE

Atlantic Ocean

GULF OF MEXICO

The Eastern Woodland Tribes

(At the earliest stages of European contact with each tribe)

0   100   200   300 Miles

The Columbian Legacy

THE EUROPEAN DISCOVERY OF AMERICA WAS A FORTUITOUS mistake, but a mistake nonetheless. Columbus was looking for something else and certainly did not expect to encounter a continental obstacle. Like any sensible Mediterranean trader, he sought the certified wealth of the Orient, with which to launch an old-fashioned crusade to liberate Jerusalem from the scimitared hand of Islam. And he went to his grave believing that the lands he had found, while new to the mapmakers, *were* part of the Far East.

With the venial hubris of hindsight, we do not hesitate to second-guess the Admiral's interpretation of his own accomplishments. We believe firmly that Columbus discovered *America,* not Japan or China or islands off the coast of India. And so we celebrate his "discovery." But we also know that his precedence is only relative and maybe specious. Nomadic hunters from Asia, the ancient ancestors of Columbus's generic "Indians," of course, were the first Old World people to lay eyes and feet on the New. Even of the Europeans who followed them tens of thousands of years later he was not the first. How easily we dismiss the Norsemen who temporarily settled the northern tip of Newfoundland around 1000 A.D., perhaps because they made their landfall so early, as if by some embarrassing fluke, but probably because they failed to stay beyond a year or two. Historians like winners, or at least the durable. By the same token, we give little credence to the Bristol fishermen who may have re-discovered the teeming waters of Newfoundland at least a decade before 1492. Their occupational reticence to leave documentary tracks does little to endear them to academic landlubbers.

To Columbus's contemporaries the discovery of America was a nautical venture of much less moment that it is to us. Much of the population of early modern England, France, Spain, Portugal, and Italy lived on or within a few miles of the sea. To them oceans were highways, familiar conduits of trade, people, and news. In the sixteenth century and well beyond, land was the obstacle, where transportation—the ligaments of empire—was expensive, inefficient, and slow. If not a Genoese sailing for Spain, sooner or later another captain in another crown's employ would have made an appropriate landfall and generated the right publicity. Whether the western discovery was seen as part of the known world or recognized as a geographical novelty made little difference, for "most of the exploration for the next fifty years was done in the hope of getting through or around it."[1]

Our excitement, by contrast, betrays our altered geographical consciousness. Most historians and certainly most of their readers today are landlocked. Our imaginations are high and dry, our point of reckoning always *terra firma*. To us oceans are moats, watery impediments to solid destinations. From such a perspective it is easy to exaggerate the novelty and precedence of Columbus's accomplishment. A fifteenth-century seaman who earned his living on the Mediterranean or the rough Atlantic would have been much less impressed.

It is not the westward journey of the *Santa Maria* itself that is historically significant, but the vast and often turbulent confluence of cultures that followed in her wake. Columbus did not so much discover a new world as bring together two worlds that were already old. As a Hispanicized Inca historian would soon write for a Spanish audience, "there is only one world, and although we speak of the Old World and the New, this is because the latter was lately discovered by us, and not because there are two."[2]

Drawing on the religious and martial energies of the *Reconquista,* with which the Spanish reclaimed their peninsula from the Moors, Columbus forged unbreakable links between four continents and three races. When he met *los Indios*—and they him—on the beaches of the West Indies, the anthropologies of Europe and America each suddenly grew by one whole race and myriad cultural variations. And when Spanish exploitation of the Indies and newly introduced European diseases decimated the native populations, African slaves were imported to take their places in mines and cities, on ranches and plantations. Thus "a new human network of points and passages" was laid between Europe, Africa, South America, and soon North America.[3] The American population quickly became a broad palette of human colors, and American society a crucible of institutions and forms, ideas and mores.

Spain's success in extracting the mineral wealth of the New World from the Indians and the earth fed the envy of her European rivals. As Spanish settlements sprang up around the Caribbean and in Florida to guarantee the safety of the royal fleets carrying Mexican and Peruvian gold and silver, French and English corsairs flew to the region to commandeer their mobile treasure. French Huguenots even tried to establish a military presence in the heart of Spanish Florida; learning from the ruthless crushing of that attempt, the English sought a haven for privateers on the farther coast of "Virginia."

Neither colony succeeded in relieving the Spaniards of a single doubloon, but they did turn Europe's attention toward the social and economic possibilities of the temperate regions of North America. The piscatorial wealth of the Grand Banks and the Gulf of St. Lawrence had already drawn hundreds of European mariners and numerous investors to its northern parts. In the seventeenth century, France and England (and less successfully Sweden and the Netherlands) planted permanent colonies on the continent north of New Spain. This opened another complex and fascinating chapter in the confrontation of cultures sparked by Columbus's fateful voyage.

The Normative Stance

CHAPTER ONE

A Moral History of Indian-White Relations Revisited

STUDIES IN INTER-ETHNIC CONFLICT ARE RIFE WITH MORAL JUDG-ments, some intended by their authors, others unnoticed. Scholarly disinterestedness seems to be especially difficult to achieve when the conflicts studied are between the (native, Native, first) Americans and (imperial, invading, intrusive) Europeans, as a sample choice of adjectives graphically shows. Recognizing in myself strong if shifting feelings about Indian-white relations over a dozen years of teaching and writing about them, I wanted to explore the philosophical status of normative judgments in historical thought to see if it was legitimate to have such feelings and to register them in writing.

The answer I came to was that moral judgments are not only inevitable, given the nature of language, but also, given the goals of humane education, desirable, if rendered subtly and sensitively as conclusions *after* mastering the historical record. My thinking about this issue was sharpened by friendly but frank disagreements with Bernard Sheehan, who kindly agreed to debate it at the 1982 meeting of the Organization of American Historians in Philadelphia. There he was joined by another friend, Bruce Trigger, a Canadian anthropologist whose roots in a democratic socialist-cultural materialist tradition gave him another slant on the question. Between these two formidable critics, the following essay was honed before being published in *The History Teacher*

in February 1983. To keep the debate alive, Professor Sheehan
has written "The Problem of Moral Judgments in History,"
which appeared in the *South Atlantic Quarterly* (Winter 1985).

IN SPITE OF THE MEDIA ATTENTION ACCORDED THE SECOND
battle of Wounded Knee, the guilt-ridden popularity of Vine
Deloria's books, and the film cult of *Billy Jack,* the history of
Indian-white relations has "arrived" in Academe. Like the
blacks and women who slightly preceded them, the American
Indians can no longer be ignored in our lectures, textbooks,
journals, or—need we say—scholarly meetings. They have arrived, not because the popular culture adopted them in the
late 1960s and '70s (as it had in other generations for other
reasons) nor because their well-publicized militancy forced
intellectual as well as political concessions, but because rank-
and-file historians in increasing numbers realize that the full
and faithful story of America cannot be told without them.
But the new arrivals are not the stereotypical "savages" of the
past, noble or ignoble. Rather than faceless features of geography or players of bit parts in a blanched scenario of nation-
building, the Indians are seen today as active determinants of
American history, at center stage, not in the wings, of our social experience and cultural identity.

The major reason for this salutary change in native casting
is the scholarly direction of ethnohistory, which since the late
1940s has forced the American judiciary and, more recently,
American historians to confront the reality of native societies
on their own cultural terms. In forcing us to recognize the
distinctive human faces on both sides of our historical frontiers, however, ethnohistorians have posed a classic problem
for historians of Indian-white relations: namely, if each society must be judged by its own standards, how do we assess
those numerous historical situations in which Indian and

white values collided? The evolution of the answers to this question that have been offered by ethnohistorians in the past twenty-five years is, I suggest, an accurate measure of the conceptual maturity of the historiography of Indian-white relations and therefore of its general value to the study of American history.

The historian who has urged us most consistently and forcefully to measure the moral dimensions of America's intercultural relations is Wilcomb Washburn. His efforts began in 1957 when he published in *Ethnohistory* a challenging article with the unprovocative title of "A Moral History of Indian-White Relations: Needs and Opportunities for Study."[1] Noting that previous histories of Indian-white relations were marred by the "one-sided moral assumptions" of their white authors, Washburn called for studies of "those aspects of culture contact in which values clash, and, in the collection and interpretation of data about which, writers tend to be dependent upon their own particular value systems," aspects such as warfare, captivities, and cannibalism. His reason was simply that a "great [literary] history" of Indian-white relations could not be written without a sympathetic understanding of the irreconcilable values at the heart of that "tragedy." In seeking an American Lecky, however, Washburn made it clear that his focus was primarily on a history of morals and values, not a moral history replete with the historian's own value judgments.

But within six months Washburn wrote another essay which inaugurated a durable interest in moral history as well as the history of morals. This essay, entitled "The Moral and Legal Justification for Dispossessing the Indians," examined "the justice or injustice of the [European] quest" to explore and colonize America.[2] As he had advocated in his previous article, he contrasted the European justifications with the realities of Indian life and showed the former to be hollow. He even wondered whether the federal Indian Claims Commission might be amenable to entertaining "broader and more fundamental moral claims," such as "the constitutional right of original Indian sovereignty in the New World." But because the problem of "the legality and morality of the expansion of one people into the territory of another" has no easy solutions, he concluded, "it [must] not be lost in the mists of history."[3] The long list of Washburn's subsequent publications guaranteed that it would not.

One of the issues that has preoccupied Washburn, perhaps because it neatly unites his interests in the history of morals and moral history, is whether "noble savages" existed in fact or only in legend. He first broached the subject in 1957 and returned to it four times by 1976.[4] In these writings, he reminded us that we must "rigorously separate the *description* of an action from the *interpretation* of that action" in historical sources. If we do so, he argued, with numerous examples, we will discover that "the early reporting from the New World" contained "a substantial amount of accurate description that [we] must be ready to respect, even while identifying and discarding the accretions and distortions of myth, ignorance, special interest, and the like." "The literature produced by those who knew the Indian best . . . provided legitimate evidence of a 'noble savage'," by which Washburn meant "a general though not uncritical admiration for Indian character and government in comparison with that of the white man."[5] As Cornelius Jaenen and James Ronda did subsequently, Washburn had re-discovered that one way to make a moral assessment of the European colonists was to have the Indians themselves make it, in word or in contrastive deed.[6]

As might be predicted, not everyone was happy with Washburn's formulation of the central issues in the history of Indian-white relations or with his normative approach. In 1969 Bernard Sheehan entered the lists with a pugnacious article in the *William and Mary Quarterly* entitled "Indian-

White Relations in Early America: A Review Essay."[7] Annoyed that historians, particularly Washburn, assumed that "the white man is guilty" for the demise of Indian culture, Sheehan reframed the proposition, with the help of the recent work of Paul Prucha and Alden Vaughan, to "diffuse the locus of guilt" by effectively blaming the Indians for their own demise. He did this by arguing that "the American aborigine was the victim of a process . . . In truth," he wrote, "as a historical phenomenon, the Indian disintegrated; as an Indian he was not annihilated but he faded culturally into another entity. The crime, if there was one, was the inexorable breakdown of the native's cultural integrity, in part the result of conscious policy"—a big admission that was not followed up—"and in part the inevitable consequence of competition between two disparate ways of life." The "fragile structure" of a "primitive" and "savage" society, "the weaker, less resilient party" "devoid of the resources for serious competition," simply collapsed in the face of a "brash and aggressive" "civilized" society full of "vitality," "a booming white America bursting out of the constrictions of its social bounds."[8]

Despite his verbal animus toward the slingers of "gratuitous slurs" against white society, and three references to the meaninglessness of "moralistic" pronouncements, Sheehan allowed that "ethics, the imputing of guilt or innocence, must *not* be excluded from the process of historical judgment." But one has the feeling that his heart just wasn't in it, for he went on to warn that moral judgments "must become much less obtrusive," indeed "must give way to an understanding of the process of cultural conflict" which allows the historian to "see all the intricate permeations of the intermeshing of disparate cultures rather than the one-to-one moral dichotomy of oppressor and oppressed."[9]

As Sheehan reinforced his early position in two articulate books and an obscurely placed article on "The American Indian as Victim," it became even more obvious that his brand

of history had no acknowledged place for normative judgments of any kind at any time.[10] First of all, Sheehan's unduly
narrow definition of ethics as "the imputing of guilt or innocence" and his disparagement of the "moral*istic* approach"
betray a serious confusion between moral*izing*—which means
"to furnish with moral lessons," according to Webster, as in a
sermon—and moral *criticism* or *judgment*. As philosophers
have known for some time, not all moral utterances are moral
rules, universalizable and prescriptive. Moral statements can
also express indignation, command or exhort, give advice,
persuade, express one's own principles, and most familiar to
historians, appraise actions, not in terms of good and bad but
rather success and failure, the compatibility of means and
ends, intentions and results.[11] And although Sheehan is right
to condemn obtrusive self-righteousness and "gratuitous
slurs," he is blind to the evidence in his own engaged writing
that "historians can make clear their moral positions implic-
itly, in terms of the language they use, and in the tone and
style of composition."[12]

Secondly, the "process" that Sheehan blames for the Indians' demise is extremely impersonal and mechanical, the
result much less of "conscious policy"—which at least implies
human agency—than of gargantuan and uncontrollable social
forces. "The major factors," he wrote in 1975, "turn out to
have been beyond the white man's control (disease), or much
too difficult to control (liquor), or so slow in working its effects
as to be imperceptible (trade), or the result of a philanthropic
effort to do good for the Indians (missionaries)."[13] The problem with his list is that it ignores war, racism, the administra-
tion of justice, and the twin contests for land and sovereignty—
issues of far greater moral substance that have been at the
center of the history of Indian-white relations from the very
beginning.

A third obstacle to the exercise of moral judgment is the
determinism that seems to dominate Sheehan's historical uni-

verse. His frequent use of "inevitable" and "inexorable" to describe the cultural process suggests that he has been blinded by hindsight. Nothing in human affairs is inevitable except in retrospect, when we look back up the stream of time and see only the unilinear progression from cause to effect, from publicly stated intention to action. But hindsight, when we allow it to impose an answer rather than use it to pose a question, tends to obscure the not unlimited but plural choices that historical actors enjoyed as they looked down the time-stream into the future. To say that their choices were inevitable, as Sheehan frequently does, is to deny the existence of free will and to drift into the bog of historical determinism.

Finally, even if Sheehan acknowledges the possibility of moral judgment in history, he postpones its exercise indefinitely by undermining the epistemological basis for understanding Indian culture on its own terms. His most distinctive argument is that white men always viewed Indian society "through the prism of their own world," with conceptions and ideas that preceded observation and changed very little with experience but at the same time lent themselves to no "general conception of those societies that can claim anthropological validity." When looking at Indians, Anglo-Americans saw only themselves. This "narcissism" prevented "even a glimmer of truth" about the "actual" nature of Indian-white relations. Jeffersonian philanthropists and architects of removal, no less than their rough-and-ready Jamestown progenitors, were guilty of a "willful failure of the intellect," perhaps, "but not of the will." Some details of native life were perceived, but such perceptions remained "dim, scattered, tentative, and invariably ethnocentric." The "full lineaments of native social order" remained hidden from white eyes until the birth of scientific Anthropology.[14]

This formulation is flawed in several parts. Basically, it commits the fallacy of historical relativism by confusing the *way* knowledge is acquired—"the prism of their own world"—

with the *validity* of that knowledge, which is characterized by varying degrees of objectivity.[15] Sheehan seems to have escaped the "intellectual suicide" that results from a "consistent relativism" only by inconsistency.[16] He begins by suggesting that *some* knowledge of the Indians is "accurate," based on an "actual perception of native life," especially that gained by bona fide anthropologists. At the same time, he strongly implies that *all* perception is a flawed, introverted, refracting medium which acts more like a mirror than a microscope. On this basis he has no grounds for declaring the superiority of modern observers, who are no more objective in the *way* they acquire knowledge than past observers. To suggest that there are such grounds smacks of ethnocentric whiggism. But to suggest that no past observers ever perceived "real Indians" because they failed to formulate a general ethnological conception of Indian societies is simply absurd and badly confuses the difference between ethnology and ethnography. Most observers of everyday life, past or present, are simply unbiased selectors of details to give adequate explanations of their subjects. They have no personal investment in their answers to most questions; as Jack Hexter has put it, "it is no skin off their noses."[17] If they do have biases, these can usually be exposed and filtered out to obtain a more-or-less objective description.

Furthermore, even if much of the initial European idea of the Indian preceded observation does not imply that subsequent experience did not alter it. Expectations are always getting shattered by the facts. Nor were those preconceived ideas necessarily founded on the white man's perception of himself; indeed most probably were not. Any idea of an Indian must have some relation to the objective reality we call Indians. If the Europeans before extensive contact had an idea of an Indian, they clearly had to get it from somebody's previous experience. They could not have fabricated the idea out of whole cloth. If someone asked an Elizabethan Englishman "What is your idea of an Indian?", to answer he would have to know as a minimum that an Indian was a human being who lived in either India or the New World, which by definition meant that an Indian was in at least some human ways similar to, and probably in many cultural ways different from, himself. His answer, therefore, would have certain defined boundaries, certain pieces of objective truth, even while its content and details might be filled with errors and half-truths. But if you then put that man on a fishing boat for Cape Sable and he encountered a village of Micmacs or Penobscots while fetching fresh water and wood, we can rest assured that his original idea of an Indian would give way to a more accurate and detailed idea of—not *an* Indian but—Indian*s* in their cultural variety and human individuality. And if by chance he happened to be captured by those Indians and adopted as a kinsman and then proceeded to live their life for a number of years, we can be even more confident that his idea of Indians would take on a quality of unusual accuracy, detail, and objectivity, even if his *interpretation* of those facts remained culture-bound and personally biased. As an informed if untrained ethnographer, he would surely know what "real" Indians were like, even if he never formulated a general ethnological theory of their cultural development and social organization. If he did not know, ethnohistorians and historians of Indian-white relations would constitute another vanishing breed.

Although Sheehan's attack on moral history was misdirected and ineffective, the normative approach advocated by Washburn and practiced by the large majority of Indian-white historians received a more serious challenge in 1975 from Bruce Trigger, who published in the following year *The Children of Aataentsic: A History of the Huron People to 1660,* what many consider to be the best ethnohistory of an Indian tribe.[18] In an article called "Brecht and Ethnohistory," Trigger described how he chose the "interest group" rather than the individual or the whole tribe as his basic unit of analysis in the book, and how he borrowed Bertolt Brecht's theatrical technique of *"distantiation"* to try to achieve "something like parity" in his treatment of Indian and European interest groups. "Whether he studies an historical situation in terms of individuals or groups," Trigger noted, "the historian is tempted to identify himself with one party or another and to seek to influence his reader to make a similar identification. Even when the historian feels no particular sympathy for either side, it is difficult for him to avoid expressing personal judgments about his subjects. Such biases may simply add harmless colour to a dry story," he warned, "but they can [also] turn an historical study into a dangerous piece of propaganda." In his search for a "genuine explanation" of Indian behavior that was logical in its own terms but also understandable to non-Indians, Trigger sought, like Brecht, to write in such a way that his audience would not "identify with a particular individual or viewpoint" but would view the "total situation" in a "detached and critical spirit." If his approach resulted in a portrayal that seemed "colder and more calculating" than many readers would prefer, he was prepared to live with the consequences.[19]

None can gainsay the brilliant success that Trigger achieved in his history of the Hurons and their interactions with the French. As a model of ethnohistory, *The Children of Aataentsic* has no peers, and Trigger should have no difficulty in living with the consequences of his approach. But I suggest that he succeeded less because he practiced what he preached than because he was and is a master ethnohistorian endowed with a sophisticated and sensitive ethnological understanding, a keen grasp of historical method, and a supple and precise literary style. In fact, he followed only one half of his prospectus—in focusing on interest groups—and effectively ignored the second moiety of advice against normative judgments. Our everyday language is morally loaded; there is no neutral vocabulary for historians that is not either "aestheti-cally void or technically esoteric."[20] Any historian who em-ploys nouns, verbs, adjectives, and adverbs to tell his story and puts them together in calculated patterns will unavoid-ably express "personal judgments about his subjects."[21] Vir-tually any page of Trigger's work will reveal such judgments being made, not because he somehow failed to maintain his cool detachment but because he succeeded in using his per-sonal human qualities to capture the objective reality of the past. Trigger worried that sympathy for one's subjects does not necessarily lead to understanding, without which respect is impossible. But as Washburn noted in 1969, "it is [also] possible to achieve detachment without understanding" by failing to grasp, with the heart as well as the head, "the *ideas* that motivate, the *passions* that impel, [and] the *love* that transmutes."[22] Fortunately, Trigger was not led by his own misconception of moral judgments to divorce his full human-ity from the search for understanding.

Added to Sheehan's confusion, Trigger's characterization of moral judgments as "harmless colour" or "partisan propa-ganda" suggests that the role of value judgments in historical writing is widely misunderstood. Some needed clarification may be gained if we consider in turn the questions: *Why* do we judge the past? *What* do we judge? and *How* do we judge?, the last of which will return us to our introductory question, How do we judge a situation in which Indian and white values clashed?

It seems clear that we judge the past for three important rea-sons. The first is to appraise actions, which function separates the work of historians from that of mere antiquarians or com-pilers. It is the historian's judgment, his interpretation, that transmutes historical documents into a vital and rounded rendition of a past event. Evaluation is *intrinsic* to the his-torical process, not an option, because the moral connotations of the everyday words we use are part of their descriptive meaning. Furthermore, historians are interested primarily in change, and changes have multiple causes. When we assess the causes of any action or event, we make value judgments about their necessity and sufficiency, and therefore place them in a hierarchy of importance. Not to make such judgments is to abandon the past to itself, rendering it unintelligible, untranslatable, to the present. To write as an historical critic, on the other hand, is "to assume an active responsibility both to a phase of the past and to a contemporary public, and to engage one with the other." But we must remember that judgments of any kind are the *end* products of understanding, not a substitute for or prelude to it; they are, as John Higham has called them, "intensive, concrete reflection[s]" upon the life of the past and, by extension, the life of the present.[23]

The second reason for judging the past is to do justice to it, a "fuller and more precisely measured justice than practical and procedural exigencies allow the law to attempt." Rendering justice is not the same as "passing sentence," however. "The serious historian may not wrap himself in judicial robes and pass sentence from on high; he is much too involved in both the prosecution and the defense. He is not a judge of the dead, but rather a participant in their affairs, and their only trustworthy intermediary." He is, in other words, "detective, lawyer, judge," and trustee rolled into one. But historical justice does not operate like the modern legal system. The historian's justice is retrospective, not contemporary, and his goal is not to punish or rehabilitate historical malefactors—who are all mortally incorrigible—but to set the record straight for future appeals to precedent. There are essentially two ways to do justice to people in the past: we can modify contemporary or historical judgments upon past malefactors, especially those who somehow were not caught in the glare of contemporary morality, or we can rehabilitate the reputations of those who have been unjustly punished for deeds they never committed or committed in extenuating circumstances. It no longer matters to the dead whether they receive justice at the hands of succeeding generations, but, as Garrett Mattingly urged, "to the living, to do justice, however belatedly, should matter."[24]

Finally, we also judge the past to advance our own moral education, to learn from and, in effect, to be judged by the past. Since we write for our own generation, "we can have judgmental effect only on ourselves. . . . The lessons to be learned from the [past] are lessons for today" and perhaps tomorrow, not yesterday. The central issue "is not whether something had to happen, but whether it has to happen again." Consequently, history becomes, in Bolingbroke's famous phrase, "philosophy teaching by examples," a "preceptor of prudence, not of principles." Like all historical judgments, moral judgments are provisional and contextual; "there is no superhistorical standard." But hindsight allows us to reflect on the whole process of action-taking in the past, from the exercise of choice through its implementation and consequences, foreseen and unforeseen. Perhaps most important, moral valuations are the *products* of understanding. We are not moral educators in our *research,* whose goal is objective truth about the past, only in our *writing.* "To describe and assess action is, in the broadest sense, to educate; and part of this is moral education."[25]

After bearing witness to the past with all the scholarly disinterestedness and human empathy he can muster, the historian then "lets himself be judged by the past as much as, or more than, he judges it." For while "we are not in a position to instruct the past . . . we may well be instructed by it." "We go to history not only to find out what has happened in human affairs, but what is possible." The historian "derives from moral criticism an enlarged and disciplined sensitivity to what men ought to have done, what they might have done, and what they achieved." But since "history is one of the disciplines most effectively organized for imparting knowledge of what it is like to be another," through its study "we can extend our own way of life," though not by "bring[ing] the other way within the . . . existing boundaries of our own" or by simply learning new techniques for doing things. "More importantly we may learn different possibilities of making sense of human life, different ideas about the possible importance that the carrying out of certain activities may take on for a man, trying to contemplate the sense of his life as a whole." If we are fortunate, we may even gain some measure of wisdom from his experience.[26]

As we learn about "what it is like to be other than ourselves," we are better able to do justice to the past. The best way to learn to make discerning moral judgments is to practice making them. To judge is human, and to judge according to the highest standards of moral judgment is humanizing. But the next best way is to observe a discerning moral critic at work. If we wish to help people, especially young people, learn to make sound moral judgments, whether of other people's lives or their own, we should provide them with the example of engaged and informed scholars making fair and humane judgments of the past.[27]

Our second question, What is it that we judge?, can be answered succinctly. Historians comment upon the moral character of whole societies and institutions or, more frequently, individuals. Unless we are rigid determinists, we assume that people in the past had choices when they came to act. "We hold people responsible only to the degree that we think them free to choose their course." Then we assess their *motives,* not only their publicly stated *intentions* but other conscious goals that they may have hidden from public view. To uncover the latter we make an assessment of the actors' *character,* the consistent pattern of their habits and will. We then examine the "quality of *actions* promoted by such intentions" and the "*consequences* of such actions to the extent that they were foreseen, or foreseeable." We should not assume, of course, that a happy consequence necessarily follows from a virtuous action or intention, or a negative consequence from a sinister intention. And we should not hold people responsible for consequences far removed from or unattributable directly to their actions. But while they cannot be expected to have foreseen all the consequences of their actions, we can legitimately hold them responsible for anticipating *some* of them. "A willful failure of the intellect" or "good intentions" is a weak defense, especially if other men in their society chose other, more salutary courses of action or, even if no one actually chose another course, the alternative was perfectly viable and possible for *that* society at *that* time.[28]

If there is considerable agreement among historians on the *subject* of moral judgments, there is even more consensus on the *standards* we should use to judge the past. One of the firmest canons of historical scholarship is that a past society must be judged first and foremost by its own values and norms. We judge the conduct of people "by their success in acting in accordance with the ideals they have chosen." "To make a moral assessment of the character of an action . . . means to assess it in its own moral context, in relation to the moral inspiration, support, education and possibilities of action actually available" to the actor. The difficulty is to ascertain as precisely and objectively as possible just what contemporary moral community a person belonged to, whether it coincided with the larger society or only some part of it.[29]

While an individual event or action should be evaluated *historically* in terms of the practices and conventions of its time, the historian may also measure it *comparatively* against similar events in other times and places, and, less effectively, against his personal scale of values. There is a critical difference between the two. Both call upon the historian's per-

sonal judgment. But the comparison of historical events of
different eras and contexts is an *interpretive* or *synoptic* judgment, which is the *result* of his research and thought, whereas
the application of a personal *moral* view may actually *precede*
the exploration and analysis of the occurrence. Expressions
of moral outrage or prejudice, therefore, are not only super-
fluous but as counterproductive as the other kinds of flagrant
bias stemming from race, sex, religion, class, or nationality.
Moral judgments, like all historical judgments, should be
made only after the historian has done his homework, and
then in a subtle, unobtrusive way that brings the reader and
the subject together rather than coming between them. "To
advance and defend our view of how things were, and why,
and what this meant to the people of the time, and what it
means"—or should mean—"to people of today" is, as Gordon
Wright said, a *"final* step," not one to be taken prematurely
or casually.[30]

The historian's obligation to judge a society by its own standards is difficult enough to fulfill when our subject is a single
society. But when we study the clash of two societies, as we
do in the history of Indian-white relations, our task is more
than doubly complicated. Of course, we must first strive to be
scrupulously fair to all parties, which is possible only after
immersing ourselves so deeply in the historical sources of
each society that we are as much or more at home in their
time and place than in our own. Because of the ever-present
dangers of moral absolutism, favoritism, and presentism, however, we will have to make a special effort to achieve parity of
treatment. I believe this can be done most successfully by
letting the conflicting societies judge each other. A sympathetic understanding of the past "can be conveyed with much
more subtlety, and ultimately more effect, if the historian, instead of pronouncing his own moral judgments speaks through
the mouths of contemporaries, using their recorded thoughts

and opinions as pieces of evidence much like any other. If he is skillful, the historian can still make us aware of his own moral position. But, because he is using contemporary utterances, he can also make us aware of the view and opinions of those whose moral positions diverge from his own. Contemporary moral judgments enable us to enter the lives of the men of the past. We begin to see 'heroes' and 'villains' in their terms, and thus to appreciate more fully not just their circumstances, but the moral choices and judgments that they themselves made."[31] By this technique, Washburn's bilateral interests in moral history and the history of morals will coalesce.

While two societies in the past may have been evenly matched in the contest for moral and cultural superiority, the surviving documentary record of their respective positions may be much less equal. If the sources for one society are slim, a sensitive application of imagination and empathy to a mastery of the available sources can often establish a culturally valid standard of judgment by which to redress the balance. To the same end, a light use of irony or gentle iconoclasm can effectively prick the pretensions and self-righteousness of a dominant society blessed with an advantage of records. If more comment or moral criticism is called for by the complexity, abnormality, or enormity of the conflict situation, we can use the standards of other contemporary societies, preferably neighbors who found themselves in similar circumstances. Beyond this kind of concrete, contextual treatment, most historians will not need or want to go. Personal preference will dictate whether we proceed to apply, as Washburn once suggested, "quasi-universal" moral standards in a "new cultural context, . . . free from the interpretations and assumptions under which [the original actions were] performed or observed by the participants."[32]

By now it should be clear that "personal preference" is the key to much of the historian's moral involvement, just as moral sensitivity, mastery of the English language, and capacity for historical understanding are unevenly distributed. Because of the normative character of our language, we are all moral historians because we make moral or value judgments merely by choosing words to convey our understanding of the past. Whether we make those infinite, ubiquitous judgments skillfully and subtly, and whether we feel called upon to make more explicit moral assessments, are matters of personal style.

A book that vividly illustrates the need and opportunities for moral style is Francis Jennings's *The Invasion of America,* published in 1975.[33] Virtually a casebook in moral history, *The Invasion of America* sought to expose the fallaciousness of the "cant of conquest," the willful propaganda-ideology mouthed by the seventeenth-century English colonists to "overpower their own countrymen's scruples" about the invasion of Indian land and sovereignty. Jennings made two initial moral assumptions: first, that "what we approve in past conduct will be repeated in the future," and second, that because "human persons . . . have some power of choice over their conduct . . . their adherence to moral standards, whatever those standards may be, is a matter of historical concern." And from his study of history, he also concluded that "conquest aristocracies" (as he called them) "reaching for illicit power customarily assume attitudes of great moral rectitude to divert attention from the abandonment" of their moral standards. At the same time, Jennings criticized the work of numerous modern historians, especially Vaughan, Prucha, and Sheehan, for accepting in various guises the colonists' "savage/civilized" dichotomy, which lay at the heart of the cant of conquest.[34]

Convinced that it would take a mighty "struggle to break the bonds of ideology so long established and so firmly fixed," Jennings armed himself with a veritable arsenal of wit and words, mounted a formidable breed of hard-nosed, keen-eyed research, and rushed courageously into the fray. Once engaged, Jennings's nemesis was never in doubt. His admittedly "strong aversion toward the Puritan gentry," which, he asserted, was "largely" acquired in the course of research, resulted in a vivid vocabulary of condemnation that left no reader unmoved, either to fist-pounding affirmation or apoplectic disapproval. Unforgettable phrases such as "masterful guile," "excruciating cant," "heedless grasping," "deed games," "missionary racket," "kaleidoscopic fanaticisms," "brutal charades," and "backcountry Euramerican thugs" not only conveyed Jennings's understanding of the colonial conflict between Indians and whites but identified his own moral position with unmistakable clarity.[35]

Predictably, the reviews of *The Invasion of America* were, like the book, "hardly neutral," and tell us something important about the need for stylistic moderation in moral history. Reviewers were unanimous that the book was strong, even angry, but then parted company over whether the author's moral indignation was "magnificent" or merely monstrous. Those who basically agreed with Jennings's exposure of the Puritans' clay feet and other "disquieting insights" tended to delight in, or at least tolerate, his explosive language.[36] But others, and not only those who were the targets of some of his barbs, lamented that his "partisan" polemics had interfered with objective social analysis and produced "a morality play," a post-Vietnam, post-Watergate "tract for the times," instead of a valid history.[37] Regardless of the justice of these criticisms, such a negative assessment indicated that many readers would not be persuaded by, perhaps not even give a respectful hearing to, Jennings's exacting ethnohistorical scholarship or his commendable moral goals simply because of the literary style in which he chose to present them.

The comment of one reviewer suggests that all historians, especially historians of Indian-white relations, should pay close attention to the rhetoric of moral judgment. In an otherwise favorable review, James Ronda characterized Jennings's language as "sometimes strident, frequently wry, and often sarcastic."[38] Two of these are obviously not complimentary. Sensitive moral history, if it is to be effective, must eliminate "gratuitous swipes," "obvious personal bias," and preachy time-outs for egregious moralizing. Equally unacceptable is *sarcasm* because it shows contempt for its objects and is intended to wound their feelings (which it cannot do since they are all dead). This leaves us with four major rhetorical devices for writing implicit moral history and balancing documentary sources to enable Indians and whites to judge each other. The first, *satire,* must be used cautiously because in holding up vice and folly for ridicule or reprobation, it too may not show sufficient respect for the people of the past or show discernment. If handled carefully and applied with a deft hand, however, satire does have its uses, especially when, as Pierre Bayle noticed, "men are such that when writing history one has the appearance of making a satire."[39]

The other three devices are, I would argue, not only available to historians of Indian-white relations but should be standard equipment. The first is *wit,* the swift perception of the incongruous. No tool is better designed for perceiving unconventional analogies between so-called "civilized" and "savage" cultures. The second device is *humor,* the perception of "the ludicrous, the comical, and the absurd in life or situations . . . without bitterness" (Webster). Since life is often comical, even in tragedy, the historian should employ humor, if for no other reason, to give a fully rounded picture of the past. Again, the touch should be light but not frivolous or flippant, lest we show disrespect to our subjects. There is no need to go for the jugular when the funnybone is so sensitive. And third, *irony* is ready-made for the historian of Indian-white relations, particularly missionary efforts, because its province is the gap between preaching and practice, all those rich areas of contact where the best laid plans of (mostly) European men produced results quite the opposite of and as if in mockery of the desired results. Perhaps, as the Canadian historian Guy Frégault said, "History does not indulge in irony," but certainly historians do and should. One reason among many is that, unlike cynicism, "irony differentiates," and moral judgment requires all the subtlety and discrimination we can muster.[40]

The pummeling the Puritans took from Jennings's pen raises a final question about the possibility of achieving strict fairness toward America's Indian and white contestants without neglecting our function as moral critics: Do the dominant European "winners" have to carry an extra "white man's burden" of being judged more frequently and more rigorously than the eventual Indian "losers"? Does the underdog, by virtue of disadvantage alone, deserve the benefit of our doubt when values clash? Do modern politics of ethnicity prevent us from giving truly equal treatment to both Indians and whites in the past? The answers will undoubtedly vary according to our moral predilections. As for pressure from modern Indian politics, it should be neutralized by a self-conscious objectivity. As long as we are sensitive to new and fruitful *questions* about the past, whatever their source, as scholars we can safely ignore any *answers* proffered by people or parties who have not mastered the documentary record.

I, for one, am persuaded that the European colonists, soldiers, and administrators in America *do* carry an extra burden—not of foreordained *guilt* but—of *responsibility,* of moral *initiative,* for three reasons. First, it was *they* who invaded the Indians' land, *they* who demanded the Indians' cultural surrender, and *they* who benefitted so richly from the Indians' losses. Perhaps more important, however, is the fact that the Europeans set *themselves* an exalted standard of morality, compounded of the adamantine demands of Scripture and the softer requirements of "civility." We can do no less than respect their choice. And last, because of the predominance of

European records, we have no dearth of white judgments of Indians and their culture. In fact, our major task is to ensure the existence of equalizing judgments in the opposite direction. James Ronda and Cornelius Jaenen have shown that such material can be found, and much more exists. But we will also have to resort to our imagination, empathy, and ethnographic sensitivity to provide plausible judgments from various Indian perspectives without succumbing to uncritical "noble savagism" on the one side or indiscriminate iconoclasm on the other. The "winners," even if they are us, deserve our respect and understanding too. Only the documentary record measured against their own exacting norms should judge their actions the object of pity or scorn.

As the burgeoning literature of the past decade suggests, historians and ethnohistorians of Indian-white relations can provide new and important insights into the origins of American culture and the distinctive moral legacy we have inherited from that formative period. Because of the increased depth of their research and the steady maturation of their methodology, they are capable of explaining better than ever before the acculturative nature of Anglo-American society and the pluralistic character of America's frontiers.[41] We can expect them to advance our historical understanding and our moral sensitivity even more in the years ahead if they stand by the ethnohistorical canon and do not desecrate the field with moralistic overkill or desert it altogether in the name of false purity.

Postscript

When this essay was first presented at the Philadelphia meeting of the Organization of American Historians in April 1982, Bernard Sheehan and Bruce Trigger made substantial comments on it, the latter *in absentia.* A brief examination of their remarks may serve to clarify the major issues separating us.

We all agree on two important points: one, that the historian's *primary* task is explanation, not moral evaluation; two, that premature *moralizing* should be avoided. Egregious intrusions of the historian's personal biases—whether moral, racial, political, or religious—are usually counter-productive and always unprofessional. But there we begin to part company.

My position is that the historian's explanatory and evaluative (or interpretive) functions cannot be neatly separated, for at least two compelling reasons. The first is that the ordinary English words we use to tell our stories and make our explanations are normatively "loaded," they carry all kinds of emotional and intellectual freight because of such things as etymology, sheer sound, and layered meanings. To choose one word over another is to make a judgment, risk an interpretation, and to blinker the reader to the possibility of others. A second reason is that evaluation is inherent not only in the individual words but in the very mode of "emplotment" we choose to structure our narrative. Moreover, if Hayden White is correct, each mode of emplotment (romantic, tragic, comic, satirical) tends to entail a specific mode of argument (formalist, mechanistic, organicist, contextualist) and, by implication, an ideological mode as well (anarchist, radical, conservative, liberal), all of which obviously are highly normative.[42] While all these choices make the writing of history an undeniably *personal* act, they do not necessarily prevent an historical interpretation from being *objective,* an accurate if incomplete report on a segment of the real past.[43] My primary aim in discussing moral or normative judgments at all is to ensure that we are fully conscious that we make them in our work almost constantly and to urge that we make them subtly and responsibly.

On three other fundamental points I part company with

one or both commentators. First, Sheehan asserts that the
basis of all moral judgments should be "universal laws," a
position consonant with his Thomistic "natural law" philosophy. On these grounds he argues that such judgments are "invariably *a priori*, abstract, and ahistorical" and therefore have
little or no place in ethnohistory, which should judge "within
the limits of the historical situation." Trigger and I, on the
other hand contend that moral standards need not be universal or *a priori* to be valid, and that moral judgments are
culturally relative—spatially and temporally localized—like
other aspects of social and cultural behavior. If past cultures
judged themselves and others at the bar of a culturally relative, non-universal standard, as Sheehan maintains, why may
we in good conscience not do the same? Since we do not pretend to write history for all time and peoples, I see no reason
why we should necessarily evaluate human behavior by a universal, immutable standard. Like humanists and moral educators of all stripes, historians make normative judgments for
the benefit of their own societies, not those of the past or even
the long-range future.

Second, we all disagree on the goals of moral history. From
all that I have read, Sheehan appears to acknowledge no goal
for historical scholarship other than understanding. Trigger,
on the other hand, in accepting a place for moral judgments
in history, seeks to harness them to the search for a more humane social order. But the shaping of a society, in which "the
exploitation of one group by another is made increasingly
difficult and ultimately becomes impossible," requires more
than moral "commentary" on the behavior of individuals or
even small interest groups. "Such moralizing has done little
to halt the brutality and exploitation in the world around
us." Instead, Trigger argues (from an avowedly "materialist"
viewpoint that has "little belief in free will"), "we must try
to understand the nature of *whole societies,* which influence
people's behavior and lead them, in self-interest, to commit

brutal and inhuman acts. . . . In this approach, moralizing ceases to be a commentary that is detached from the concrete practice of everyday living" and "becomes an integral part of the search for *knowledge* on which effective social action can be based." While I wholeheartedly agree with Trigger's social goal, I, a firm believer in free will and personal responsibility albeit in a socially limiting context, think that only individuals can improve social morality, either with power exercised through socal institutions or with the authority of group leadership. I also believe that we can morally profit from the past experience of individuals and small groups. Because history translates past experience to the present not only in the form of rational explanation but also affective understanding, we can empathize with other individuals more easily than with impersonal institutions and complex societies.

Finally, I disagree with both Sheehan and Trigger on the nature of culture. Both tend to view culture (or in Trigger's case, the economic base) as a severe constraint on individual freedom and initiative, though for different reasons: Sheehan because he is philosophically repelled by what he calls "historical Antinomianism" or ("solipsism"), Trigger because he is a materialistic determinist. While we all agree that "culture establishes boundaries" around individual freedom, the commentators find those limits tightly drawn while I see more room for choice. Our disagreement is one of emphasis, but in historical interpretation as in philosophy, emphasis can be everything. I like to think that we are engaged in a common historical pursuit but that we have agreed to disagree, if only in small measure, over our methods and our meaning.

CHAPTER TWO

Forked Tongues: Moral Judgments in Indian History

AFTER THE PREVIOUS ESSAY APPEARED IN PRINT, I RECEIVED AN opportunity to practice what I preached. Mildred Alpern, co-editor of an historical column devoted to classroom applications, invited me to write about teaching moral judgments in undergraduate classes in Indian history. So I sat down to analyze how I dealt with value judgments—those of the historical sources, the students', and mine—in my own classes in ethnohistory. The following essay, minus one paragraph, was published in *Perspectives: AHA Newsletter* in February 1987.

As might be expected, ordinary words—nouns, adverbs, and adjectives—provide the most numerous and most fruitful sources of exercise. The normative resonance of *savage* is quite different from that of *sauvage; invaders* packs more wallop than *strangers* or even *intruders. Shot* and *slain* convey moral messages different from those emanating from *murdered* or *massacred.* From analyzing individual words it is a natural step to distinguishing *observations* (more or less objective) from *interpretations* of the objects or events observed. To note that the Montagnais did not practice regular field agriculture is correct; to conclude from that fact that they did not have a concept of private or communal property is erroneous. Finally, students need to grapple with the normative implications of different narrative "emplotments," the larger structures of meaning that all viable histories must have.

A history of Indian-white relations played as romance or tragedy is clearly different from one cast in a comic or satirical mode. Complications arise when sub-plots play different themes for the sake of ironic contrast or simply because the writer did not complete his literary tasks, and students should be enabled to cope with them.

Most of the words we use in history and everyday speech are like mental depth-charges. When heard or read they quickly sink into our consciousness and explode, sending off cognitive shrapnel in all directions. On the surface they may look harmless enough, or resemble something equally benign. But as they descend and detonate, their resonant power is unleashed, showering our understanding with fragments of accumulated meaning and association.

In our search for professional disinterestedness, fairness, and objectivity it is easy to give our students and readers the impression that words are strictly denotative (rather than detonative) instruments of scientific precision and emotional neutrality. Nothing could be farther from the truth. There is no neutral vocabulary for historians that is not either aesthetically void or technically esoteric. Any historian who employs nouns, verbs, adjectives, and adverbs to tell his story and puts them together in calculated patterns of meaning will unavoidably express moral or value judgments about his subjects.[1]

Teaching the history of Indian-white relations, whether independently or as part of an American survey course, quickly brings us face to face with some of the classic problems posed by our loaded vocabularies. The first problem is shared by all students of history: the tendency to apply our own limited range of modern meanings to words we share with the past but which may have meant different things to the historical actors who used them. Here the *Oxford English Dictionary* or its American equivalents are needed to clarify the usage of each age and to prevent anachronism.

Francis Jennings is particularly adept at this kind of semantical sleuthing. In *The Invasion of America* he used the *OED* to probe such elements of the English "cant of conquest" as *king, pagan, heathen, peasant, savage, and filthy*.[2] Neal Salisbury, on the other hand, was caught by a generally complimentary reviewer in the act of giving a seventeenth-century word a twentieth-century meaning. In the space of twenty pages, Salisbury referred three times to the Massachusetts Bay Company's plans in 1629 to purchase land from any Indians who *"pretend* right of inheritance" so as to "avoyde the least scruple of intrusion." He concluded (not wholly without reason) that the English colonizers were utterly contemptuous of Indian land rights. But, as Alden Vaughan pointed out, "the standard seventeenth-century meaning of *pretend* was *claim,* without modern implications of deception."[3]

Another problem faced by many historians, particularly those who study the history of native peoples largely through the documents produced by European invaders, is the tendency to adopt uncritically the intruders' descriptions and value judgments of the natives as their own. Despite our best efforts, we are all, to some extent, the unwitting dupes and victims of our sources. It is all too easy to accept as objective description the colonists' unflattering characterizations of the natives, particularly when we happen to share the writers' race, religion, or nationality. While we teach our students to be critical of every source they use, we tend to drop our own guard when a source seems relatively familiar and intellectually congenial.

A third problem, related to the first two, is our tendency to make moral judgments without admitting that we do or without sufficient attention to the normative content of the words we use in making them. Some historians have no trouble with either issue. Jennings, for one, writes unabashedly moral history because he fears that "what we approve in past conduct will be repeated in the future." Assuming that "human persons do have some power of choice over their own conduct and that their adherence to moral standards, whatever those standards may be, is a matter of historical concern," he does not hesitate to use highly charged language to describe and interpret the past.[4] The Puritan clergy "thundered their wrath and called it God's." Colonial leaders resorted to "mendacity extraordinary even among adepts" to "put a fair face on fraud," and shamefully played "deed games," the "missionary racket," and "brutal charades." The colonists' "heedless grasping and bellicosity" were spearheaded by "mercenary buccaneers" and "backcountry Euramerican thugs," who resembled nothing so much as "great [feudal] hulks on horseback." No reader has any difficulty interpreting Jennings's moral stance or recognizing that he has one.

But most historians are, by nature or nurture, more judicious in their use of overtly moral language. Yet they do not fail to make normative judgments all the time; often they are blissfully unaware that they are doing so, or they try to wrap them in the cloak of professional objectivity or the mantle of esoteric dullness. Even seemingly mild unpointed words are capable of carrying a great deal of moral freight. Take, for instance, the following two passages:

> One [of the two competing societies in colonial New England] was unified, visionary, disciplined, and dynamic. The other was divided, self-satisfied, undisciplined, and static. It would be unreasonable to expect that such societies could live side by side indefinitely with no penetration of the more fragmented and passive by the more consolidated and active.[5]

> The second moral issue raised by the scalp bounties is not that Europeans taught the Indians how to scalp—they already knew how—but that Europeans adopted the Indian practice of scalping even though their cultures offered no moral or

religious warrant for it and the traditional standards of Christian behavior condemned it.[6]

When asked to choose the least "moral," most "objective" passage, students invariably pick the first because the adjectives seem temperate and disinterested; it helps that they are also polysyllabic and abstract (the warp and woof of scientific "objectivity"). The second passage, by contrast, is sprinkled with normative-*sounding* words, such as *moral, religious, standards, Christian,* and *condemned.* But in fact, as students realize after a brief session of Socratic questioning, the first passage is much more "personal" and value-laden than the second, which simply describes, without judgment, the historical status of a moral issue raised by contemporaries themselves. The first passage is objectionable, not only because we cannot define or describe a person or society by negation (divided vs. unified, etc.), but because the unconscious sexual metaphor that concludes it betrays the male Eurocentric bias of its author.

In attempting to teach students to be fair to both Indian and white cultures and sensitive to the normative challenge of our historical vocabularies, I spend considerable time making them watch their words in speech and in writing. As we read the materials of the course together, I draw their attention to words commonly used to describe native peoples. Some of them, notably in the newer ethnohistories, are unobjectionable to Indians and historians alike. But most of the descriptive nouns and adjectives used by historical contemporaries and even modern historians to portray native life are biased, pejorative, demeaning, or simply inaccurate.

So pervasive is our literary bias against Indian people and culture that perhaps the best way to spend the few class hours we devote to the Indians in our American survey courses is to attack head-on our students' stereotypes. Asking for a list of words to describe "Indians" (tribe and time unspecified) will usually provide more than enough to work with. Another source is the collection of colonial documents in my *The Indian Peoples of Eastern America: A Documentary History of the Sexes* (New York, 1981). Then the list can be attacked, item by item, with reliable ammunition from books such as Jennings's *The Invasion of America* (particularly the first ten chapters), Gary Nash's *Red, White, and Black: The Peoples of Early America* (Englewood Cliffs, N.J., 1974; 2d ed., 1982), Robert Berkhofer's *The White Man's Indian: Images of the American Indian from Columbus to the Present* (New York, 1978), Wilcomb Washburn's *The Indian in America* (New York, 1975), or my *The European and the Indian: Essays in the Ethnohistory of Colonial North America* (New York, 1981).

Many of the words we use to describe native people and culture are relative, having no concrete reality in themselves; their meaning depends on other words that are equally slippery. Take, for instance, the following:

Savage: In European writings this is the most common synonym for 'Indian.' It is based, of course, on an ethnocentric ranking of societies, with those of Western Europe at the top. Derived from the Latin word for 'forest' (*silva*) through the French word for 'wild' or 'untamed' (*sauvage*), *savage* by the late sixteenth century had come to mean 'an uncivilized, wild person' in 'the lowest stage of culture.' The key term of reference is *civilize,* which by circular definition means 'to bring out of a state of barbarism.' *Barbarism,* as one might guess, means a 'barbarous social or intellectual condition.' And *barbarous* is defined no more helpfully as 'rude, savage,' the opposite of 'civilized.' In other words, the meanings of all these terms depend on an imaginary construct, a social-evolutionary hierarchy in the speaker's mind which has no objective or historical reality.

Understandably, the criteria for this ranking of societies are never stated explicitly because they are the familiar prod-

ucts of cultural habit rather than the earned results of philosophical analysis. From early documents it is relatively easy
and very useful for students to discover some of the unarticulated standards by which European observers judged a "savage" American society. Consonant with the definition of
savage as '*un*civilized,' these benchmarks are usually stated as
deficiencies: *lack of* clothing; large towns and cities; statutory
law; centralized and compulsory forms of government; literacy and printing; draft animals and fences; iron, cloth, and
glass; scriptural and ecclesiastical religion.

Primitive: In the discussion surrounding these social judgments, this word usually appears. Derived from the Latin
primus ('first'), *primitive* in the late seventeenth century
meant 'having the quality or style of that which is early or
ancient; simple, rude, or rough.' But since then it has acquired more pejorative connotations from social evolution-
ists. Sensitive anthropologists recently have urged their colleagues to expunge the word from their vocabularies, because
the concept is as value-laden and descriptively useless as *savage*.[7] When so-called "primitive" or tribal societies are examined carefully, usually the only thing remotely "simple" or
"rude" about them is their technology. While the North
American Indians had no wheels, ships, paper, guns, compasses, or cathedrals, some of the shrewdest students of society
have struggled mightily to plumb the complexity and sophis-
tication of their polytheist religions, kinship systems, "barter"
economies, suasive governments, arts of war and peace, and
languages.

Once the last vestige of crude evolutionism has been disposed of, students should be urged to consider more worthy
criteria for comparing human societies, namely those things
that contribute to the *quality* of life. Without succumbing to
"noble savagism," our classes are likely to give the Indians
higher marks than did their colonial predecessors by measur-

ing native and colonial societies—all members of them—
against standards of health, life expectancy, physical security,
individual freedom, personal fulfillment, leisure, emotional
support, and aesthetic and religious expression.

Pagan: With the exception of kinship, religion was the
least understood aspect of Indian life. Seeing no familiar
churches, crosses, clergymen, or Scripture, Europeans concluded that the natives were "without faith," godless, "pagan."
But of course *pagan* (and its synonym *heathen*) is simply a
Christian definition of—or rather epithet for—a *non*-Christian,
one who 'does not worship the *true* God.' To the natives who
worshipped them, Indian deities were no less 'true.'

Superstition: Instead of "true religion," Indian religion
was thought to be devil-worship and rank "superstition."
From the early sixteenth century, Englishmen used *superstition* to denote 'religious belief or practice founded upon fear
or ignorance.' In the next century, however, Thomas Hobbes
reminded his countrymen that "fear of things invisible, is the
natural seed of that, which every one in himself calleth religion; and in them that worship, or fear that power otherwise
than they do, superstition."[8] Students of history can use the
same reminder.

Even well-meaning modern historians occasionally use
terms that are inappropriate or vaguely insulting.

Red Man and *Redskin* are inappropriate for two reasons.
First, because they refer to a physical characteristic, they lend
themselves to racial stereotyping and discrimination, as does
(upper case) "Whites" to denote Europeans or Anglo-
Americans. Historians should be discriminating only in their
respect for cultural and human diversity. Second, the color is
objectively wrong. As Alden Vaughan has shown, the colonists described the Indians' pigmentation as brown, copper,
olive, black, tawny, and even white, but not red. When *Red*
slowly came into use in the second half of the eighteenth cen-

tury, the color referred to the Indians' warpaint and, by extension, their allegedly ethnic or racial antipathy to the "White Man."[9]

Brave is a nineteenth-century word for an Indian warrior of the Plains, so it is inappropriately used to describe a warrior of an Eastern Woodland tribe or an Indian male who did not join war parties.

Squaw, a neutral Algonquian word for 'woman,' quickly acquired pejorative coloration from European descriptions of native women as "drudges" and "slaves" who did most of the farming, transported lodge material and household items in their travels, collected firewood and water, and hauled game home from the spot where it was killed by their menfolk. Indian people today eschew it for that reason.

Half-breed: Miscegenation (there should be a better word) between Europeans and Indians produced numerous descendants who were often referred to, pejoratively, as *mixed bloods, half-breeds,* or simply *breeds.* Objectively, of course, the blood of members of two different ethnic or racial groups does not "mix" except in a genetic sense, at the chromosomal level. In order to unload "the freight of a phony and damning folk biology," therefore, we should use the neutral French term *métis* for 'mixed.'[10] The original *Métis* were the nineteenth-century descendants of French and Indian parents from the Red River settlement in Manitoba. But today the term applies more generally to any person of mixed Indian-white ancestry, particularly in Canada and in the northern border states of the United States. (In areas settled by the Spanish the equivalent term is *mestizo*.) Jennings has coined the uneuphonious term *synethnic* for such people, but historians should avoid such cumbrous jargon like the plague.[11]

Almost invariably our textbooks commit three other verbal *faux pas,* to which students should be alerted.

Prehistory is used to describe the Indian past before the arrival of Europeans and written records, as if the natives had no real history until the white man gave it to them. Such a condescending attitude does an injustice to the historical value of archaeology, glottochronology, and oral tradition. *Precontact* is a better word.

Massacre is typically what Indians (i.e. "savages") did to (innocent) white folks, as in the Virginia "Massacres" of 1622 and 1644 when the Powhatans surprised the encroaching colonists and in brilliant coordinated attacks claimed nearly 850 victims. The English attack on the Pequot Fort in 1637, on the other hand, is rarely described as a massacre, although between three and eight hundred men, women, and children lost their lives in the fiery onslaught. If there is to be an historical standard of judgment, it should not be double.

French and Indian War appears in nearly every American history textbook—and should give way to "Seven Years' War" (even though in America the war lasted nine years, thanks to George Washington). Indians fought on both sides in that and every other *intercolonial war*. From the French perspective, the encounter could have been seen as the "English and Indian War." To the Indians it was simply another "French and English" or (by that time) "White Man's" War. Contemporaries, of course, called it none of these. To them it was just "the war" or "the last war." The "French and Indian" tag apparently was hung by Anglo-American historians in the nineteenth century.

As they move through texts and documents, students will discover that other words bear watching. Buffalo, not Indians, "roam." The "nomadic" Indians of the Eastern Woodlands did not wander; they commuted on an annual cycle between familiar residences. By the same token, the American environment was a "wilderness" only to the European newcomers, not to the natives who called it home. And only the rare certifiable homicidal maniac sought to commit "genocide" upon the Indians. The vast majority of settlers had no interest in killing Indians and those who did took careful aim at temporary political or military enemies. *Genocide* was coined in 1944 to denote the systematic "annihilation of a *race*," and the settlers' animus was directed at *cultural* or *social* foes.

Virtually any course will provide abundant materials for the teacher and student interested in exploring the moral dimensions of history. But the history of Indian-white relations offers a particularly rich field because it features five centuries of sustained, sometimes deadly, combat over the most basic cultural values. The moral complexion and complexity of the contest for the continent provides students with an historical experience which raises the full range of normative issues in the relative safety and quiet of the past, but also reminds them that few of those issues are dead. And to prepare them to deal sensitively and intelligently with the moral dilemmas of their own time is, after all, the main purpose of moral history.

New World Crusades

Northeastern North America:
The Theater of Competition

SILLERY — Catholic Indian reserves
NATICK — Protestant Indian towns

0   100   200   300 Miles

CHAPTER THREE

Some Thoughts on the Ethnohistory of Missions

WHILE ENGAGED IN LONG-TERM PROJECTS, SCHOLARS—UNLESS THEY have preternatural reservoirs of patience—often get the itch to write something finite. Usually a request comes over the transom about that time for a conference paper, a guest lecture, or an article to fill the thematic issue of a journal. With alacrity he accepts and bolts from the library to the typewriter to write what is half-affectionately known as a "spin-off," a piece that can be ripped from or is suggested by a problem or theme in the larger work.

"Some Thoughts" was born of such tergiversation during the twelve-year gestation of *The Invasion Within*. It was first given as a paper at the Conference on Iroquois Research (which has long tolerated my non-Iroquoian forays) in Rensselaerville, N.Y., in October 1976. Five months later, it withstood the scrutiny of the Chicago-area Early American History Colloquium at the Newberry Library. In November 1980 it was recycled again for the first Wilfred Laurier Conference on Ethnohistory and Ethnology, which met in Waterloo, Ontario. Finally, in 1982, its peripatetic phase was brought to a close with publication in *Ethnohistory*, in a number devoted to several papers from the Laurier Conference. I have altered the text slightly and updated the footnotes.

Those who read the essay immediately before *The Invasion*

Within may discover that, while I tried mightily to follow the spirit of my own prescription for mission history, I did not always manage to obey the letter.

IN THE COURSE OF WRITING THE INVASION WITHIN, AN ETHNO-history of the French, English, and Indian efforts to convert each other in colonial North America, I encountered an interpretive problem that has not been handled particularly well by ethnohistorians or by historians of religion.[1] And that is, What are the criteria for judging the success or failure of a missionary program?

Most writers simply do not stop to consider the question. They just plunge in and with an unarticulated set of assumptions proceed to judge the mission efforts from the perspective of the missionaries. The judgments they pass are usually of two kinds. First, if the writer is a Christian missiologist, say a Jesuit historian or missionary, the mission effort is judged to be some kind of semi-success, semi- because of the trying "pagan" or indelibly "primitive" circumstances under which it was conducted. Conventionally, such an assessment turns out to be a numbers game in which numbers of baptisms, communicants, marriages, apostates, perhaps native priests, nuns, and catechists are subjected to a kind of clerical calculus and then, somewhat mysteriously, made to reveal a success quotient that only a papal nuncio could understand.[2] But the lay reader is left in some doubt as to the criteria being used, or at least their value for historical understanding.

The second kind of judgment has come more recently from lay historians, who also size up the conversion attempts by peering over the missionaries' shoulders.[3] But almost invariably their judgments have been negative because, while they still tend to take the missionary goals as the standards for judgment, they switch focus in the end to assume that the results in the native society being *acted upon*—passively—are more important. These historians, often with counter-cultural tendencies of their own, commiserate with the natives over the tragic loss of their cultural integrity and curse the black-robes whose ethnocentric intolerance and muscular evangelizing forced the Indians into such a compromised position. Partly because they no longer share the Christian belief that pagans and infidels should be converted wherever they flourish, and partly because they have borrowed a dash of the anthropologist's cultural relativism (which in practice means that they bend over backwards for the natives without performing the same gyration for the Europeans), the historians writing mission history have come up with the wrong conclusion for reasons that are more than half right.

One way to approach the general question of missionary success is to ask: Why did the Indians convert to Christianity? Discounting Christianity's "inherent rational superiority" over other religions, the answer must be that Christianity provided a better—comparatively better—answer to the urgent social and religious questions that the Indians were facing at that particular juncture in their cultural history. Of course, the questions as well as the answers varied from person to person, but for the sake of simplicity I refer only to social groups, such as bands, villages, or tribes.

In the English colonies, the most obvious examples of Christian success (from the missionary viewpoint) were the "praying towns" of eastern Massachusetts, founded almost single-handedly by John Eliot and Daniel Gookin.[4] Before King Philip's War largely nullified their efforts in 1675–76, they had founded 14 praying towns, 7 "old" and 7 "new," with a population of 1100 souls. Excluding the new towns (because they were founded too recently to bear spiritual fruit), the old towns totalled 500 persons, of whom about 125 were baptized and another 70 or so were in full communion.[5] This means that about 15 percent were full or "elect" members of the church, and nearly 40 percent belonged to the church as full members or as baptized "children," figures that compare favorably with the older church-oriented English towns of the Bay Colony.[6] Moreover, before the American Revolution, there were 22 Indian churches in New England, 91 praying towns or reservations, and 133 native preachers and teachers.[7] These statistics require an explanation, especially in light of the traditional historian's conclusion that the Christian program was a failure of the worst sort. Even from the missionary viewpoint, it cannot be said to constitute a failure; the numbers are too impressive.

I suggest that mission history simply adopt a good working principle from ethnohistory, namely that each side of the Christian curtain has to be viewed from its own perspective. Thus far, historians have judged the missionaries by the missionaries' criteria, but then have judged the Indians only from their *own* contemporary perspective as champions of the underdog, defenders of the weak, and protectors of the ethnic enclave. Of course, the Indians come off very badly indeed, as do the missionaries who started it all. But if we ask whether the *Indians,* from *their* point of view, were successful or not in adopting or adapting Christianity, I think we arrive at a somewhat different measure of success for the following reasons.

In large part the praying towns of New England were erected on or very near the natives' homeland; the natives did not wish, or were physically unable because of surrounding enemies, to go elsewhere to try to revitalize their culture. And disease, particularly the plague of 1616–19 and the smallpox epidemic of 1633, made it imperative to revitalize. The adult generations had been sharply reduced—in many of the coastal tribes by as much as 90 percent—and severe economic, social, and religious dislocation had set in, followed hard by political subjugation to the English. Reduced to begging in

English houses and menial servitude, the eastern bands of Massachusetts had no other alternative but to revitalize on the spot or to die as a people. So in large numbers, led in many cases by traditional leaders of the "blood," they converted to Christianity and the English way of life that accompanied it. Rather than achieving a nativistic revitalization at the hands of a charismatic prophet, they used the religion of Christ to the same end. Even though it entailed wholesale cultural changes from the life they had known before contact, it preserved their ethnic identity as particular Indian groups on familiar pieces of land that carried their inner history. At the cost of a certain amount of material and spiritual continuity with the past, their acceptance of Christianity—however complete or sincere—allowed them not only to survive in the present but gave them a long lease on life when many of their colonial landlords threatened to foreclose all future options. Ironically, the acute English sense of cultural superiority—which was colored by racism before the eighteenth century—helped the Indians to maintain the crucial ethnic core at the heart of their newly acquired Christian personae. In colonial eyes, they were still Indians and always would be, no matter how "civilized" or "Christian" they became.

The elemental fact of ethnic survival is all-important in assessing the success or failure of mission efforts from the native perspective. From an English or missionary perspective, the praying towns were quite successful, but not totally because the converts were still biologically Indians and never fully assimilated into English society. But from an Indian perspective, the towns were an equal if different kind of success because they ensured some future of native communities on home ground with native leaders. The more desperate the Indians' social-cultural situation (as in seaboard Massachusetts), the greater the possibility of physical annihilation of the group and thus the greater the efficacy of life-giving conversion and revitalization, which Anthony Wallace defines simply as "any conscious, organized effort by members of a society to construct a more satisfying culture."[8]

It would be easy—and foolish—to lament this particular revitalizing break with their pre-Columbian past as a tragic loss of innocence for the Indians. It was indeed a loss for them, but not necessarily a tragic one. Only if we continue to see the precontact Indian as the only real Indian, as the "noble savage" in other words, can we mourn his loss of innocence. Only if we persist in equating courage with mortal resistance to the forces of change can we condemn the praying Indians as cultural cop-outs or moral cowards. For life is preferable to death, and those who bend to live are also possessed of courage, the courage to change and to live in the face of overwhelming odds as well as the contempt of their brothers who died with stiff necks.

In *Death and Rebirth of the Seneca,* Wallace has shown how Christian missionaries helped to revitalize the Seneca—again on their own (albeit circumscribed) lands—in the early years of the nineteenth century.[9] Because this occurred two centuries after contact, we are apt to find the Senecas' adaptation of Christianity more acceptable to our view of the noble savage. After all, the Europeans polluted and corrupted them so much over 200 years that a European religion was scarcely all that could have saved them at that point. Yet only a romantic view of precontact innocence prevents us from seeing a much earlier acceptance of Christianity as morally acceptable. For traditional historians, looking over the missionaries' shoulders, the offer—or, as they would see it, imposition—of Christianity by the "invaders" is seen only as religious insult added to cultural injury. I suggest that we see it through Indian eyes as a powerful and effective new answer—however distasteful, grieving, or upsetting—to the urgent and mortal problems that faced them.

There is no doubt that English diseases, armies, attitudes,

rum, and land greed "reduced" the Indians of Anglo-America to "civility"—as the missionaries phrased it with unintended irony—in other words, presented the natives with a wholly new set of cultural problems and imperatives. But at the same time, the English, especially the subculture of missionaries and philanthropic laymen, offered their hapless "victims" a colonial Marshall Plan, an "Eliot Plan" if you will, for their moral rearmament, social reconstruction, and religious revitalization. If colonial racism, disease, lawlessness, and hypocrisy eventually spelled the demise of many Christian Indian groups—as they certainly did, Natick, Massachusetts, being a prime example—the *initial* effectiveness of the Christian mission program cannot be denied for those Indians faced with accommodation or annihilation.

But a second question suggests itself: Were all the Christian missions equally successful? How do the eighteenth-century missions in Maine, Connecticut, and New York stack up with the seventeenth-century Massachusetts praying towns? The key to the answer lies in the widespread colonial belief that "civility must precede Christianity," that is, the Indians must adopt an English lifestyle before they can be trusted with the Christian sacraments.[10] For the English this was not just an ideological statement but a statement of fact because the English Protestant version of Christianity was bound up with a version of English cultural style. For a variety of reasons having to do with national insecurity, the Reformation, and the nature of reform Protestantism, the English had translated many Biblical injunctions, once applicable only to the ancient Jews, into their own cultural imperatives and had thoroughly scripturalized other secular cultural habits.[11] It was therefore not possible to accept their brand of Christianity without the accompanying cultural baggage. Understandably, this made for an impossibly difficult standard of conversion (from the missionary perspective), to say nothing of the strictly religious requirements for church membership.

Despite these cultural difficulties, however, actually *because* of them, conversion was a tailor-made remedy for the Indian groups *most* endangered by the English presence, those closest to or surrounded by the colonial juggernaut. For these peoples, the Eliot Plan—as a complete social and cultural system—held out some hope of survival as Indian groups and some lease on the future, however uncertain.

But those tribes who could still put a piece of forest between themselves and the long arm of the invaders, those who escaped the worst maladies of European contact, had little need of the full "civilized" cure offered by the Christian doctors. To have accepted it would have brought on premature cultural suicide. But the complete prescription did contain some useful ingredients, such as political and military alliance, guaranteed land, economic aid, and trade advantage. If to obtain them the Indians had to swallow the bitter pill of religious conversion, the sacrifice was small enough, considering that Christianity might truly satisfy some new intellectual or emotional hunger. If there was none to be satisfied, the convert could simply, in time-honored Indian fashion, add the power of the Christian God to that of his own deities and proceed to syncretize the beliefs and practices of the new religion with the deep structures of his traditional faith. By accepting the Christian minister or priest as the functional equivalent of a native shaman and by giving traditional meanings to Christian rites, dogmas, and deities, the Indians ensured the survival of native culture by taking on the protective coloration of the invaders' religion. Obviously, this brand of Christianity often lay very lightly on the surface of their lives, its acceptance largely expedient to ensure their independence and group identity.

Since native needs varied from group to group over time, the success rates of the missions appear to vary as well. From the missionary perspective, this was no doubt true: Christian wares sold better in some places (Massachusetts and Martha's

Vineyard) than elsewhere (Ohio and Maine). But from the viewpoint of the Indians, the cultural customers, the Christian missions, it could be argued, were uniformly successful because the Indians used them to fulfill their needs in just the amounts necessary to maintain their cultural integrity and ensure their survival. The natives may have made individual or short-term miscalculations of their own best interest, white strength, and policy direction—no group is capable of a perfect functionalism—but in general they took what they needed for the resistance and accepted only as much as would prolong their existence and independence. On this scale, then, those who accepted only political alliance or economic aid from the missionaries, while paying lip service to their religion, were as successful as their more beleaguered brothers in Massachusetts who opted for the whole Eliot Plan.

At the same time, we are confronted by a double paradox. The first is that the missionaries were most successful when less benign elements of their "civilized" society had most decimated and endangered the very survival of the Indian groups being proselytized. In other words, the Eliot Plan sold best among the remnant brands of eastern Massachusetts staggering from twenty-five or thirty years of the colonial onslaught. The second paradox is that the Indians were most successful when they accepted the least amount of Christian "civility" or the most, that is, when their cultural resources and sovereignty were so unimpaired that they could refuse or pick and choose from the missionaries' offerings, or, at the other end of the scale, when their cultural and social needs were so great that they opted for the life of the group by forming a praying town, rather than splintering into vulnerable fragments or resorting to arms in a futile effort to stem the colonial tide.

But Indians, like their colonial neighbors, seldom acted in concert, either within villages or tribes. Indigenous factionalism can be explained by differing native perceptions of need and solution. Roughly speaking, when the members of a native group perceive the need for revitalization differently—some seeing no threat as yet, others more certain that change is needed—the time is ripe for the growth of traditionalist and Christian or pro-European factions. When the group as a whole perceives the need for revitalization but members differ on the best solution, the growth of nativistic, Protestant, and/or Catholic factions is likely. Of course, this scheme can become infinitely complex for any one group, as Robert Berkhofer has shown for the Senecas.[12] But in general, it has the virtue of placing the generation of native factions squarely in native culture, rather than assuming ethnocentrically that all Indian actions were simply passive reactions to European stimuli.

The general implication of all this is that we should begin to assess the intercultural contests in North America by two basically different criteria. As ethnohistorians we should no longer accept the Western assumption that one standard is sufficient for everyone, especially when so much of the contact in North America was competitive, if not overtly military. Therefore we should judge the European colonial cultures in *offensive* terms, as societies on the muscle. How well did they succeed in changing the native cultures to their cultural goals and style? How effective were they in persuading the natives to accept their offer of Christian "civility"? How successful were they in undermining native culture and institutions so as to create a crisis in which the natives would have to turn to their brand of cultural religion as a solution?

At the same time, however, we should judge the Indian cultures in *defensive* terms, largely because they were tolerant of other people and their religions and were, in fact, the targets of the European invasions. How well did they succeed in minimizing the impact of invasion, in maintaining their cultural vitality, integrity, and independence? How effective were they in accepting only as much of the Europeans' offerings as helped them to survive and prosper in their own terms? How successful were they in forestalling a crisis in which they might be forced to choose the Christian way as a solution?

As we ask these questions, we should remember that to be on the defensive does not imply the total loss of initiative. Although the Indians were incredibly tenacious of their culture and lifestyle, their traditionalism was neither blind nor passive. Like any good basketball team, they knew that sometimes the best defense is a good offense; witness their surprising capture, adoption, and conversion of hundreds of European colonists in wartime.[13] And as the history of the missions clearly shows, the native peoples of the eastern woodlands were equally resourceful in forging as well as adjusting to new conditions, especially in using elements of European religious culture for their own purposes and in designing alternatives to them.

By now it will be obvious that my suggestions rest on one large assumption, namely, that cultures should be free to define their own goals, set their own course, and to survive in any way they can—and that ethnohistorians should honor those rights in their scholarship as well as in everyday life. If one culture tries to infringe the rights of another, we are at least allowed, if not obligated, to condemn the practice. But we should first see how successfully the invaded group defended its own terrain and turned what may at first glance appear to be a social defeat into a cultural victory. In our histories as in our own world, underdogs often do need champions. But I suspect that they possess more cultural resources and stronger instincts and capacities for survival than even their friends have tended to allow.

CHAPTER FOUR

The Scholastic Frontier in Western Massachusetts

THE FOLLOWING ESSAY IS A TRUE SPIN-OFF FROM *The Invasion Within*. In 1985 *The Massachusetts Review* invited me to contribute an article to a special double issue they were planning on New England. Their nominee was "Dr. Wheelock and the Iroquois," an iconoclastic look at the fashionable myth that Dartmouth was founded as an "Indian college," which I had given at the Iroquois Conference in 1977 and at Dartmouth in 1978. But it had already appeared in *The European and the Indian* and in a festschrift for William Fenton, "Mr. Iroquois," and was about to reappear in a somewhat new guise in a chapter on English schools for Indians in *The Invasion Within*. The deadline they gave me was too short to write anything new, so I offered them another piece on New England from the same chapter. It was published in the summer of 1986 as "The Rise and Fall of the Stockbridge Indian Schools."

This little-known episode in the history of colonial education seems to me an apt symbol of the failure of the English to convert Indians over whom they did not have considerable political and economic power. It also documents the utopian foolishness of the English in believing that they could convert the relatively independent native peoples of western New England and eastern New York by sending their children to rigid and loveless English grammar schools.

THE GOAL OF THE ENGLISH MISSIONS IN NORTH AMERICA WAS to convert the Indians from a traditional to a totally new way of life and thought. No aspect of native life, no native person, was too small to ignore. Throughout the colonial period, missionaries tried to reach Indian children and adults at the same time. But when the English became frustrated in their attempts to convert native adults, their emphasis shifted perceptibly toward the young. This was a logical emphasis because from the beginning the English hoped to train native preachers, teachers, and interpreters to assume the task of converting their brethren to civility. The only feasible way to train this cadre of native agents was to catch Indian children early in their development, before the hereditary stain of "savagery" became indelible, and "bring them up English."

According to the book-learned ministers and officials who designed the missions, conversion was essentially a form of education—re-education—and education was something that transpired largely in formal institutions of learning. The best way, then, to "reduce" Indian children, primarily boys, to "civility" was to send them to English schools and colleges—sexually segregated, morally guarded, classically oriented, rigorously disciplined, patriarchally dominated and, until the eighteenth century, located in English territory, far from the contagion of traditional habits, families, and friends.

The English reliance on formal institutions was safe and convenient, but it failed to capture the imagination or the allegiance of the Indians. In stressing structure over example, compulsion over persuasion, duty over love, schools could never attain the influence wielded by charismatic missionaries living among the Indians. The English resort to schools constituted a surface attack on native habits, manners, and words, but not a deep thrust for conviction and loyalty. Schools touched the intellects of a few, but not the hearts of the many. Predictably, they failed.

One of the longest but least known experiments in native education in the eighteenth century was mounted in Stockbridge, Massachusetts, which lay astride a principal warpath from Canada. But a flawed design, the "prevalence of party," and English land hunger doomed it to mixed failure.

During the peaceful interlude between Queen Anne's and King George's War (as the English knew them), Massachusetts farmers and speculators received from the General Court and purchased from the Indians most of the southwestern corner of the colony. The native Housatonics, who had suffered severe depopulation from smallpox and had incorporated into their number many Mahicans from the upper Hudson Valley, retained four villages, the most important of which were Skatekook and Wnahktukook. But boundary disputes with New York and the presence of Dutch farmers in the Housatonic Valley forestalled extensive English settlement until after 1736, when the mission town of Stockbridge was laid out on six square miles at a bend in the river. To give the ninety Indian townsmen visible models of civilized piety and industry, the government encouraged four English families to join John Sergeant, the resident missionary, and Timothy Woodbridge, the Indian schoolmaster. Almost inevitably, the advent of English farmers, led by the ambitious Ephraim Williams, resulted in the alienation of the Indians' land, the frustration of designs for their education in "civilized" ways, and their eventual removal to New York.

Stockbridge was founded largely to assist the missionary labors of Woodbridge and Sergeant, who since 1734 had divided their attentions between the two main Indian villages. Sergeant, a small, energetic man with a keen mind, lively black eyes, and a withered left hand, had been plucked from a comfortable tutorship at Yale College to answer the Housatonics' call for Christian succor. Blessed with a "catholick temper" and a "guileless spirit," he sought to avoid partisanship of any kind and to befriend everyone, Indian and white.[1] When he married Abigail Williams, the accomplished young daughter of Ephraim, however, he allied himself with one of the colony's most powerful and clannish families, thereby inadvertently raising the devil for his native neophytes and his ministerial successor. Unlike his son-in-law, Williams kept a sharper eye on the Indians' soil than on their souls. From an initial homestead of 150 acres, situated symbolically on a proud eminence overlooking the native village along the river, Williams parlayed his position as town moderator and selectman into 1,500 acres by the time he left Stockbridge in 1753. Most of it was acquired after the 1744 separation of Indian and English precincts, in which the natives—for whom the town ostensibly was founded—received less than a third of its land.[2]

Despite the unsavory machinations of his father-in-law and his own post-marital move from a plain cottage among the Indians to an imposing Georgian pile on the hill, Sergeant seems to have maintained the trust and affection of his native congregation throughout his ministry. A major spring of their regard was his constant concern for their secular education as well as their spiritual welfare, which manifested itself even before he was ordained and installed as their missionary. When Sergeant was invited by the New England Company to assume the Housatonic post in September 1734, he wished to guide his senior class through commencement before leaving Yale. As a compromise, he visited the Housatonics for two months that fall, preaching and teaching with Woodbridge at a site midway between the two main villages. Returning to Yale in December, he was accompanied by two Indian boys, the eight-year-old son of "Lieutenant" Umpachenee, the headman of Skatekook, and the nine-year-old son of "Captain" Konkapot, the chief of Wnahktukook. Two years later these men would lead their tribesmen to Stockbridge and become its dominant Indian selectmen; although the Mahicans were matrilineal, Sergeant sought to equip their sons for future leadership roles by sending them to the New Haven free school. Living with Sergeant in college, these "very likely lads" learned English by day and taught an Indian dialect to their host by night. When their parents came to retrieve them in May, they must have been pleased to show off their new tongue, along with the college's library and "rareties." So promising was Konkapot's son that he was allowed to remain in school all summer, at the conclusion of which he had "learnt to speak and read English very well."[3]

After Sergeant settled among the Housatonics in July, he and Woodbridge both taught English and religion "in a catechetical way" to about forty children and a number of adults who wished to prepare for the brave new English world. As soon as the Indians moved to Stockbridge in 1736, however, the educational program received a tremendous boost from Isaac Hollis, a London clergyman whose recent inheritance allowed him to indulge his passion for missionary philanthropy. Hollis made a long-range commitment to underwrite the cost of lodging, diet, clothing, and tuition for twelve Indian boys. And about the same time another English benefactor contributed £100, which Sergeant earmarked for the domestic education of native girls.[4]

Within two years Sergeant had spent only £5 to board two young girls, one of them Konkapot's eldest daughter, with English families, because "thro' a childish fondness for home," as he called it, "they would not be contented to stay long enough where I sent them, to obtain any good by it."[5] The Hollis grant, on the other hand, helped to solve the serious problem of native absenteeism. For several weeks in late winter the Housatonics traditionally left Stockbridge and repaired in family groups to sugar camps in the bush to collect and boil down maple sap. In the summer similar migrations took them to planting grounds around their old villages or to work for Dutch farmers in New York. Hunting expeditions in the fall and late winter also removed children from school. The lack of continuity in their English lessons, the frequent and often lengthy intervals of traditional living and speaking, and the daily influence of Indian-speaking parents at home conspired to minimize the impact of Master Woodbridge. Hollis's benefaction made it possible for the English to tuck at least a dozen students firmly under their pedagogical wing for most of the year.

In January 1738 Sergeant took the twelve new Hollis scholars into his new bachelor's quarters, overseen by an Indian housekeeper, and began to instruct them in reading and writing. But the care and feeding of such a youthful horde severely taxed the preacher's domesticity, so after a year he placed them in English families, paying their living expenses from the Hollis fund while continuing to teach them. Those who could not or would not live with the English received only their clothes and were sent to the town school with Master Woodbridge. In the end, it was thought, "those who liv'd in English families made much the best progress in their learning, beside the benefit of gaining the English language."[6]

By 1741 Sergeant realized that the placement of Indian children in a variety of unsupervised English families might not improve the natives' moral or social fortunes as much as their language. In a letter to the Reverend Benjamin Colman of Boston, one of the commissioners of the New England Company and a staunch advocate of the Stockbridge mission, Sergeant proposed the establishment of a "Charity-House for the instruction of our Indian children, both boys and girls, in business and industry, as well as in reading and writing and matters of religion." Because such a plan would require the donation of two hundred acres of unappropriated Indian land, the missionary rightly "suppos'd the jealousies [suspicions] of the Indians would be a bar in the way," so for two years he kept it to himself. But by 1743 a "more than ordinary spirit of religion" appeared among his native congregation. Symptomatic (to Sergeant's thinking) was the personal request of two Stockbridge girls to be placed in English families to learn the English language and manners. As Sergeant explained to Colman in a letter that was soon published as a prospectus, his missionary goal was to change the Indians' "whole habit of thinking and acting," to "raise them as far as possible into the condition of a civil, industrious and polish'd people," to instill the "principles of virtue and piety," and "withal to introduce the English language among them instead of their own imperfect and barbarous dialect." For this he sought to build a boarding school, on the lines of an "Irish Charity School," to remove boys between ten and twenty years old from the corrupting example of their parents and friends. Under the direction of a study master and a work master, they would have their congenital "idleness," "vicious habits," and "foolish, barbarous and wicked customs" rooted out of them, the whole enterprise supported eventually by the profits from their own stock raising and farming.[7]

Hollis, of course, was enthusiastic about the scheme and doubled his support. But the public subscription launched by Colman was a limited success. A number of English dignitaries responded generously, but in the colony only ten English inhabitants of Stockbridge and Colman himself came forward with cash. Four American gentlemen subscribed but never paid, probably because the whole affair was thrown into doubt by the outbreak of King George's War in 1744. When that conflagration died on the frontiers four years later, Sergeant returned to the task. Hollis was champing to have his new donation spent specifically on twelve additional boys of "heathen parents, such as are not professors of Christianity," which effectively eliminated most of the local Housatonics. With Colman now dead, however, Boston was even cooler to the idea of supporting an expensive boarding school for distant and dangerous savages, and gave nothing. Only a testamentary bequest and two church collections in Connecticut raised enough money to enable Sergeant to complete the construction of his boarding school in the summer of 1749, days before he died of a nervous fever.[8] Although he had lived to see his educational dream materialize, death spared him the cruel sight of its misuse and eventual destruction at the hands of the master he had appointed and his own relatives.

Even before the frontiers were completely safe, however, the importunity of Isaac Hollis had persuaded Sergeant to send twelve boys of "heathenish" proclivities to the relative security of Newington, Connecticut, to be schooled for a year in civility by Martin Kellogg, a sixty-year-old army captain, farmer, and interpreter. When the boarding school was completed the following summer, Kellogg was persuaded to transfer the boys to Stockbridge and to assume their direction for another year. Had he lived through the summer, Sergeant also planned to visit the New York Mohawks in the company of Kellogg, who spoke their tongue after being twice captured by the Caughnawagas, to invite them to send children to the new Hollis school.[9] A number of Mohawk children—and their relatives—eventually moved to Stockbridge to board on the Hollis bounty, but the pedagogical incompetence of Kellogg and the internecine infighting of the English over the control of the town's various Indian schools soon drove them away.

At the unlikely center of this educational imbroglio was Abigail, the brilliant and beautiful widow of John Sergeant. In the eyes of her father, Ephraim Williams, her taking of a new husband would perpetuate the Williams dynasty in Stockbridge, particularly if the lucky man also happened to be Sergeant's successor as Indian missionary. Obligingly, Abigail cast her eye first on Ezra Stiles, a Yale tutor (as Sergeant had once been), though five years her junior, who proved acceptable to the Indians and the Williams side of the church. But Stiles had doubts about his own religious orthodoxy and

sensed that a hornet's nest of intrigue awaited him in Stockbridge. When he announced to Abigail his withdrawal from
ecclesiastical (and, by implication, marital) consideration in
the fall of 1750, her anguished response must have confirmed
the wisdom of his decision. She revealed that Deacon Woodbridge, a religious New Light, was pushing to have the Indian missionary post given to Jonathan Edwards, the brilliant
theologian who had recently been ousted from his Northampton pulpit by another branch of the Williams clan. Her father and Captain Kellogg, of course, were "very Bitterly
against" his appointment. But the crowning blow, she confessed, was that Woodbridge had told the Indians that "they
must not have a young man, [for] if they do he will likely
marry in to my fathers famely and then Be under his Direction."[10] Thanks to Stiles, and much to the chagrin of the Wil-
liamses, the elderly Edwards was duly installed nine months
later.

Frustrated in love, Abigail sought to build her own Indian
fiefdom by becoming mistress of the Indian girls' school,
which did not yet exist. Although various English benefactors had contributed toward the education of girls, little had
been done and their monies had been diverted. But in April
1750 her father had persuaded the General Court to spend
annually £150 for seven years to educate twelve Indian girls,
six Housatonics and six Mohawks, "according to the Plan of
the late Reverend Mr. Sargeant." Although another Williams
was to administer the funds, the legislators asked Colonel
Williams and Captain Kellogg for their opinion of the plan
and to inform the Mohawks, about twenty of whom had recently moved to Stockbridge at Sergeant's earlier invitation.[11]
Apparently, the colonel successfully presented his daughter's
credentials for the job. The following summer Elisha Williams, an American member of the London Board, persuaded
the New England Company to pay his cousin Abigail £30 a
year to serve as schoolmistress to not more than ten native

girls, each of whom would also be credited with £7.10s for clothes and lodging. An extra £10 was drafted to enable Mrs. Sergeant to put her already impressive house in order.[12] Clearly, a widow with three children could do worse than to set herself up in the Indian business.

Abigail did even better in 1752 when she married Joseph Dwight of Brookfield, a forty-nine-year-old politician, speculator, brigadier general, and recent widower. They had undoubtedly come to a meeting of minds during the previous winter, when Abigail took some of her Indian girls to Brookfield and put them out to service rather than teaching them herself. From then on the Dwights moved to monopolize Indian affairs in Stockbridge, with no little hope of personal profit. The general assumed charge of provincial affairs in the west, the Hollis foundation, and the business of the New England Company, bypassing Edwards, the Company's missionary, at every turn. Edwards could only conclude that the proud and domineering Abigail had twisted her courtly consort around her finger; nothing else seemed to explain the abrupt reversal of Dwight's lifelong admiration for Edwards.[13] It looked to Edwards as if the Williams clan was trying to duplicate its Northampton victory in Stockbridge. Although the stakes were much less theological, the aging missionary was determined not to lose another round. He unleashed the only weapon at his command—verifiable truth—in a barrage of letters to officials in London and Boston. In unambiguous detail, he described how the Dwight-Williams ring had wasted the Hollis fund, wrecked the promising Mohawk mission, and made a mockery of the girls' school.

The Dwights' interest in the Indian girls' school, Edwards revealed, was little more than a brazen attempt to pervert the public trust for personal profit. With funds and materials provided by the General Court, they proceeded to build a schoolhouse on the widow Sergeant's land, hoping eventually to sell the parcel to the province at a "high rate." In the mean-

time, two of their sons were maintained and educated at public expense, two daughters similarly enjoyed free rides in the
girls' school, a Dwight relative served as Abigail's usher, their
family servants were disguised as the school's workmen, and
the whole family eventually moved into the school, which
drove the remaining Mohawks straight back to New York.
Although Abigail did provide a certain amount of care to the
native girls, her three batches of children—his, hers, and
theirs—monopolized her time and energies, just as Edwards
warned the commissioners it would. And superintending all
of this chicanery was the province's resident trustee of Indian
affairs and two commissioners of the Boston Board—her husband, her father, and her cousin.[14]

The Hollis fund and boarding school were equally mismanaged, which in turn undermined the province's efforts to
secure the Mohawks' critical allegiance through education.
By the end of King George's War, if not long before, it became clear to New Englanders that their exposed northern
frontiers could not be guarded without the keen eyes and ears
of native allies, preferably those living in English territory.
The Mohawks fit the bill nicely because they enjoyed an en-
viable reputation for martial prowess, had relatives in Canadian *reserves* who might act as unwitting spies or refuse to
fight, could influence the other five nations of Iroquois to
sever their French connections or at least to remain neutral,
and were located nearby in eastern New York. If a substantial
number could be induced to relocate in Stockbridge, western
Massachusetts would have not only a mobile force of experienced guerilla warriors but a collection of young hostages to
ensure the right behavior of countrymen at home. In the
boarding school and the ample funds provided by Hollis and
the General Court, the material means existed to attract the
Mohawks to Stockbridge. All that remained was to give their
children an educational experience that did not alienate their
affections but also had some discernible payoff in improved

behavior and literacy. This the aggrandizing army of General Dwight, Colonel Williams, and Captain Kellogg could not provide, no matter how earnestly they sought the Mohawks' allegiance.

The heart of the matter was the indisputable incompetence of Kellogg. Even Sergeant who had appointed him recognized his mistake, but he died before he could find a suitable replacement. Since the new boarding school was largely finished, Kellogg returned the Hollis boys to Stockbridge and carried on there as best he could. His best was simply not good enough for the parents of the few boys who remained in his charge. Early in 1750 twenty Mohawks who had moved to town for the sake of their children's education left, complaining that the boys were "not cloathed so well as they are at home." Only a great deal of verbal and material persuasion by provincial agents brought the Mohawks back to Stockbridge. In October 1751 nearly a hundred arrived to settle on prepared farm land around the boarding school, partly on the strength of Kellogg's promise that he now had clothes in abundance. What he meant was that he had clothes and room for twenty-four boys on the Hollis fund but not for the other Mohawk children, who numbered thirty-six by January. When the provincial committee asked him to take all of the Mohawk boys until a separate schoolhouse could be built, he refused, saying "he was Independent in his School, and inclined to keep it separately," conveniently forgetting that "his" school was built partly with government funds. Accordingly, Benjamin Ashley, Kellogg's assistant and brother-in-law, was ordered to teach the other boys.[15]

After watching Kellogg rapidly alienate the Iroquois, Edwards could hold his peace no longer. Speaking for the vast majority of Indian and English townsmen as well, he penned a series of frank letters to Hollis and various Boston officials exposing Kellogg's utter unfitness. First, as even the long-house-dwelling Indians noticed, the boarding school was in a "miserable state"—unfinished, too small, and ill-equipped. Ceilings in two of the five rooms and a staircase were missing, as were adequate beds, writing tables, benches, and bedclothes. Still worse was Kellogg's care and government of the boys. Although he drew full pay from the Hollis fund for two years, he never made an accounting of his expenditures to Hollis or to Dwight, apparently with good reason, for the boys were poorly "dieted" and their clothes cost "but a trifle." Furthermore, he spent a third of the year away from school pursuing more pressing "avocations," which was perhaps just as well because when he was present his teaching and discipline left much to be desired. Barely literate himself, Kellogg managed to teach only mindless memorization. The children merely learned to attach sounds to clusters of marks "but know not *the meaning* of the words," said Edwards, "and so have neither profit nor pleasure in reading, and will therefore be apt soon to lose even what they have learned." And even though the Mohawks gave their children over for English-style "Correction & Discipline" as well as instruction, Kellogg's scholars made "no progress in civility & vertue," the townsmen accused, "but have rather declin'd, living an idle life, and much without government." Understandably, parents complained loudly of the "increase of unrulyness & disorder in their children" and would have withdrawn them and moved from Stockbridge altogether had Edwards, at the request of the Boston Commissioners, not hired in February 1752 an able master to teach the Iroquois not enrolled in the Hollis school.[16]

The new master, Gideon Hawley, was a twenty-four-year-old Yale graduate with a "happy talent in teaching" and a "good spirit of government." Within weeks of his arrival he was diligently teaching the colonial 3Rs to about thirty-six pupils, several of them lured away from Kellogg. In addition, he was learning an Iroquois tongue (Mohawk or Oneida) and teaching it to a couple of English boys whom the province had placed in the school to prepare for future work as missionaries or interpreters. Perhaps most pleasing to the Iroquois parents, who "strengthen[ed] his hands" whenever possible, was his regulation of the children's "manners" and establishment of "good order."[17]

The advent of a successful rival soon drove Kellogg, Williams, and Dwight to distraction. Not only had their nemesis Edwards made the appointment, but Benjamin Ashley had been permanently assigned to Hawley as an assistant master and all three had advised the Iroquois in an open meeting to remove their children from the captain's ill-run school, which seven of them promptly did. With only a handful of students left, Kellogg took to coming into Hawley's school and acting as though the boys were his. In his most imperious manner Dwight did the same thing, sometimes removing boys for several days to teach himself. Since the Indians disliked a man of his "sovereign & forbidding aers," they were especially disgusted by his treatment of their young master after Hawley had castigated a Williams associate for coming into his school and caning one of his students, the son of an Oneida chief, without just cause. In response, Dwight flew into Hawley's classroom and, before the alarmed children, berated him for a full three hours. Some of his anger was undoubtedly stoked by the frustration of having watched Hawley appointed just days before he could intrude his own son Henry, a Harvard student, into the school. For the next several months the general kept threatening to underwrite a rival school with Kellogg as steward and young Henry as master, a threat which came to naught. For his part, Ephraim Williams made the most manic gesture of all. One October morning, in an effort to undercut Edwards's base of local support, he literally tried, cash in hand, to buy out every English farmer in Stockbridge. Needless to say, he too failed and was soon laughed out of town.[18]

The Williams family's search for autocracy in Stockbridge

Indian affairs died in one final act of desperation in 1753, shortly before the colonel moved to Deerfield. After the boarding school had been sufficiently repaired, Hawley had moved in in the fall of 1752 to be near his young linguistic informants. On a bitter New England day in the following February, the school, "in a way unknown, took fire, and was reduced to ashes," along with Hawley's furniture, books, and clothing. Hawley had no doubts that the school had been fired "by design"—and not by the faction adhering to Edwards and Woodbridge. Early in April two-thirds of the Mohawks returned to New York, thoroughly disenchanted with Dwight's stonewalling techniques and the nasty turn of events in the life of their school; the rest followed a year later, ironically, only two weeks after Edwards had been given complete control over the town's Indian affairs. On April 9, 1754, eight days before the Seven Years' War effectively began at the forks of the Ohio, the General Court wrote the epitaph to their long, frustrating experiment in native education by referring to the "late Mohawk School at Stockbridge."[19]

CHAPTER FIVE

White Legend:
The Jesuit Missions
in Maryland

THE BIGGEST SURPRISE I RECEIVED IN RESEARCHING *The Invasion Within* was to learn that, deprecating Puritan opinion notwithstanding, the Jesuits of New France were the best prepared, most adaptable, and most successful missionaries in eastern North America. They clearly outshone their English Protestant rivals and their Catholic rivals in Canada and Louisiana. I was therefore interested in comparing them with their English brethren in Maryland, about whom precious little had been written.

I soon discovered why when I wrote the essay that follows for delivery at a conference on "Maryland: A Product of Two Worlds," held in St. Mary's City in May 1984. Simply put, the English Black Robes left a paucity of documentation on their short-lived and ill-fated activities in the New World. Even the newly catalogued archives of the *Propaganda Fide* in the Vatican produced little new information. It therefore happens that the most interesting aspect of the Maryland story is the sharp contrast it offers with the Jesuit experience in Canada, where superior numbers, wealth, and skills brought them thousands of *bona fide* converts before 1763.

"White Legend" was published in the *Maryland Historical Magazine* in the spring issue of 1986.

THE HISTORY OF JESUIT MISSIONS TO THE INDIANS IN COLONIAL Maryland is quickly told and, it must be said, merits little space in the history of the colony or of English colonization in general. Even in the larger history of the Society of Jesus it warrants only a small footnote and, given the amount of documentation we have, perhaps an even smaller one in the ethnohistory of the coastal Algonquians. But it is not totally without interest, particularly when we compare it with the longer and more remarkable experience of the Jesuits in New France. The strong contrasts in personnel, means, and results between the English Jesuits in Maryland and their French confrères in Canada do much to illuminate the history of both.

The *Ark* and the *Dove* were carrying two Jesuit priests and a lay brother when they tacked up the Potomac in the early spring of 1634. Another priest and brother followed close behind to help begin the hopeful work of inducing the natives of Maryland to "civility," seducing them to Christianity, and reducing them to allegiance to the English crown.

The Black Robes played a not unimportant and altogether characteristic role in the opening scenes of settlement. After erecting a cross on Blakiston's Island to take "solemn possession of the Country," the Jesuits—probably Father Andrew White, at fifty-five one of Leonard Calvert's wisest heads—advised the governor to confer with the "emperour" or tayac of the Piscataways, the Indian overlord of the region, before striking settlement. So a party set off in a pinnace to pay a courtesy call some 120 miles upriver. One reason for the small size of the delegation was to allay the fears of the natives all along the river, who had been told by William Claiborne, a Virginia councillor with a fur trade empire on the upper Chesapeake, that the Spanish were coming with six ships to destroy them all and possess their country. While it was politically astute, White's tactic was also consonant with

Loyola's *Constitutions* for the Jesuit order, which instructed missionaries to begin their labors with "important and public persons" whose conversion would "spread the good accomplished to many others who are under their influence or take guidance from them."[1]

On their way to Piscataway, the party called on the acting headman at "Patomecke town," where Father John Altham lectured the man on some of the many errors in native religion. According to the Jesuits, the werowance "seemed well pleased" with his first lesson in Christian etiquette, perhaps because it was subtly modified by their indispensable but untrustworthy Protestant interpreter from Virginia. The response of Wannas, the tayac of Piscataway, was slightly less encouraging. When Calvert asked permission to settle within the tayac's domain, the Indian allowed "that he would not bid him goe, neither would hee bid him stay, but that he might use his owne discretion." Again, the tayac's words may have lost something in the translation. The interpreter Calvert found at Piscataway was Captain Henry Fleet, a sometime associate of Claiborne and a former captive "excellent in language, love, and experience with the Indians." As a Virginian and a fur trader, he was disposed no more than Claiborne to encourage the invasion of his commercial turf by rival Englishmen, no matter how well connected in Court circles they might be.[2]

To remove the interlopers from his best source of furs, Fleet cagily persuaded them to settle far downriver at what became St. Mary's. There Calvert "bought" some thirty miles of ground and a village from the Yoacomacoes, the local natives, for axes, knives, hatchets, hoes, and cloth. Though the English were grateful for the "miracle" of getting temporary housing, land, and cleared fields for what they considered a "trifle," it was actually the Indians who made out like bandits. For a trove of valuable trade goods, they gave up an old village that the previous year they had decided to abandon to escape the raids of the Susquehannocks, a fierce tribe living at the head of the Delmarva Peninsula. Thus an Algonquian longhouse came to be the Jesuits' first residence in Maryland.[3]

The settlers' initial good fortune in avoiding conflict with the Indians owed less to the ethnographic sensitivity of the Jesuits than to three preconditions over which the settlers had no control. The first was the widespread fear among the region's inhabitants of Susquehannock attacks, which caused the natives to welcome the well-armed colonists as potential allies and protectors. Secondly, having been introduced to the cloth and metal trade goods of the Virginia traders, the Indians welcomed the Marylanders as future and more reliable sources of the same. According to Father White, the natives "exceedingly desire[d] civill life and Christian apparrell." The tayac of Piscataway wanted an English house built for him, and the chiefs of Patuxent and Portobacco affected English clothes and wanted some of their children to be educated at St. Mary's, no doubt to cement their new commercial alliance in traditional native fashion. While the Indians were familiar with some aspects of English material culture, they were more deferential toward Calvert's crew because of larger products of their technology, namely huge floating "islands" that obviously were not made of one piece like the natives' dug-out canoes, and heavy cannon at whose thunderous roar the natives "trembled." As in Canada, the natives' initial awe of European technology went some way toward gaining receptive audiences for the missionary message.[4]

But for nearly five years the message was not delivered. Part of the problem was personnel. By 1638 the Jesuits numbered only four priests and a lay brother. At least as many had come and gone after short stays, and two other Black Robes had succumbed to yellow fever in the late summer of 1637. A larger problem was their deployment. Governor Calvert and probably Provincial Secretary John Lewger prevented the Jesuits from living among the Indians ostensibly because of fear of sickness and native hostility; an English trader had recently been killed and a general "conspiracy" against the English seemed to be brewing. Moreover, there was more than enough to do around St. Mary's. Catholic settlers needed spiritual sustenance, and the large number of Protestants who arrived in 1638 needed to be saved from heresy, as they all were, along with several servants and craftsmen hired in Virginia. The Jesuits' only preparation for Indian missions took place between weekly catechism and feast day sermons to the colonists when a few of the priests put their tongues to school in the native dialect. But without immersing themselves in the living language of an Indian village, progress was extremely slow and awkward.[5]

The following year they got their first chance to exercise their evangelical talents upon native souls. When the Indian "conspiracy" failed to materialize, all the Jesuits but one moved out of St. Mary's to carry the Gospel into the enemy camp. Ferdinand Poulton, the new superior, and a lay brother maintained the mission "storehouse" and fields at Mattapany, a plantation across the peninsula near the mouth of the Patuxent River given by Maquacomen, the "king" of the Patuxents. Father Altham lived sixty miles away on Claiborne's Kent Island, to which large numbers of Indians from the north and west resorted to trade. And Father White was well accepted by Kittamaquuund, who had assassinated his older brother Wannas to become tayac of the Piscataways. White had first attempted to work with the more proximate Patuxents, and had succeeded well enough to be given the Mattapany farm for the Society. But for some reason the chief's initial ardor for the English had cooled, and Calvert removed Father White to avoid having him held hostage in the event of war.[6]

Kittamaquuund would have Father White live no where else but in his own lodge, where the priest was plied with cornbread and meat by the tayac's wife. Part of the reason for Kit-

tamaquund's affection was his need for English support
against tribesmen who resented his bloody usurpation of
office. Another reason was two dreams or visions he and his
late brother had had, which featured Fathers White and
Altham, the governor, and a beautiful god of unimaginable
whiteness "who gently beckoned the Emperor to him." After
his dream Wannas called Father White "his parent," perhaps
adopting him in the process, and tried to give the Jesuits his
much-loved son to educate for seven years. Father White
gained even more influence over Kittamaquund when the
latter fell extremely ill and the ministrations of forty shamans
brought no relief. When the Indian fully recovered after
White bled him and administered a concoction of herbal
powder and holy water, he resolved as soon as possible to lead
his family into the Christian fold.[7]

While Father White instructed the royal family in the precepts of Roman Catholicism, Kittamaquund began to reform
"the errors of their former life" in accordance with the priests'
cultural and religious expectations. He exchanged his skin
garments for clothes made in the English fashion, and made
some effort to learn the English language. He also moved to
monogamy by discarding what the Jesuits called his "concubines" and living contentedly with one wife. Delighting in religious conversation and prayer, he abstained from eating meat
on fast days, and even told Governor Calvert, who was trying
to sell him on the value of a healthy fur trade, that he esteemed earthly wealth "as nothing" compared with the riches
of heaven. From the Jesuit point of view, the tayac's most significant act was to abjure before a large assembly of the confederacy the stone, herb, and other amulets that the natives
traditionally "idolized" in favor of the one true Christian
God. After such a hopeful sign, the priests were convinced
that after the baptism of his family the conversion of "the
whole empire" would "speedily take place."[8]

While their hope was never realized, it was not misplaced.

The following summer (1640) the tayac, his wife, their infant daughter, a leading councillor, and his little son were washed in the holy waters of baptism in a bark chapel constructed for the occasion. Surprisingly, the reborn were given common English names rather than appropriate names of saints or biblical characters. To celebrate the importance of the first native baptisms in Maryland, the governor, his secretary, and many other English notables attended and shouldered a great wooden cross in procession. Unfortunately, the weight of the occasion soon fell on two of the priests. In performing the long ceremony of baptism in the mid-summer sun, Father White contracted a chilling fever that sent him to St. Mary's and plagued him off and on for nearly a year. Father John Gravener developed a severe foot problem and could not walk; when he recovered, he died of an abscess in a matter of days.[9]

The hand of death lay on the new mission throughout the winter. An extreme drought the previous summer spread famine among the Piscataways. Though the Jesuits were sorely pinched themselves, their farm at Mattapany having been confiscated for constitutional reasons by Lord Baltimore, they considered it necessary to succor the Indians' bodies with cornbread lest they lose their souls. Father White had a relapse when he returned to Piscataway in February, which put the mission in danger of losing its best linguist. The tayac was not as fortunate. Perhaps weakened by the famine, he died in early March, before the new year's crops could even be planted.[10]

The prospects for the Maryland mission seemed so dim that Father Poulton had to pull out all stops to convince some of his superiors not to dissolve it. Apparently they were affected by his heartfelt preference to "die lying on the bare ground under the open sky, than even once to think of abandoning this holy work of God through any fear of privation," but not enough to send reinforcements. Even a petition from "the Catholics of Maryland" asking for a dozen priests and a prefect received no action until Father Poulton was accidentally shot in July 1641 and a single priest was sent to replace him at year's end. The plea of the chief of the Anacostans to have a Black Robe live in his village near the present site of Washington, D.C. was a sad impossibility with only three priests. The missionaries rightly felt that it was "not right to be too anxious" to bring others into the fold lest they seem to abandon prematurely their "present tender flock."[11]

Unable with only three priests to maintain permanent missions in key native villages, the Jesuits after 1641 were forced to mount a series of flying "excursions" in search of souls. With only a servant and an interpreter, a priest would row a pinnace upriver to the Indians, camping ashore in a tent and living off wild game and a few staples carried in one of four small chests. At the targeted village, the priest erected an altar from a slab of wood he carried and dressed it with sacred vessels from one chest and bottles of baptismal water and sacramental wine from another. To attract an audience, he distributed gifts from the third chest, such as hawk's bells, combs, knives, and—with appropriate symbolism—fishhooks.[12]

Then he catechized the listeners and conducted mass through the interpreter, for none of the Jesuits had mastered the native dialect sufficiently to discuss the mysteries of Christianity. For that matter, neither had the young interpreter— there seems to have been only one; even his employers admitted that he sometimes reduced the Indians to laughter with his strange accent and flawed grammar. Father White eventually wrote a native dictionary and grammar, but there is no evidence that he was ever fluent. The best linguist seems to have been Roger Rigby, Father Poulton's replacement. Despite a three-month bout with fever, the 34-year-old Rigby, who had been considered an excellent student by his superiors, was reported in early 1643 to be making good progress toward "ordinary" conversation with the Patuxents and had composed a short catechism with the help of the interpreter.[13]

The language barrier was not insurmountable, to judge by the number of Indian converts. In 1642 the missionaries added to their growing register of baptisms the headmen and chief councillors of several villages along the Patuxent and upper Potomac. Susquehannock raids kept the priests away from Piscataway, but most of the residents of Portobacco received the holy waters. In all, more than 130 pagans were added to the Church, which is the more remarkable because, like their Canadian brethren, the Maryland Jesuits administered baptism to healthy adults only after considerable instruction and testing in the doctrinal elements of the Faith. Their fear of apostasy was stronger than their desire for converts.[14]

Catholic ceremonialism undoubtedly helped to bridge the cultural gap when language was inadequate, as did political and economic self-interest. And the Jesuits' "shamanic" power to cure did its part to supplant the native priesthood. The day after Father White took from his necklace a piece of the original cross, applied it to a deadly arrow wound in the side of an Anacosta warrior, and recited the Gospel prayer for the sick and the litanies of the Blessed Virgin from the Holy House of Loretto, the man was briskly paddling a canoe with only a small red spot to show for his pains. In gratitude, he soon joined the ranks of the native converts who had prayed for his deliverance.[15]

We would like to know what happened during the next two years, but the annual reports to London and Rome apparently did not survive. We do know that two young priests of mediocre talent arrived early in 1643, and that some thought was given to sending missions into "Virginia" and "New England," the ill-defined territory south and north of the "island" of Maryland (as the *Propaganda Fide* still called it in the eighteenth century).[16] But as for the number and behavior of Indian converts, we are completely at sea—with one prominent exception: the seven-year-old daughter of Kittamaquund. Shortly before her father died in 1641, she was brought to St. Mary's, baptized 'Mary,' and placed under the gentle guardianship of Margaret Brent, a pious and wealthy Catholic lady. In an imposing brick house pitched on a hill called "the Lyon of Jude," the "Empress" of the Piscataways acquired the best of English manners, dress, and speech. She must have learned quickly and well; before she reached the age of consent, she had turned the head of Giles Brent, her guardian's brother, and married him. When the shockwaves of the English Civil War washed over Maryland, the Brents moved across the Potomac to northern Virginia, where they raised a numerous brood of *métis* children. Although by her marriage Mary had abdicated any claim to Piscataway land or office, a Virginia gentleman married her eldest daughter with one eye on her supposed "inheritance." He was as disappointed as Giles had once been in the quest for a huge chunk of Maryland, and "parted civilly" from her when his jig was up. Such a lesson must have completed Mary's education in the finer points of English "civilization."[17]

Whatever happened after 1642, the Jesuit mission to the Indians came to an ignominious end in 1645 when Virginia Protestants invaded the colony and turned out the Calverts. Fathers White and Copley were packed off to England in chains, where they spent three years in prison. Their three younger colleagues were taken to Virginia, where a year later they all died of unspecified causes; their superiors had no doubts that the cause was the murderous "cruelty of heretics."[18]

Obviously, the truncated mission was not able to accomplish much in only eleven years, particularly when the first five years were needed to launch it and the restored Jesuits were never numerous or interested enough to renew it. Compared to the Canadian missions, which were nearly contemporaneous, the effort in Maryland was modest indeed. By 1643 the French Jesuits had baptized some 2700 natives, a third of them at death; the English Jesuits in Maryland had baptized fewer than 150.[19] Why were the results so modest? The answer, I suggest, lies in personnel and resources.

In the eleven years after 1632, the year in which New France was restored by the English, the French provincial sent to Canada 40 priests and 13 lay brothers—53 highly educated masters of philosophy, divinity, and rhetoric, men of robust constitution and iron will, the cream of Europe's intellectual class. The embattled English province, which needed the best of its 338 members to serve the houses and clandestine chapels of the Catholic gentry, sent only 11 priests and 3 brothers in the same period, four of whom stayed very briefly. Eight of the remaining ten died by 1646, at an average age of 41. The brittle cold of Canada's snowy forests was clearly healthier for missionaries than the steamy heat and fever-ridden damp of the Chesapeake; only three French missionaries died in Canada before 1643, and only one of those from natural causes. Thus the Maryland mission never had more than five workers at one time; New France always had twenty to thirty.[20]

The contrast in material resources was equally stark. Maryland's Jesuits were doing moderately well until Lord Baltimore decided that the Jesuits could receive land only from himself, not from grateful Indians, and confiscated the mission "storehouse" at Mattapany. The drastically reduced acreage they were eventually granted elsewhere was never sufficient to their needs, which included numerous gifts and food for their native audiences. The Catholic population of the colony was too small and too poor to make up the difference in alms, and wealthy English benefactors were few if any. The most reliable supply came from trade with the Indians, with whom the Jesuits—through two agents—were al-

lowed to barter in the absence of currency and as long as they
paid Baltimore one-tenth of all beaver for the privilege.
When funds ran dry, they had to depend on loans or gifts
from their English provincial.[21]

By contrast, the French missions were comparatively flush.
The first two French estates liberally subsidized the Canadian
missions, inspired often by pleas from the field published annually in the Jesuit *Relations*. The Society also received rich
endowments of land at home and in seigneury along the St.
Lawrence, and later annual subventions from the king. And
like their southern brothers, the Jesuits of Canada dealt in
Indian furs, but mostly as gifts from generous neophytes who
also wished to decorate the mission churches in Baroque
splendor. Maryland had no mission churches and certainly
no Baroque splendor.[22]

One final contrast between the Canadian and Maryland
Jesuits is suggested by the great differences in their long-term
results. To this day, the vast majority of Algonquian and Iroquoian peoples converted by the French missionaries have
retained their Catholicism, despite numerous attempts by
traditionalists and Protestant preachers to effect a change.
With the premature withdrawal of the Jesuits in Maryland,
however, the Piscataways had little way to maintain their new
faith and perhaps less need. As James Merrell has shown, the
Piscataways were able to avoid the brunt of English colonization for so long that accommodations with the new order
could be made largely on their own terms in their own time.
Although they were tributaries of the Maryland government,
this critical distance allowed them to chart their own course
for most of the seventeenth century, and Christianity was simply not on the itinerary.[23]

It may be hazarded that one reason for these contrasting
results was a relatively minor but still significant difference
in the length and quality of catechizing required for baptism
and church membership. Two pieces of evidence speak to the

point. First, Father White instructed Kittamaquund, the crucial first neophyte of the new mission, for little more than a year to prepare him for baptism. In Canada the French Jesuits would not admit their first important candidate to the sacrament for more than three years of extremely rigorous testing.[24] A second suggestion that the admission standards of the English may have been somewhat low is the admittedly hostile observation of a Puritan minister detained in Maryland by contrary winds. When Thomas James landed in 1643, he saw "forty Indians baptized in new shirts, which the Catholics had given them for their encouragement unto baptism. But he tarried there so long for a fair wind," wrote his correspondent John Cotton, "that before his departure, he saw the Indians (when their shirts were foul, and they knew not how to wash them) come again to make a new motion, either the Catholic English there must give them new shirts, or else they would renounce their baptism." Canadian converts also received gifts to commemorate their baptism or first communion, but after their long immersion in the Faith they would never mistake them for bribes or pledges of sincerity.[25]

A second, and I believe more important, reason for the French superiority as missionaries was their superior knowledge of Indian culture and mastery of native protocol. With the possible partial exception of Father White, the Maryland Jesuits never got inside native culture far enough to be accepted as bona fide members, the social and spiritual equivalent of the shamans they were trying to supplant. Such penetration was simply impossible because the English never became fluent in the native language or lived in native villages long enough to be adopted, given Indian names, or accepted as "men of sense." Their French brothers did, and reaped a rich harvest of souls as a result.[26]

CHAPTER SIX

The Power of Print in the Eastern Woodlands

ONE OF THE FRENCH JESUITS' KEYS TO EVANGELICAL SUCCESS WAS their early appreciation that the natives, members of an oral culture, were extremely impressed by printed books and the Europeans' ability to read and write. They quickly turned this phenomenon to their advantage by awing the Indians with their "shamanic" powers to "read minds at a distance." Since natives all over the eastern woodlands were initially impressed by literacy, books, and writing, I wondered why the English missionaries had not been able to capitalize on the natives' astonishment to the same degree. "The Power of Print" was the result.

The French material had been discussed in *The Invasion Within* in the context of Jesuit methods of conversion, but the English and Indian data were largely new. In the fall of 1985 I vetted a version before the Iroquois Conference, an Institute of Early American History and Culture colloquium, and the annual meeting of the American Society for Ethnohistory in Chicago. It was published in the *William and Mary Quarterly* in April 1987.

Since the late 1960s I have been interested in the contrast between oral and print cultures and in the origins of literacy in Classical Europe. It is pleasing to think that the following essay adds at least a footnote to the exciting work of Marshall McLuhan, Walter Ong, Eric Havelock, Elizabeth Eisenstein, Jack Goody, Natalie Davis, Harvey Graff, and David Hall. Much more, of course, needs to be done on the nature of Indian orality and the cultural and mental changes attendant upon the natives' transition to various degrees of literacy.

I T WAS NOT LOST ON THE IMPERIAL RIVALS FOR NORTH AMERICA that whoever solved their "Indian problem" first stood the best chance of winning the continent. Early in the colonization of eastern America, therefore, the French and the English each enlisted black-robed missionaries, as well as honey-tongued traders and hardened soldiers, to compete for native souls, land, pelts, and allegiance. The French began by recruiting the Recollects, a mendicant Franciscan order, in 1615. But poverty, lack of manpower, and an obdurate philosophy of "civilizing" before Christianizing hamstrung the friars and led them to call for Jesuit assistance ten years later.

The Jesuits, by contrast, were numerous, financially well-endowed, highly educated, and culturally flexible. By 1640 they realized that the attempt to turn Canada's Indians into sedentary farmers was not only impossible but foolish in a colonial society whose lifeblood was the furs trapped, processed, and transported by native hunters. So they adopted a philosophy that subordinated cultural change to religious conversion and set out to win the confidence of the natives. While their Protestant counterparts suffered from the general reputation of Englishmen as land-grabbers, remained tied to their colonial congregations, and refused to budge from their civilizing priorities, the Jesuits fanned across Canada, Acadia, and later Louisiana in search of converts and, thereby, trading partners and military allies for New France. Without condemning everything native as deficient or sinful, they insinuated themselves into native life in hopes of supplanting traditional shamans as spiritual counselors to people who seldom distinguished the religious from the secular. When they succeeded, they either converted large portions of tribes and villages to Catholicism, often through leading families and headmen, or gathered their neophytes into one of seven *reserves* along the St. Lawrence. Until the Seven Years' War, which opened a much larger theater of combat, it was these faithful guerilla fighters who often maintained the military balance between the tiny French colony and the prolific English colonies to the south.[1]

By contrast with the tens of thousands of Jesuit converts, only some of whom died shortly after baptism, English Protestant missionaries were singularly unsuccessful outside of southern New England. There, by 1674, John Eliot, the Mayhews, and a number of colleagues had gathered some twenty-three hundred "Souls yielding obedience to the gospel" from local tribes that had been battered by disease, frightened by English power and population, and increasingly deprived of their land by fair means and foul. Perhaps three or four hundred of these "praying Indians" had been baptized or admitted to full membership in highly selective Indian churches, having been nurtured on the Bible and other devotional works translated into an Algonquian dialect. But in the other colonies missionary efforts had been halfhearted, nonexistent, or frustrated by colonial injustices that had pushed the natives into sullen resistance, open rebellion, or exile. Beyond any doubt in the minds of English or French observers, the French had won the contest for converts in North America.[2]

While the Jesuit missionaries enjoyed many advantages over their Protestant rivals, the major key to their success was something they shared with the English—their ability to read and write, and their possession of printed books. The Jesuits' use of literacy did not by itself secure the natives' conversion, but it allowed the Black Robes to get a foot in the native door faster and much farther than the Protestants ever did. That edge contributed in no small way to the decisive Jesuit superiority in the European search for American souls and allies.

The first European to describe the Indians' reaction to the printed word was not a Jesuit but Thomas Harriot, the ethnological expert aboard the second Roanoke voyage in 1585. The natives of coastal North Carolina, he noticed, were dazzled by the products of European technology, such as the sea compass, the telescope, clocks, guns, and, not least, books. These artifacts the Indians thought were "rather the works of gods then of men," or at least had been given to the English by the gods. When Harriot sought to catechize the natives on the central tenets of Christianity, he felt that he was given "greater credite" for religious wisdom because of his possession of such minor miracles of technology. The Indians' reaction to his printed Bible was especially noteworthy. Although Harriot tried to tell them that "the booke materially & of it self was not of anie such vertue . . . but onely the doctrine therein contained," many of them were "glad to touch it, to embrace it, to kisse it, to hold it to their brests and heades, and stroke over all their bodie with it."[3]

The natives of southern New England were also impressed with the invaders' products. Roger Williams, who lived among the Narragansetts for many years after his exile from Massachusetts, noted in 1643 that "when they talke amongst themselves of the *English* ships, and great buildings, of the plowing of their Fields, and especially of Bookes and Letters, they will end thus: *Manittôwock* They are Gods."[4] Since Williams was unwilling to convert Indians until he had received a divine appointment to an apostolic ministry, however, he never discovered how his possession of books and literacy might have furthered his missionary efforts.

Catholic missionaries, on the other hand, were able to observe the natives' unacculturated responses to writing and print in numerous situations as they spread across New France. When Gabriel Sagard, a Recollect priest, ministered to the Hurons in 1624–1625, the Indians would have spent "whole days and nights," if allowed, counting the pages of the

French books and admiring the pictures in them. Such frequent handling of the books, Sagard complained, "which they constantly were asking to look at, one after another, especially the Bible on account of its size and illustrations, ruined them and reduced them to tatters."[5]

Sagard was much happier about the Hurons' reaction to writing. On his way back to Quebec, when he and his Huron companions discovered that one of their canoes was leaky, he sent a note to his colleague back in the village asking him to send a fresh canoe. "When our canoe arrived," Sagard remembered, "I cannot express the admiration displayed by the natives for the little note I had sent to Father Nicolas. They said that that little paper had spoken to my brother and had told him all the words I had uttered to them here, and that we were greater than all mankind. They told the story to all, and were filled with astonishment and admiration at this mystery." As soon as Sagard reached Quebec, he turned the Hurons' admiration to practical advantage. When he sent a package of necessities (including edible communion wafers) to Father Nicolas, he attached a note telling the canoemen that "if they did any harm to these things the little paper would accuse them." The package arrived safely and unopened.[6]

When the Jesuits followed the Recollects to Canada in 1625, they inherited the natives' respect for writing and the writer's mantle of spiritual power. As elsewhere in the eastern woodlands, the natives in New France seemed to worship the written word upon first acquaintance as a kind of talisman or amulet. One Algonquin neophyte of the Jesuits was so taken with the litanies he had heard sung at Quebec that he asked for them in writing, although he could not read. The Jesuits obliged him with a selection of verses on a piece of paper. When he returned home, "he assembled his neighbors every day in a large cabin, hung this paper to a pole, and all stood around it, singing what they knew of these Litanies." Later in the year, when he went into the woods to hunt, he took the paper and offered it to God in lieu of the Christian prayers he had not yet memorized. He and his people enjoyed an abundance of game, he told the Jesuits, because they had prayed: "If we knew what is in this paper, we would all say it to thee; but since we are ignorant, be content with our hearts and have pity on us."[7]

In native eyes, men so strangely powerful were, like traditional shamans, also capable of malevolence. Since all spiritual power was double-edged, the white *manitous* and their mysterious "talking papers" were often blamed for the inexplicable epidemics that sliced through native villages in the early years of contact. When Father Paul Le Jeune attributed the deaths of natives around Quebec in 1636 to immoderate consumption of brandy, one Indian stoutly defended his right to drink and laid the blame elsewhere. "No," he said, "it is not these drinks that take away our lives, but your writings; for since you have described our country, our rivers, our lands, and our woods, we are all dying, which did not happen until you came here."[8]

A small band of Algonquins who wintered near the French at Quebec the following winter feared writing in much the same way. Their explanation for their own extraordinary mortality was that a Basque in the early days of settlement, repelled by their greasy odor, spat on the ground and told them to be gone. "Yet he wrote our names upon a piece of paper," said their spokesman, "and perhaps by this means he has bewitched us and caused us to die."[9]

During the horrendous smallpox epidemics of the 1630s and 1640s many Hurons also found in the Black Robes and their strange writings the causes of their misery. The winter of 1640 was particularly lethal for the people at the newly baptized Mission of St. Jean Baptiste. As fear and despair swept through the cabins, stubborn traditionalists reported dreams in which the Jesuits unfolded "certain books" on the shore of Lake Huron, "whence issued sparks of fire which spread everywhere, and no doubt caused this pestilential disease."[10] Even converts could entertain suspicions about the Jesuits' books. In 1644, as Father Francesco Bressani was being taken to Huronia by six native Christians, his canoe was overturned by a companion who stood to shoot an eagle. "The Hurons took this accident for a bad omen," which it soon proved to be. Two days later the whole party was captured by an Iroquois war party. On route to Iroquois country, his Christian companions, Bressani reported, "commanded me to throw into the water my writings . . . as if these had been the cause, as they superstitiously believed, of the wreck of our canoe" and their subsequent ill fortune.[11]

Why were the Indians of the eastern woodlands so impressed by European books and literacy? The answer lies in the nature of the natives' oral culture and their shamanic religion. In the absence of alphabetic writing and print, native life revolved around the spoken word. Theirs was a predominantly voice-and-ear world in which a word was a real happening, an event of power and personal force. Because sound is evanescent and irretrievable, words while they are being spoken are precious, mysterious, and physically efficacious. Contrary to the children's jingle about sticks and stones, words can hurt, even kill, in the form of charms, spells, and hexes. In oral cultures like the Indians', sound is more real or existential than other sense objects. It registers an immanent, personal *presence*—a speaker—who, like all beings or "souls" in the native cosmology, is complicated and unpredictable. This, in turn, demands alertness and commitment from the listener. Indian speakers were respected and never interrupted, and the art of public speaking was regarded as an important qualification for social leadership. Even Europeans who did not yet understand the native languages were impressed by the dignified character of Indian councils and by the respectful silence between one speech and the next.

Words did not come cheaply to people for whom speaking was as real as shooting a deer or lifting a scalp.[12]

On one level, the Indians' "admiration" of the Europeans' printed books was simply an appreciation of the sheer technological novelty of thinner-than-birchbark paper, uniform typefaces, gold-stamped bindings, and illustrations of strange faces and unfamiliar places. A book was a totally foreign object, complicated in craftsmanship and thus obviously the work of a *manitou* or great-spirited being. That books stood beside a host of other marvelous artifacts in the European cabinet of curiosities only enhanced their reputation and reception.

But books were less amazing as objects than for what they enabled the Europeans to do. The ability to read and write was awe-inspiring to the Indians largely because it duplicated a spiritual feat that only the greatest shamans could perform, namely, that of reading the mind of a person at a distance and thereby, in an oral context, foretelling the future. Native shamans possessed powerful souls which, it was thought, could sometimes leave their bodies and travel in space and time to discover the outcome of future events. During a self-induced trance or a shaking tent ceremony, the shaman's soul might discover lost objects in faraway places or predict the success of war or hunting parties. His greatest skill was his ability to detect the identity of witches who had magically intruded a small item into a victim's body or had captured a victim's soul in a dream, thereby causing illness or death.[13] This required the ability to see inside the witch's mind, to expose its evil intentions, and only the most singular shamans were so endowed. Yet every European who could read a handwritten note from a distant correspondent could, in effect, read the writer's mind. Small wonder that the natives who first witnessed this amazing feat regarded the literate Europeans as "greater than all mankind."

The Indians' identification of the Europeans with tradi-

tional shamans had another cause and two important consequences. Almost without exception, the Europeans whose
literacy first impressed the Indians were missionaries, men of
religion whose faith was anchored in a holy book and sustained by other books. When these missionaries told the natives that their books contained the word of the Great Spirit
himself, the natives lost little time in realizing that writing's
ability to communicate over time and space made it more effective as "a way of getting in touch with distant deities."[14]

Since the eclecticism of native religion readily allowed the
incorporation of such a novel technique, literacy became
firmly identified with religion. This had two consequences.
One was that the Indians expected the literate European
"shamans" to be able to perform other traditional shamanic
feats, malevolent and benevolent. Thus the native belief that
the Black Robes had inflicted them with deadly epidemics by
bewitching them with books or writing, and the correspondent
belief that they or their leaders could cure them just as easily.
In 1637 an Algonquin captain sought to visit Gov. Charles
Huault de Montmagny because "he is considered a grand per-
sonage in our country; they say he is a great friend of the Sun,
and that he gives letters which prevent one from dying, at
least soon."[15] The natives also expected the missionaries to
predict and control the weather, and to procure for the wor-
shipers practical dividends of a social and economic sort.
When a Montagnais captain wished to impress a group of native visitors with the spiritual prowess of his French allies, he
called Father Jacques Buteux into his lodge and asked him
to write down the names of twelve or thirteen small tribes
toward the north which the captain pronounced quickly.
When Buteux duly impressed the assembly by reading aloud
the names in order from his *massinahigan* or notebook, one
of the visitors asked if he could also tell "how deep the snow
would be the next winter."[16]

Nearly a century later, when the evangelizing trader Alexander Long told the Cherokees that their religious beliefs were all false, the Indians replied that the fault was not theirs because they did not have the ability to learn from reading and writing. "If we had," their spokesman said, perhaps with a hint of sarcasm, "we should be as wise as you . . . and could do and make all things as you do: [such] as making guns and powder and bullets and cloth . . . and peradventure the great god of the English would cause us to turn white as you are."[17]

For the oral cultures of the eastern woodlands, the magic of the written word derived from its practical value as a means of communication with the natural and supernatural worlds (a distinction Indians did not make), from the prestige and technological achievements of the culture from which it came, and particularly from its close association with a priesthood. When reading and writing were primarily religious activities, the instruments of writing—books and handwritten notes—became invested with supernatural powers in their own right. Writing, therefore, did not banish magic from the native world, but enhanced and extended it. The native headmen who agreed to send their children to schools in Europe or colonial towns were induced partly by a desire to acquire the new magic through the younger generation. But a second consequence of the natives' belief in the shamanic quality of writing was their gradual acceptance of the religious systems associated with it. The magic of literacy rather than the touch of cold theology first led the Indians to Christianity.[18]

The missionaries who best capitalized on writing's potential for religious conversion were the Jesuits. The Recollects who preceded them by ten years were simply too few and too poor to spend enough time in any one place to master the native languages, without which they could not hope to tout the virtues of their own written words. Having acquired Indian tongues by immersion, the Jesuits lost no time in arguing the superiority of their religion. Their first and seemingly irrefutable argument was that Christian doctrine was immutable, and therefore superior to native religious traditions, because it was preserved in a printed book as it had been delivered by God. The transmission of God's word to the French appeared so direct that the Montagnais imagined that the Bible had been let down from heaven on a rope. In 1637 Father Le Jeune argued with a Montagnais band that the French version of the story of the Flood "could not be mistaken" because "[we have] the same belief as our ancestors, since we see their books." The Indian version, by contrast, had been garbled into "a thousand fables."[19]

Wherever they went, the Jesuits hammered home the point that "the Scripture does not vary like the oral word of man, who is almost by nature false." Huron converts had been so persuaded by their resident Black Robes that they could interrupt the traditional history recitations performed at council elections to make the same argument. In 1646 one old Christian man stopped a narration of the tortoise-Creation story, replete with one-inch mnemonic straws, to ask: "Where are the writings which give us faith in what thou sayest? . . . [E]ach one is permitted to invent what he will . . . But the French do not speak by heart; they preserve from all antiquity the Sacred books, wherein the word of God himself is written, without permission to any one to alter it the least in the world." Fifty years later, Father Sébastien Râle was still cutting off his Abenaki opponents with the same sharp weapon. After explaining the essential articles of Catholic faith, Râle told a group from the lower Kennebec: "All these words that I have just explained to you are not human words; they are the words of the Great Spirit. They are not written like the words of men upon a collar [wampum belt], on which a person can say everything that he wishes; but they are written in the book of the Great Spirit, to which falsehood cannot have access." After such an onslaught, the natives were hard pressed (as the priests put it) to "confuse their fables with our truths."[20] When Father Joseph Le Mercier reported to his superiors in 1638, he drew up a list of what inclined the Hurons to Christianity. At the top of the list was "the art of inscribing upon paper matters that are beyond sight."[21]

When the Jesuits' success with the Hurons was repeated elsewhere in New France, the priests drew on their shamanic reputation as readers of minds to insinuate themselves into native society and thereby to continue the conversion of the people to Catholic Christianity. To judge by the thousands of bona fide adult baptisms they performed and the number of rock-ribbed Catholic *reserves* they founded along the St. Lawrence, their use of books and writing for evangelical purposes was little short of inspired.[22]

The obvious question that arises is, why did Protestant missionaries not cash in on literacy's preternatural power? After the testimony of Harriot and Williams, there can be no doubt that the native peoples of the eastern woodlands equally were dazzled by the power of print and the lure of books. A partial answer is that at least one Protestant *did* attempt to proselytize by resorting to the virtues of print. John Eliot's arguments, presented by lightly fictionalized Natick Indian missionaries in 1671, struck the same chords that the Jesuits did. To a village of Nipmucks, who suspected that the Christian stories of heaven and hell were invented by Englishmen to drive them from their lands, Eliot's alter-ego replied that "the Book of God is no invention of Englishmen. It is the holy law of God himself, which was given unto man by God, before Englishmen had any knowledge of God." On another occasion, King Philip of the Wampanoags asked what Scripture is. The native missionary Anthony responded that it was "the word and will of God written in a book. . . . And this is a great benefit to us . . . ," he continued, "for a word spoken is soon gone, and nothing retaineth it but our memory. . . . But when this word is written in a book, there it will abide, though we have forgotten it." Finally, to dismiss

the competition from the north, Anthony boasted that, unlike
the Catholics who "wickedly wrong the scriptures, especially
by adding to them, . . . we teach nothing but that which is
noted in, and grounded upon the scriptures of truth."[23]

It is also clear that Protestant missionaries in the English
colonies made little headway against the tide of traditionalism
in the native East. Some of the many reasons for the Protestant failure were clearly out of the hands of missionaries. And
yet we must still ask why the English missionaries, with the
partial exception of Eliot, did not choose to profit from books
and writing in their quest for native converts.

Three reasons suggest themselves. First, even in New England, the Protestant missions were mounted too late by too
few. For many years, Eliot worked virtually alone, in the in-
terstices of his obligations to his own congregation in Roxbury. He did not begin preaching to local tribesmen until
1645, by which time the Plymouth pilgrims had been established for twenty-five years and the Puritans of Massachusetts
Bay for at least fifteen. The natives' acquaintance with some
15,000 nonclerical settlers, nearly half of whose adults could
read and write, simply eroded the novelty and magic of
print.[24]

A second reason is that Puritan missionaries like Eliot, unlike their Jesuit counterparts, were culturally inflexible. They
were totally incapable of assuming the role of shaman for
purposes of infiltrating native society, as their Jesuit rivals
were.[25] Instead, they sought to destroy it. In their eyes, native
religion, like most other facets of native life, was a foul and
devil-ridden sink of iniquity, which had to be scoured and
reamed before the Indians could receive new anglicized personae and be reborn as "new men" in Christ. Even if the acculturated New England natives had credited the literate
ministers with shamanic power, playing the part of satanic
Indian priests found no favor in the Puritan company.

Finally, the Protestant belief in the priesthood of all be-

lievers and the need for each Christian to confront the scriptural message directly led the English missionaries to translate
their religious writings into native languages as quickly as
possible and to open schools to teach Indian children to read
and write.[26] This, of course, diminished the mystery of the
foreign language and the exalted status of the priestly caste of
literate guardians and interpreters of God's Word.

The Protestant failure to capitalize on the power of print
helped the Jesuits to win the contest of cultures in colonial
North America. Their victory in turn helped New France
endure in the face of overwhelming odds until 1759, when
Montcalm's military ineptitude virtually handed the colony
to Wolfe's isolated, ill-equipped troops on the Plains of
Abraham.

CHAPTER SEVEN

Were Indian Conversions Bona Fide?

A SHORT CONFERENCE PAPER IS A GOOD PLACE TO TRY OUT ONE'S conclusions about a subject, but a poor one for trying to prove them; twenty minutes sandwiched between other presentations is not sufficient. I rediscovered this in November 1986 when I read a nine-page version of the following essay at the annual meeting of the American Society for Ethnohistory in Charleston. The reaction to my paper from the two respondants and some of the audience was, to put it nicely, skeptical. So I went home determined to make my case at greater and more convincing length. The following essay was written for this volume to accomplish that end.

I continue to be fascinated by the variety of reasons why normally sensible scholars so strongly resist even the possibility that Indians in the seventeenth century could convert to Christianity, sincerely and in good faith. I suspect that they would have much less trouble crediting the conversion of nineteenth- or twentieth-century Africans or Asians. I certainly hold no brief for Christian missionaries, as a glance at any of my work will show. But I am persuaded by the evidence, and by the history of Christianity around the world, that many Indians—certainly not all of them—were receptive to the solutions offered by the new religion and were capable of taking the decisive step from their old religions to the new, without deceiving themselves, the missionaries, or us.

In MUCH OF THE RECENT HISTORIOGRAPHY OF COLONIAL MIS-
sions, the conversion of Indians to Christianity has received a
poor press. In the past fifteen or twenty years, historians and
ethnohistorians of both Protestant and Catholic missions have
cast aspersions on the quantity, quality, and longevity of native conversions to the intrusive religions. They have sought
not only to deflate the numerical success of the colonial missionaries but to ridicule their cultural goals and methods and
to minimize their spiritual results. The effect of all this debunking has been to paint the missionaries either as evil tools
of imperialism or as naive fools, and their Indian neophytes
as hapless victims of clerical oppression or as cunning Br'er
Rabbits of the forest.

The Puritans, those favorite whipping boys of the enlight-
ened, predictably fare the worst, particularly "Apostle" John
Eliot of Massachusetts. According to Francis Jennings and
Neal Salisbury, Eliot's goals were so tainted by a barely hidden political agenda and his methods so "repressive" that his
religious results must be drastically discounted. Only after
the Massachusetts Bay Colony had been founded for sixteen
years did Eliot decide to get into what Jennings calls the "missionary racket," largely for the annuity offered by an English
noblewoman to encourage American missions. He used an
Indian "slave" (a war captive) as a language teacher, and in
1646 talked the colonial "oligarchy" into outlawing the practice of native religion under pain of death and into setting
aside some land, purloined from the Indians, as bribes to converts seeking "secure habitation" in the chaos of the Puritan
land-grab. These reservations or "praying towns" became the
major Puritan institution of "cold war" against the natives.
When surrounding tribes would not voluntarily submit to
English dominion, Eliot sent faithful warriors from these
towns, armed with guns and ammunition purchased with mis-

sionary funds, to "compel them to come in." Moreover, in his
published reports abroad, Eliot cooked his results and inflated
his own role in converting native New England. Although
Eliot claimed that some 1100 Indians had been "subjected to
the gospel" by 1674, Jennings could find only seventy-four in
full church communion and another forty-five who had been
baptized, a total of 119 or just over 10 percent of those
claimed for Christ's battalions. Richard Bourne of Plymouth
and especially the Thomas Mayhews, Junior and Senior, of
Martha's Vineyard "outperformed Eliot in almost every respect," largely because of Eliot's "authoritarian and repressive" methods and corrupting political ends.[1]

In 1974, Neal Salisbury took the indictment one step farther by questioning the quality of Eliot's native conversions
as well as their quantity. The public narrations of the saving
grace they had experienced, given by Indian neophytes to
gain admission to a Congregational church, contrasted with
those of their English brethren in two decisive ways. First, as
far as Salisbury could see, they contained no evidence that
the Indian converts "understood either the [biblical] Word
. . . or the most basic tenets of Puritan theology." Second,
the confessions were also bereft of evidence "that the missionaries expected their [Indian] saints' conversion experiences to measure up to those of the English." Furthermore,
the few Indians who converted to Christianity were "respond-
ing to the crisis posed by English expansion into their lands"
and sought, "albeit unconsciously, to invest the imposed religion with traditional meaning." In the end, they were "left
suspended between two cultures," without a spiritual home
or a social identity.[2]

Historians of Catholic missions are not much more san-
guine about Indian conversions in Canada. But rather than a
story of crushed cultures and religious dragonnades, David
Blanchard, Cornelius Jaenen, and Bruce Trigger tell of the
tenacity of native traditions and the gullibility of French mis-

sionaries. Unlike the New England praying towns, which Blanchard said were "regarded as cesspools for storing the remnants of societies now lost to war, disease and migration . . . internment camps for the vanquished," the Catholic *reserves* along the St. Lawrence were populated by natives of strength and integrity, who "manipulated the French and the English to gain the best advantage over both." One of the strongest *reserves,* Caughnawaga across from Montreal, was virtually a "traditional Iroquois settlement," where neophytes took on the protective coloration of Catholicism while going about their lives much as before contact. The Mohawks of Caughnawaga, Blanchard argued, "were not witless followers of the Jesuits. They used the Jesuits to gain advantageous trade concessions from the French" and gave up very little in return. Contrary to Jesuit belief, the inhabitants did not relinquish their traditional religion and beliefs but merely "modified their religious practices and developed a syncretistic system of ritual that yielded the desired affect."[3]

Jaenen took a different, less speculative, route but ended up in the same place. In casting his eye over the whole religious terrain of New France, he marshaled several contemporary reasons for skepticism about the quality of native conversions to Catholicism. Among the most telling were the existence of native apostasy and backsliding; conversions—or at least baptisms—procured by economic inducements, force, or the childish attraction of colorful ceremonies; the lack of native clergy, except a few nuns and *dogiques* or teaching assistants; clerical accusations that competing religious orders were not nearly as successful as their propaganda would have us believe; and, of course, the existence of syncretism, the "incorporation of pagan and pre-Christian elements" in Catholic Indian belief and ritual. Even in the *reserves,* Jaenen admitted, Jesuit success "was not always as sincere a case of acculturation as the missionaries hoped it would be. Rather, it was often a mere addition of Catholicism as a cultural overlay." And the Recollects and Sulpicians were "no more successful than the Jesuits." While Jaenen admitted halfheartedly that "numerous Amerindians became zealous Catholics," he argued that conversion "could only be a disruptive factor" in an already chaotic situation and that the missionaries made "more gains for the church triumphant than for the church militant."[4]

Bruce Trigger also doubted that the Jesuits managed to convey an "accurate understanding of Christianity" to their early converts, even though the Black Robes were astute pedagogues and masters of native tongues. He based his skepticism on an "anthropological" understanding of social typology. The Indians of New France were members of *egalitarian* societies governed by consensus, "in which one human being did not have the right to command another." Christianity, on the other hand, was "a creation of *hierarchical* and coercive societies." "Obedience to God and to his earthly representatives, within society and the family, was central" to its teachings. Consequently, native societies had to be socially transformed before their members were capable of receiving the hierarchical Christian message. As Allen Trelease put it in 1960, "true conversion of the Indians . . . depended on their prior submission to the white man, with the attendant disintegration of their own culture."[5] Trigger could find "no evidence that the Jesuits or any other Christian group in the seventeenth century was able to make Christian doctrine comprehensible to people who lived in a self-sufficient tribal society." The crux was political and economic power, for until native groups had been subordinated to European power, they stood no chance to grasping the "meaning and spirit" of Christianity.[6]

In short, says the new wisdom, not only was the number of Indian conversions in the Northeast small, certainly much smaller than contemporary boasts would suggest, but many, perhaps most, of them were not even made in good faith.

It is not difficult to see where this kind of thinking comes from. Some of it is inherited from contemporary Protestant and Catholic rivals who sought to denigrate one another's missions by doubting all estimates of evangelical success but their own. New England Puritans sought to puncture the Catholics' record in New France by ridiculing their alleged propensity for baptizing natives sunk in pagan ignorance or on their deathbeds—the thick and the dead.[7] Jesuits fired a double salvo by suggesting that Protestant "depravity" made such a mockery of the labors of the Recollects that in the friars' first ten-year stint in Canada "almost no progress" was made.[8] To which the Recollects—or their hired pens—retorted that even the English and the Dutch were doing better than the Jesuits, who, since they joined the Recollects in 1625, had propagated "scarcely any Christianity among the Indians, except some individuals in very small number."[9] And to top it off, an anticlerical Canadian officer thought that both Catholic orders had "lavish[ed] away all their Divinity and Patience to no purpose" because they refused to recognize "the (almost) invincible Aversion of the Indians to the Truths of Christianity."[10]

But most of the new debunking comes from modern historians who began their studies of Indians in the chaotic '60s and '70s, as the latest wave of Indian activism was receiving widespread media attention. These historians are—or were (for historians change as much as "times")—basically of two types: those of a secular, agnostic, or atheistic disposition for whom religion, past or present, is largely irrelevant; and those of a "liberal," anti-Establishment, or pro-underdog persuasion who think—or rather hope—that inscrutable Indian protagonists and "patriots" have an infinite capacity for putting one over on the white man.

Whatever its source, the new iconoclasm has something to be said for it. Many of the Indians who were counted as converts in the Northeast were not given adequate instruction in the Christian mysteries, morally tested to ensure that their outer lives reflected their inner grace, or sustained by established churches, sacraments, and ecclesiastical discipline. Jessé Fléché, a secular priest who accompanied the sieur de Poutrincourt to Acadia in 1610, baptized twenty members of a sagamore's family within the first month and eighty more tribesmen within the year, without knowing a word of Micmac. The two Jesuits who arrived in 1611 were appalled that the Indians were ignorant of the most elementary tenets of Christianity and began the conversion process all over again.[11] Similarly, in the midst of widespread epidemics, Catholic priests baptized hundreds of natives who lay at death's door, after only a modicum of instruction and the most circumscribed assent of the stricken. Perhaps a third of the 16,000 natives anointed by the Jesuits between 1632 and 1672 soon expired, often from imported European diseases.[12] In the eighteenth century, for political reasons, Protestant missionaries sometimes rushed to baptize neophytes who had not demonstrated convincingly their rejection of "pagan" ways. One of the best Anglican missionaries to the Mohawks folded his tent in despair after six frustrating years when most of his converts returned to "their former Evill practices," as he said, "like a dog to his vomitt."[13]

Sooner or later, it was apparent to the missionaries themselves that some Indians professed interest in baptism solely for the material advantages that would accrue from alliance with the newcomers. These "wheat-and-eel" Christians (as they were called at Quebec when they presented themselves at the Hôtel-Dieu in search of food) were—and are—characterized as beggarly hypocrites who would grunt assent to the missionaries' preachments as long as they were offered a pipe of tobacco, a nip of brandy, a new shirt, trading privileges at the company store, or military protection. In the face of great need or desire, some Indians were capable of masterly dissembling, even over long periods. A major source of this ability was the native "secret weapon," a generalized mode of civility in the presence of strangers. The majority of Protestant and Catholic missionaries considered the greatest obstacle to America's conversion to be what they called native "indifference" to doctrinal purity. "The Indians very seldom contradict those who speak to them," wrote a Jesuit in 1673, "and, when they are taught, they approve everything. This gives the missionaries much trouble in distinguishing those who believe sincerely."[14] One Huron leader confounded his persistent but linguistically still novice priest even further by drawing out his verbal "yes's" (which normally were cut short) in a way that really meant "I will do nothing of the sort," enabling the man to remain a "rebel soul" a quarter of a century after receiving baptism.[15]

Native converts fell from grace—usually temporarily—not because the Indians were congenitally "fickle and irresolute," as the Rev. John Sergeant accused in 1747, but from an understandable desire to cling to familiar cultural habits.[16] It is no coincidence that missionary handwringing over "apostasy" increased during the winter, when converts often left the supervision of Christian settlements and retired to the woods to hunt. One reason the Recollects and early Jesuits were keen to restrict their neophytes to sedentary agricultural villages was their fear that "even those whom we have long catechised, except a very small number, are not to be depended upon if they return for ever so short a time to the woods."[17] Out of the moral ken of the Black Robes, the Indians could divorce their spouses, take up with "concubines," drink to excess, resort to "jugglers" and shamans for cures, and sing and dance in satanic abandon. In the dark woods the devil lay waiting to ensnare the new Christians, using, a French physician said, "the lack of Faith of their relatives or friends, the weakness of nature, [and] the despondency caused by all their troubles, showing them the solace of their ancient superstitions."[18] Small wonder that the missionaries had "greater trouble in keeping [their] Christians than in acquiring them."[19]

Despite the plausibility of the new debunking, it is essentially polemical and incorrect. Take the number of converts involved. The propaganda figures offered by contemporaries can certainly be revised downward, but not by much. For example, Jennings accepted John Eliot's word that some 1100 Indians—about 500 in the seven older, established praying towns and another 600 in the newly founded Nipmuck towns to the west—were "subjected to the gospel" and interpreted that phrase to mean that they were *converted*. But clearly the Nipmuck towns should not be included in any meaningful search for converts because they were so new that they did not have churches or ministers by which to gather converts; they merely had English-appointed Indian magistrates and an occasional teacher. Moreover, Jennings failed to add the number of *baptized* natives in Natick, the oldest and largest praying town: some 80–100 people. This would bring the total of full church members and baptized neophytes to between 190 and 220, or well over 40 percent of the towns' populations.[20] By the same token, even though we should not count the moribund baptisms of the Jesuits as true converts—as even they did not—we are left with at least 10,000 healthy adults who were baptized in just one forty-year period. And as Father Francesco Bressani observed in 1653, the priests might have baptized the whole country had they been interested only in "number and name."[21]

Furthermore, we should not exaggerate the extent of apostasy, even in the Canadian woods. Apostates were very few in the praying towns of New England, largely because traditionalist alternatives were few after the onslaught of European diseases, English settlement, and militant Puritanism. In New France, apostasy was a problem mostly in the early decades of missionization, partly because after 1640 the Jesuits concentrated on Christianizing rather than "civilizing," partly because several of the first converts were former shamans of strong habits, and partly because several natives who were baptized in a hurry on their deathbeds recovered and became technical "apostates" in the eyes of the French for resuming their traditional ways. While the most notorious apostates were given considerable coverage in the Jesuit *Relations* to edify European readers, the Jesuits were not unduly concerned about their numbers. From disease- and war-torn Huronia in 1645, Jérôme Lalemant admitted that not all of his Christian neophytes were exemplary. Some "fall into sin, and have disastrous relapses; some lose heart in mid-course; all are not strong in the spirit of holiness. But," he continued, "I know not in what spot on earth we can find every one perfect. . . . It is sufficient that a portion comes to maturity. . . ."[22]

To make further sense of native "apostasy," we must see it in context. Before we can appreciate what it meant for a native to apostatize, we must understand the Christian norm to which he was expected to conform. In New England throughout the colonial period and in New France until 1640, the major missionary goal was that of "civilizing" the natives before or while converting them to Christianity. Because the Indians were strange, numerous, independent, and unpredictable, they stood as a tremendous potential obstacle to the colonial goals of the European intruders. Their friendship and loyalty were essential. Particularly in the early stages of settlement, when the Europeans were greatly outnumbered, Indians were needed as military allies against rival Europeans and hostile tribes, suppliers of food, sources of knowledge about the American environment, and labor in the hunting and processing of furs.

But in the English colonies, as the colonial population swelled, the natives stood in the way of agricultural expansion. So the missionaries sought to confine them to modest praying towns, thereby freeing vast tracts of real estate for the "civilized" use of the English. Even in New France, where the Algonquian tribes on the intemperate north shore of the

St. Lawrence had little or no experience of horticulture and were essential to the fur trade, the Recollect and early Jesuit missionaries sought to solve their perceived "Indian problem" by inducing the natives to trade their roving ways for sedentary life in European-style villages, their hunting for farming, and their "godless" liberty and pride for due subordination to French law and Christian morality.

Resettlement in a New English praying town or a New French *reserve* was only the beginning of the changes expected of native neophytes. Understandably, the missionaries interpreted "civility" in the familiar terms of their own Western European cultures, indeed usually according to the standards of their own upper-middle, educated class. Virtually nothing was left unscrutinized and untargeted for reform. Happy-go-lucky children and "liberated" wives were to be subordinated to their fathers and husbands. Female farmers were to exchange their hoes for spinning wheels and brooms; their menfolk were to drop their bows and fishing nets and pick up hoes, axes, and slop buckets. Male and female "nakedness" of limb and breast was to be covered in modest, fitted fashions from urban or peasant Europe. Long, proud hair was to be cut. Moccasins were to be replaced by cobbled shoes. Menstruating women, alleged to be spiritually powerful at such times, were no longer to be secluded in special huts in the woods to protect their "superstitious" menfolk from illness or bad luck in the hunt. Unruly children were to be birched or cuffed rather than allowed to "run wild"; as many children as possible, certainly the offspring of leaders, were to attend school to learn the art of sitting, obedience, and the 3 Rs—reading, writing, and religion. Native gutturals were to give way to the smooth sibilants and languid labials of French and English. Solid frame or log houses with chimneys were to supplant bark wigwams and longhouses with mere smokeholes. Tame beef and pork was to replace wild game, and to be eaten on plank tables rather than dirt floors. The unwritten custom of the tribe was to give way to the written laws of the town, enforced for the first time by courts, police, and jails. Even time was to be regimented by church calendars and mechanical clocks rather than the natural rhythms of the sun and moon.[23]

Even when the strictures of colonial culture were not fully imposed, as they largely ceased to be in New France after the Jesuits altered their methods in 1640, the demands of Scripture and catechism were exacting. Ten Commandments, Seven Deadly Sins, and as many as seven sacraments (only two in Protestant New England) could put a severe crimp in traditional native consciences and behavior. The Christian abhorrence of gluttony, for example, effectively proscribed native "eat-all" feasts, given to cure the sick, fulfill a premonitory dream, or honor a "pagan" deity. The first two commandments against "idolatry" outlawed resort to shamans, powwows, amulets, and dreams; the fourth, declaring one day in seven a workless sabbath, made a hand-to-mouth existence in the forest all the riskier. In Catholic Canada the sacrament of marriage forbade divorce and mandated monogamy to natives long used to plural wives, easy separations, and no-fault divorce. "Of all the laws which we propound to them," a Jesuit reported to his superiors in 1644, "there is not one that seems so hard to them as that which forbids polygamy, and does not allow them to break the bonds of lawful marriage."[24]

Measured against the adamantine standards of a new culture and a new religion, it is small wonder that a number of native converts backslid into apostasy. Even more remarkable, however, was the paucity of permanent apostates and the correspondingly vast majority of converts who kept the new faith in the teeth of powerful temptations, habits, and scorn. Four reasons account for the missionaries' success and the good faith of their native converts.

First, at least the first two generations of missionaries were well qualified for the task of conversion. The Jesuits especially

and several Puritans, including John Eliot, were spiritually
elevated men, products of the best educations in Europe, linguistically gifted, extremely motivated, indefatigable, and
pedagogically astute. After years of working among the white
"pagans" of Europe, following the writings of their brethren
in other parts of the world, and long apprenticeships among
the Indians, they were shrewd students of human nature in
much of its cultural variety and sensitive judges in "cases of
conscience," the classical way for priests and ministers to learn
to handle spiritual difficulties. They were definitely not easy
to hoodwink or hornswaggle. Deservedly, they were confident,
as a Jesuit superior said, that "it is easy to recognize in a continued instruction whether or not the heart agrees with the
tongue."[25] Yet they remembered—as should we—that *bona fide*
conversion *was* a matter of the heart, a secret transaction between the self and the soul, but that the only way to measure
it was by outward behavior. For the missionaries, action—cultural reform and "right living"—spoke louder and more truth-
fully than words.

All the talent and education in the world were wasted unless the missionaries gained the sustained attention of their
native targets. In eastern Massachusetts and on Martha's Vineyard, Eliot and the Mayhews had relatively captive audiences
for their proselytizing; they could usually get a hearing, if not
always the results they desired. In Canada the Jesuits had to
work harder to gather audiences of independent villagers and
mobile hunters. They did this by attaching themselves to native groups, by being adopted and given Indian names, by
patiently and thoroughly learning native dialects and the
elaborate art of council oratory, by acting generously and
honestly, and by following native custom as long as it did not
compromise their religious scruples. Once they had passed
these exacting tests, the Black Robes were accepted as "men
of sense" who thought and acted like "real people" (the name
most native groups gave to themselves). It also worked to

their advantage that by profession they showed no lust for Indian women, land, or furs.

Having gained a respectful hearing, the missionaries proceeded to draw their audience toward Christ with a variety of pedagogical techniques learned in Europe but adapted for America. Whenever possible, they adapted the natives' metaphorical style of speaking to Christian uses. Instead of peddling abstruse theological niceties, they taught only the essential articles of faith from catechisms familiar to Europe's children. While Puritan missionaries were content with time-tested catechizing, the Jesuits appealed to native senses as well as intellect with beautiful polyphonic music, richly decorated altars and vestments, wafers stamped with Christ's initials, incense, solemn rituals and processions, pictorial renditions of Christian events carefully modified to Indian tastes, crucifixes, rosaries, and rings and medals bearing hearts, Madonnas, or Christ on the cross. All were designed to inculcate the new faith indelibly and to sustain it communally.

If the listeners balked or wavered, the Jesuits enlisted Western technology to give credence to the superiority of their message. Mechanical clocks that "spoke" on command (on the hour), accurate predictions of eclipses, chunks of sulphur that burned and stank like the fiery ground of Hell, metal-moving lodestones, compasses, prisms, and particularly the ability to "read minds at a distance" by reading written notes or printed pages all bespoke the priests' standing as *manitous* or spiritual experts whose powers rivaled those of native shamans. The force that did most to undermine the Indians' faith in their shamans and healers was European epidemic diseases. Lacking acquired immunities to the new microbes, native populations were often decimated by onslaughts of small-pox, measles, and influenza. When native shamans proved powerless to stop the carnage, much less to explain it, they rapidly lost credibility to the new black-robed shamans, whose prayers, nursing, and palliative medicines often brought recovery and whose religious explanations usually made simple if disturbing sense.[26]

The missionaries' third key to success was that both Puritans and Jesuits held the Indians to a high standard for baptism and church admission, indeed higher than that set for their own countrymen. Contrary to Protestant mythology (which still infects modern histories), the Jesuits were as hardnosed about admission to baptism as the staunchest Puritan. Only the dying were sprinkled without extensive instruction, in order to ensure their salvation. In Canada the first adult Huron was admitted to the rite only after three years of careful catechizing and testing. And some candidates, after as long a period, never made it. One priest explained why: "We were not willing to receive a single adult, in a condition of perfect health, before we were very well informed about the language; and before we had—after long probation, sometimes for whole years—judged them constant in the holy purpose not only of receiving the Sacrament of Baptism, but of punctually observing the divine precepts."[27]

Puritan missionaries put their candidates to an equally hard test. Eliot's flagship church at Natick was not formally gathered until nine years after the town was established and Eliot began to preach and catechize there regularly. In 1652, the second year of his ministry there, Eliot asked his most promising neophytes to make "preparatory confessions" to him, which he then read to the elders of neighboring English churches. A month or two later, the candidates made full "public confessions" before a panel of visiting clergymen. The following year Eliot and Thomas Mayhew published both sets of confessions in London in order to gather the opinion of English clergymen on the sincerity and suitability of the Indians as potential Christians. In 1654, after assurance from England had arrived, eight natives were given a final grilling before Eliot's Roxbury congregation. Although their answers to 101 questions on Scripture, Protestant belief, and the conversion experience were entirely satisfactory, Eliot weighed their knowledge and behavior for another six years before allowing them to subscribe to a covenant of faith and to become a true church.[28]

The informed specificity and emotional depth of these early confessions simply cannot sustain Salisbury's suspicions about their quality in comparison with those by colonial candidates. They are not only as probing of the inner "morphology of conversion" as English confessions, but they contain distinctively Indian elements that should allay fears that the minister was merely dictating, or that the Indians were merely parroting, a standard form of confession. As to the natives' knowledge of Scripture and Puritan theology, the better place to look is not in the confessions but in the searching questions the Indians asked during instruction or following sermons. Many of the questions drove right to the heart of Christianity's historical and philosophical contradictions, pushing the missionaries to the walls of their knowledge. The Indians' ready "faculty to frame hard and difficult questions" demonstrated their grasp of the intricacies of Christian theology and European arts and sciences. When they plunged into queries about biblical history, death, and the problem of evil, the missionaries often must have wished that they were dealing with English parishioners who took more for granted.[29]

The irony of Salisbury's second complaint, that the missionaries did not expect the conversion experiences of their native neophytes to measure up to those of the English, is that the admission standards of the Indian churches not only began higher than English colonial standards but remained higher throughout the seventeenth century. By the early 1650s white New Englanders, quite unlike the Natick candidates, no longer sought church admission by making personal relations to the whole congregation of their full realization of "saving grace," but only of their desire for salvation, of their spiritual progress to date, and of their moral conduct.

Owning a covenant of faith—promising to work for grace with
the help of the church—was more important than being able
to give a convincing narrative of achieved grace.[30] When congregational admission standards were again lowered after the
Half-Way Covenant of 1662 and the anglicizing temper of the
1690s, Indian churches continued to admit members "according to the manner of the churches in primitive times." As late
as 1705, native candidates were still required to make "large
and particular" declarations of their Christian knowledge,
past sins, and spiritual "convictions, awakenings, and com-
forts" before the assembled congregation.[31]

The final reason for the quality of Indian conversions in
the Northeast was that both Puritans and Jesuits continued
to nourish their converts within and without. Both evangelical groups built churches and meetinghouses in the physical
center of their praying towns and *reserves,* symbolizing the
place of the new religion in the natives' lives. Since Puritan
missionaries in the seventeenth century were primarily responsible to their own colonial congregations, they trained a
cadre of native preachers and teachers and installed them in
the native churches, with full rights and responsibilities for
guiding their brethren in the new ways, usually in an Indian
tongue.[32] The Jesuits, on the other hand, were corporately
wealthy and numerous enough to supply the Indian churches
themselves, though they employed native *dogiques* to assist
them in catechizing and enforcing Catholic morality. The
Black Robes also fostered sexually segregated choirs and so-
dalities of the faithful to nourish the spirit and help the community.[33] Since many natives had been converted along with
family and other kinfolk, the missionaries spliced institutional
and biological bonds to gently but firmly tie their converts to
the faith.[34]

Even when forced to acknowledge numbers of Indian converts, the new skeptics immediately question the sincerity of
their conversions by resorting to the hobgoblin of "syncre-

tism." The praying Indians of New England, Salisbury asserted, "*unconsciously* sought to invest the imposed religion with traditional meaning." Blanchard went even further in arguing that the Caughnawaga Mohawks were altogether conscious of taking on the protective coloration of Catholicism in order to obtain a number of socio-economic advantages from the French. They merely "modified" their religious practices in (we are left to assume) minor ways and developed a "syncretistic system" of ritual. Jaenen seems to have agreed. Even in the *reserve,* he wrote, acculturation amounted to a "mere addition of Catholicism as a cultural overlay," implying that the new religion lay very lightly on the surface of native life.

In the hands of the new critics, syncretism is a red herring dragged across the discussion of the quality of native conversions. First, at this remove, historians are in no position to know if converts *unconsciously* interpreted the new religion (solely, largely?) in traditional terms, or for how long. Second, if they *consciously* did so, we must have some kind of documentary proof; Blanchard and Jaenen provide none. Proof exists, but it does not support those who assert the perdurable traditionalism of two-faced converts. The Jesuits, for example, were well aware of a certain amount of syncretism on the part of their *neophytes,* less often of their *converts.* In fact, they approved, encouraged, and initiated the moderate use of it in order to ease the Indians' transition to the new faith. Traditional naming and adoption ceremonies and feasts of all kinds were given Christian purposes, as were dreams and dream-guessing. Tobacco sacrifices were made to the new God rather than local deities; Christian sacramentals—rings, medals, crosses, rosaries, and relics—assumed the instrumental function of traditional charms and amulets. And in the most significant replacement of all, Jesuit priests accepted the spiritual mantle of shamans, conjurers, and healers until they could educate the natives in the true office of a Catholic priest.[35] Most ritual bridges spanned similar functions in both religions. The natives sought some carryovers because they bore expressive rather than instrumental value and helped the natives maintain their social identity as Indians. Still others were essentially cultural rather than religious in nature and were preferred to European equivalents, which were often offered or imposed by the missionaries as planks in the "civilizing" platform.[36]

However syncretic the early converts tried or proved to be, we should realize two important facts. First, the missionaries dominated the conversion process, monitoring every stage and guarding the gates of admission. If traditional or "pagan" elements were carried over, they were translated piecemeal as isolated elements rather than religious complexes or systems, and it was the missionaries who allowed them to pass. Once the missionaries gained the religious initiative in native villages and began to proselytize, increasingly they defined the relevant concepts, delineated the proper stages of spiritual growth, installed the new pantheon, and set appropriate moral standards. And second, the missionaries regarded syncretic practices as temporary expedients, until they could persuade the natives of their inefficacy or impropriety and could show them a "purer" way. For prophetic, world religions like Christianity are essentially dogmatic and intolerant of other visions of the world. They are simply not capable of giving up their exclusive claim to truth. The alternative perspectives offered by tribal religions, which feature a host of local deities concerned mainly with particular communities and their environments, have no validity in the eyes of those who worship a supreme deity of universal pretentions.[37]

The new skepticism errs also in reducing religion, in the manner of cultural materialists, to a mere epiphenomenon of socio-economic realities. Indians in the Northeast "converted," the critics believe, because they were forced to take on protective coloration by the harsh realities of imperial subjection. This assumption is misleading in three ways: (1) it is unwarrantedly reductionist and belied by countless historical examples, (2) it confuses the *social* functions of conversion for *groups* with its *emotional* and *intellectual* meaning for *individuals,* and (3) it confuses the *explanation* of conversion with the *validity* or *quality* of the result.

Trigger commits another error by reifying societies into crude social types—egalitarian and hierarchical—and then obliterating the human individuality and will of their members. Moreover, he is incorrect in thinking that Algonquian and Iroquoian societies were utter strangers to hierarchy and obedience. Although most of these groups eschewed corporal punishment and compulsion most of the time, at least two Algonquian groups—the Mohegans and the Powhatans—were led by chiefs whom even the rank-conscious English regarded as "despotic." The natives of the Northeast, like most societies, always had ways of compelling their children to behave properly, often by shaming them but sometimes with physical punishment.[38] These lessons in obedience served them well when Iroquois clan matrons led workbees of women into the corn-fields and war chiefs coordinated guerilla raids or mass assaults on enemy villages. Indian people also understood hierarchy because, like most people, they enjoyed different statuses and reputations, they recognized the superiority of certain tribesmen and women (civil chiefs, war chiefs, shamans, healers, clan matrons, orators), and they differentiated their deities similarly.

Perhaps more to the point, even if the Indians had no concepts of hierarchy and obedience, the missionaries would have indoctrinated them with such ideas, as indeed they did historically. The difference between European and Indian ideas of hierarchy was one of degree, not of kind or of existence vs. nonexistence. Therefore, for several reasons, individual Indians were capable of converting to Christianity in good faith without waiting for their whole society to be hammered out of its "egalitarian" shape.

As history has shown many times over, the true "meaning and spirit" of Christianity were accessible to all kinds of people universally, regardless of the societies from which they came. The tribal peoples of the Northeast were no exception. Those in the first generation who formally converted did so for many reasons, most of which went to the grave with them. But in general, they turned to Christianity because that world religion satisfied new emotional needs and intellectual hunger. Those needs were created by the advent of the European strangers, their marvelous technology, and their deadly diseases. The ablest native minds could simply not explain—much less predict—the origins of white men and black, the geographies of continents beyond their own "island on the turtle's back," the lethal etiology of smallpox, the arts of metallurgy and papermaking, alphabetic literacy, or lunar eclipses. Nor could native societies control even their own circumscribed worlds as before. The invaders put so much pressure on native America, some of it deliberate, some inadvertent, that traditional culture was sooner or later thrown into disarray. Understandably, Indians whose lives were most affected by the colonial juggernaut were the likeliest candidates for conversion. For Christianity (and its attendant culture) offered answers to their most urgent questions, balm to their frayed emotions, and techniques of prediction and control to replace those they had lost.

It should therefore come as no surprise that thousands of natives who survived the new epidemics placed themselves under the spiritual tutelage of the black-robed spokesmen for a greater God. Certainly the missionaries were not surprised. Nor did they worry about the quality of their native converts. The missionaries' answer to the modern critics would be both the number *and permanence* of their converts—the thousands of Indians who drastically altered their lives to become "new men" for a new God; the hundreds who voluntarily left their "pagan" brethren to live in Christianized praying towns and *reserves;* the native nuns, preachers, teachers, *dogiques,* and celibate imitators who spread the "good news of the gospel" at home and in "pagan" country with evangelical pertinacity; the adamantine souls who kept the faith in the face of traditionalist ridicule, threats, torture, and martyrdom; and particularly those who formed churches that have resisted the blandishments of rival religions and denominations until the present day. The most eloquent testimony to their evangelical success and to the *bona fide* character of their native converts are the Protestant congregations of Mashpee and Martha's Vineyard and the Catholic parishes of Saint Francis and Caughnawaga.

Confluences

CHAPTER EIGHT

Through Another Glass Darkly: Early Indian Views of Europeans

By THE PRINCIPLES OF THEIR CRAFT, ETHNOHISTORIANS SOONER OR later get around to examining both sides of their various cultural frontiers. For a long time, anthropologists dominated the discipline and devoted most of their attention to the study of Indian groups, past and present. With the increasing participation of historians in the early 1970s, ethnohistory has expanded its purview to treat the other side of the frontier, but somewhat more critically than Western or Turnerian frontier historians of previous generations were wont to do.

One group of historians who have shown a sustained interest in Indians, or at least the *idea* of Indians, are intellectual historians, who have written extensively on the changing views of Indians held by European and American observers. But until the mid-'70s, they did not write systematically about Indian views of the white man. Cornelius Jaenen broke this impasse in 1974 with an article on "Amerindian Views of French Culture in the Seventeenth Century," published in the *Canadian Historical Review*. It was soon followed by James Ronda's " 'We Are Well As We Are': An Indian Critique of Seventeenth-Century Christian Missions," which appeared in the *William and Mary Quarterly* in January 1977. It is no coincidence that both authors are ethnohistorians, for only ethnohistorians know the Indians, as individuals, well enough to imagine that they, as well as whites, had an intellectual history worth reconstructing.

"Through Another Glass Darkly," a playful allusion to one of my earliest essays on Indians,* was written initially as a brief talk for a conference on "Early American Encounters with the Americas," held at Ohio State University in October 1986. It has been considerably expanded and illustrated for this volume.

For CENTURIES, EUROPEAN EXPLORERS AND SETTLERS HAVE taken their lumps from historians for having mistreated the Indians of North America. Much of the indictment, some of it written by contemporaries of the actors, has stood up well even on appeal to modern historical judges. But recently the indictment has taken a new twist in which the invaders are accused of not even having *seen* the Indians clearly and realistically. Instead, the critics charge, they saw them at best (in Shakespeare's overworked phrase) "through a glass darkly"; at worst, they never saw them at all but only tawny reflections of their own self-projections and neuroses, as in a mirror. In any event, the Europeans' "ethnocentrism," their monolithic concept of "savagism," whether noble or ignoble, so clouded their vision that the human and cultural reality of native life was almost never recognized and less seldom acknowledged. Inevitably, this ethnological blindness led to constant misunderstanding and violence.[1]

Exploration of the various conquest mentalities is all to the good, provided we do not commit the fallacy of intellectual determinism, of attributing historical change solely to ideas.[2] But we should also realize that such a procedure is only half that required by the working principles of ethnohistory. If ideas have consequences when they are translated

---

* "Through a Glass Darkly: Colonial Attitudes toward the Native Americans," *American Indian Culture and Research Journal,* 1 (1974), 17–28.

by will into action, it is imperative that we examine the reigning ideas of all parties, European *and* native. For if the intruders were driven to act partly by their particular mental constructs of the natives, the natives' behavior in turn must have been similarly motivated by their mental images of the Europeans. If we do not have some idea of what was in the Indians' minds and imaginations as they confronted the intruders, we will never fathom why they acted as they did in different circumstances. The consequence of that ignorance will be to reduce them to inscrutable inhumanity, without feelings, ideas, or expectations. But we must avoid the lazy and unhelpful tactic of attributing their behavior to an indigenous brand of "ethnocentrism." As members of cultures, *all* people are ethnocentric. Our task is to discover the particular configuration of ideas and values that makes each culture distinctive.

We must be equally careful to speak of plural Indian perceptions and not to homogenize them prematurely into a stereotypical "Indian" response. The natives, no less than the Europeans, were divided by politics, gender, age, rank, and status. And they met Europeans at different times in different places under different circumstances. The perception of a young Iroquois girl whose first white person was a gentle missionary walking alone and unarmed into her village was obviously different from that of an older Micmac warrior who was greeted by cannon shot from the first sailing ship he ever saw.

Nevertheless, while it may no longer be permissible to speak of "the primitive mind," as previous generations of anthropologists were wont to do, the various Eastern Woodland groups who met the earliest waves of Europeans shared enough mental habits and conceptual modes to give their responses a striking degree of similarity. Undoubtedly, tribal reactions to the intruders differed, but largely as a result of specific and immediate socio-cultural circumstances rather than conceptual frameworks. So we are as justified in generalizing about a century of Eastern Woodland—"Indian"—views of intrusive Europeans as we are about "European" views of the New World and its inhabitants.

Yet our evidence for native views poses special challenges. Since the Indians of North America had no writing systems, they have left us virtually no first-hand accounts of their early perceptions of white men. But they did not fail to register their views for later historians. The first source is the descriptions of early European explorers and colonists, who witnessed—through their own distorting lenses—the Indians' behavior toward them, from which we can cautiously deduce certain attitudes and emotions. Second, these same Europeans and later ethnographers recorded native myths and stories about the Indians' first meetings with Europeans. Even when collected long after the event, oral traditions accurately convey cultural details and the emotional ambience of those initial encounters. Related to oral tradition are the first names given by the natives to the white men. The characteristics highlighted by these names are a valuable index to native images and values. Europeans also made an appearance in native art, where the material projects images as vividly as words do. And finally, the White Man appears in native humor, which reflects persistent attitudes and durable stereotypes.

Indians formed opinions about Europeans not only in North America but in Europe as well. From Columbus's first voyage onward, European explorers had a propensity for plucking human souvenirs from the beaches and riverbanks of the New World. A few were taken to the slave markets of Spain, others to the monasteries of France, some to audiences with heads of state, others to learn a language to enable them to serve as interpreters upon their return, all to satisfy the curiosity of the homebound and to be impressed in turn by the splendors of "civilization."[3] Those who survived the round trip had strong feelings about their experiences and their hosts or captors. These feelings they conveyed to their countrymen, and we are fortunate to be able to eavesdrop on a few of their frank relations.

Even before the first white men appeared they may have impressed themselves upon the Indian imagination. Shamans who were thought capable of seeing into the future and other prescient people may have prophesied the coming of the Europeans. I say "may have" because these prophecies were recorded only after contact with the newcomers. A Powhatan shaman in Virginia predicted that "bearded men should come & take away their Country & that there should none of the original Indians be left, within an hundred & fifty years."[4] During the lethal plague that preceded the arrival of the Plymouth pilgrims in 1620, a Nauset Indian on Cape Cod dreamed of the advent of "a great many men" dressed in what proved to be English-style clothes. One of them, dressed all in black, stood on an eminence with a book in his hand and told the assembled Indians that "God was *moosquantum* or angry with them, and that he would kill them for their sinnes. . . ."[5]

More prevalent were oral traditions regarding the Europeans' arrival, a few collected shortly after contact, most of them several centuries later. In 1633 a young Montagnais related the story his grandmother had told him of the Indians' astonishment at seeing a French ship for the first time. Like many natives before and after, they thought it was a "moving Island." Having seen the men aboard, however, the Montagnais women began to prepare wigwams for them, "as is their custom when new guests arrive," and four canoes bade the strangers welcome. The French gave them a barrel of ship's biscuits and probably offered them some wine. But the natives were appalled that these people "drank blood and ate wood" and promptly threw the tasteless biscuits into the St. Law-

rence. Obviously more impressed by French technology than
cuisine, the Montagnais henceforth called the French *oue-
michtigouchiou,* "men in a wooden canoe or boat."[6]

The Micmacs were equally unimpressed by French fare.
When the first Frenchmen arrived in the Gaspé, the Micmacs
"mistook the bread which was given them for a piece of birch
tinder." When wine was proffered, the natives became convinced that the strangers were "cruel and inhuman, since
in their amusements . . . they drank blood without repug-
nance. . . . Therefore they remained some time not only
without tasting it, but even without wishing to become in any
manner intimate, or to hold intercourse, with a nation which
they believed to be accustomed to blood and carnage."[7]

Further west, an Ojibwa prophet dreamed that

> men of strange appearance have come across the great water.
> They have landed on our island [North America]. Their
> skins are white like snow, and on their faces long hair grows.
> These people have come across the great water in wonder-
> fully large canoes which have great white wings like those of
> a giant bird. The men have long and sharp knives, and they
> have long black tubes which they point at birds and animals.
> The tubes make a smoke that rises into the air just like the
> smoke from our pipes. From them come fire and such terrific
> noise that I was frightened, even in my dream.

At once a flotilla of trusted men was sent through the Great
Lakes and down the St. Lawrence to investigate. On the lower
river they found a clearing in which all the trees had been cut
down, which led them to conjecture that "giant beavers with
huge, sharp teeth had done the cutting." The prophet dis-
agreed, reminding them of the long knives in his dream.
Knowing that their stone-headed axes could not cut such
large trees as smoothly, they were "filled with awe, and with
terror also." Still more puzzling were "long, rolled-up shav-
ings" of wood and scraps of "bright-coloured cloth," which

they stuck in their hair and wound around their heads. Further down the river they finally came upon the white-faced, bearded strangers with their astonishing long knives, thunder tubes, and giant winged canoes, just as the prophet had predicted.

Having satisfied their curiosity and fulfilled the prophet's dream, the Indians returned home with their trophies; each villager was given a small piece of cloth as a memento. To impress their neighbors, the Ojibwas followed an old custom. Just as they tied the scalps of their enemies on long poles, "now they fastened the splinters of wood and strips of calico to poles and sent them with special messengers" from one tribe to another. Thus were these strange articles passed from hand to hand around the whole lake, giving the natives of the interior their first knowledge of the white men from Europe.[8]

The Indians regarded the Europeans' ability to fashion incredible objects and make them work less as mechanical aptitude than as spiritual power. When the Delawares, who once lived along the New Jersey-New York coast, met their first Dutch ship, they concluded that it was a "remarkably large house in which the Mannitto (the Great or Supreme Being) himself was present." Thinking he was coming to pay them a visit, they prepared meat for a sacrifice, put all their religious effigies in order, and staged a grand dance to please or appease him. Meanwhile, the tribal conjurers tried to fathom his purpose in coming because their brethren were all "distracted between hope and fear." While preparations were being made, runners brought the welcome news that the visitors were humans like themselves, only strangely colored and oddly dressed. But when the Dutchmen made their appearance, graced the assembly with a round of liquor, and distributed iron and cloth gifts, the natives were confirmed in their original belief that every white man was an "inferior Mannitto attendant upon the Supreme Deity"—the ship's captain—who "shone superior" in his red velvet suit glittering with gold lace.[9]

The earliest French and English explorers who were the objects of native awe corroborated native testimony, despite some suggestion that the Indians were struck most forcefully by other European characteristics. Some Indians appeared to be fascinated by the whiteness of European skin. On Arthur Barlowe's reconnaissance of Roanoke Island in 1584, the natives "wondred mervelously when we were amongest them, at the whitenes of our skinnes, ever coveting to touch our breastes, and to view the same."[10] Sixty years earlier, one of Verrazzano's sailors was nearly drowned trying to swim with some small gifts to a group of Indians on the same Outer Banks. Before returning him safely to the ship, the natives "placed him on the ground in the sun . . . and made gestures of great admiration, looking at the whiteness of his flesh and examining him from head to foot."[11]

The close examination the Indians occasionally gave the explorers' chests, faces, and arms, however, may have been focused on the skin's hairiness rather than its pallor. Mariners, after all, were likely to be deeply suntanned after a spring or summer cruise of several weeks. Most Indians, by contrast, were relatively hairless, and the little they grew was assiduously plucked or singed. Understandably, European beards and tufted chests held an ugly fascination for them. Before they laid eyes on a white man, the Potawatomis and Menominees around Green Bay believed the French to be a "different species from other men" because they were "covered with hair," not because their skin was a shade or two lighter.[12] By the same token, the caresses Jacques Cartier received from Algonquians on the Gaspé in 1534 were given less because he was white-skinned than to thank him for the presents he had just given. By the time he reached the Iroquoian village of Hochelaga on Montreal Island the following year, he had learned that "rubbing . . . with their hands" was a traditional native greeting, not one reserved for white visitors.[13]

The first Europeans, however, were no ordinary guests, and their friendly reception owed much to the native belief that they were spiritually powerful men, gods (as the Europeans put it) or *manitous* (in Algonquian parlance) like the Indians' own shamans and conjurers. The sources of their power were chiefly two. The first was their reputation among the Indians as purveyors or preventers of disease, exactly comparable to native shamans, who were also thought to wield powers of life and death. Jacques Cartier was asked to lay hands on all the sick and handicapped of Hochelaga as if, he said, "Christ had come down to earth to heal them." In 1665 a Jesuit priest found himself held in similar regard by the natives of Michigan and Wisconsin. When he advised a Fox man to have his dangerously ill parents bled, the man poured powdered tobacco over the priest's gown and said, "Thou art a spirit; come now, restore these sick people to health; I offer thee this tobacco in sacrifice."[14] The priest at least came off better than the first French captain who sailed to the Menominees on Lake Michigan: he had tobacco ground into his forehead.[15]

At the same time, the Indians believed that all spiritual power was double-edged: those who could cure could also kill. Only powerful "spirits" possessed the ability to bewitch or to counteract another's witchcraft. When they inadvertently carried deadly European diseases into the North Carolina coastal region, the English colonists at Roanoke were deified by their hosts for their ability to kill Indians at a distance and to remain unscathed themselves. "There could at no time happen any strange sicknesse, losses, hurtes, or any other crosse unto [the natives]," wrote Thomas Harriot, the expedition's Indian expert, "but that they would impute to us the cause or meanes therof for offending or not pleasing us." The Indians had extra cause to worry when four or five

towns that had practiced some "subtle devise" against the
English were ravaged by an unknown disease shortly after the
colonists' departure. The English allies under chief Wingina
deduced that the havoc was wrought by "our God through
our meanes, and that wee by him might kil and slaie whom
wee would without weapons and not come neere them. . . .
This marvelous accident in all the countrie," explained Harriot, "wrought so strange opinions of us, that some people
could not tel whether to thinke us gods or men," particularly
when no Englishman died or was even especially sick.[16]

The second and more important source of the white man's
power in native America was his technological superiority.
The Indians' acquaintance with it began well before 1524,
when Verrazzano cruised the eastern waters from the Caro-
linas to Maine. On an "Arcadian" coast somewhere south
of New York harbor, a handsome, naked Indian man ap-
proached a group of the French sailors and showed them a
burning stick, "as if to offer us fire." But when the Europeans
trumped his hospitality by firing a matchlock, "he trembled
all over with fear" and "remained as if thunderstruck, and
prayed, worshiping like a monk, pointing his finger to the
sky; and indicating the sea and the ship, he appeared to bless
us."[17]

Not without reason, European iron weapons continued to
impress the natives who saw them in action for the first time.
When Pierre Radisson and Nicolas Perrot traveled among
the Indians of Wisconsin in the middle years of the seventeenth century, the natives literally worshipped their guns,
knives, and hatchets by blowing sacred smoke over them, as
a sacrifice to the spirits within. To Perrot the Potawatomi
elders said, "Thou art one of the chief spirits, since thou usest
iron; it is for thee to rule and protect all men. Praised be the
Sun, who has instructed thee and sent thee to our country."[18]

Weapons were of paramount importance to the feuding
native polities of North America, but metal objects of any

kind, cloth goods, and cleverly designed or sizable wooden objects also drew their admiration. Thomas Harriot put his finger on the primary cause of the Indians' initially exalted opinion of the white strangers when he noted that

> most things they sawe with us, as Mathematicall instruments, sea compasses, the vertue of the loadstone in drawing iron, a perspective glasse whereby was shewed manie strange sightes, burning glasses, wildefire woorkes, gunnes, bookes, writing and reading, spring clocks that seeme to goe of themselves, and manie other thinges that wee had, were so straunge unto them, and so farre exceeded their capacities to comprehend the reason and meanes how they should be made and done, that they thought they were rather the works of gods than of men, or at the leastwise they had bin given and taught us of the gods.[19]

The Sioux, Illinois, and Seneca Indians among whom the Recollect priest Louis Hennepin journeyed during the early 1680s frequently clapped their hands over their mouths in astonishment at such things as printed books, silver chalices, embroidered chasubles, and iron pots, all of which they designated as "spirits."[20] In the 1630s the natives of southern New England considered a windmill "little less than the world's wonder" for the whisking motion of its long arms and its "sharp teeth biting the corn," and the first plowman "little better than a juggler" or shaman. Being shown the iron coulter and share of the plow, which could "tear up more ground in a day than their clamshells [hoes] could scrape up in a month," they told the plowman "he was almost Abamacho, almost as cunning as the Devil."[21]

The white man's varied powers were celebrated in the generic names given to him by different native groups. The Narragansetts of Rhode Island called all Europeans "Coatmen" or "swordmen." The Mohawks of New York referred to the Dutch as "Iron-workers" or "Cloth makers," while the Hurons called the French *Agnonha,* "Iron People." In northern New England the Pocumtucks knew the French as "Knife men," just as the Virginians and later all Americans were known as "Longknives." The long-robed Recollect missionaries obviously made less impression on the Montagnais, who referred to them as "Those dressed like women." Their evangelical rivals, the Jesuits, were known less derisively as "Black Robes," and by the Hurons as "The men called charcoal."[22]

Native characterizations of Europeans also received material expression in Indian artifacts, particularly effigy combs and pipes and wampum belts. Probably in the seventeenth century, the Iroquois made a belt to mark the sight of the first "pale faces." (Samuel Champlain and two consorts clashed with a war party of Mohawks on Lake Champlain in 1609, but they were probably not the Europeans commemorated.) Unlike several eighteenth-century belts, it does not feature European figures. Rather it consists of four groups of three purple-beaded, diagonal lines, indicating props or supports of the Longhouse, the symbol of the League of Five Nations. The tradition that has come down with the belt suggests that either the Dutch or the English pledged military support to the Iroquois against their enemies, and perhaps vice versa.[23]

Throughout the colonial period, most belts employed geometrical shapes as a cultural vocabulary of mnemonics—diamonds, squares, and pentagons as tribes or nations, diagonals as agreements and mutual aid pacts, long lines as paths or messages. But by the eighteenth century the colonists were occasionally pictured as recognizably human figures. Missionaries invariably held or stood near crosses, but most Europeans wore frock coats and tall, wide-brimmed hats. A few of the purple-beaded newcomers were distinguished from their Indian companions on the belts by their white hearts.[24]

The Senecas of western New York fixed the image of the white man (never woman) when they carved delicate antler combs and molded clay pipes. The first European to make his

A Delaware Indian and a European wearing a tall hat and perhaps a frock coat hold hands on this early wampum belt to signify their treaty of friendship. The treaty was one of the early land cessions from the Delawares to William Penn, perhaps the famous one under the elm tree at Shackamaxon in 1682. In 1857 Penn's great-grandson presented the belt to the Pennsylvania Historical Society, by whose courtesy it is reproduced here.

appearance on a Seneca comb was probably a Dutchman, who was carved in frock coat and hat at the Steele site, where one village of Senecas lived between 1625 and 1645. Most of the trade goods reaching the Senecas at this time came from Dutch traders at Fort Orange on the Hudson. On a site occupied about thirty years later, the natives had begun to sculpt men in Dutch-style hats on pipes, carve mounted Europeans on antler combs, and cast lead in the shape of behatted Dutchmen. At the nearly contemporaneous Boughton Hill site, Europeans on horseback were favorite features on antler combs. Standing or mounted, most white men by then held long guns at their side, symbolizing their technological superiority as well as their potential threat to native sovereignty.[25]

The threats to native land and liberty came from many different directions. The white-hearted or guileful white man on wampum belts had analogues in Indian humor. Most of these stories are found in colonial or early national collections of American folk anecdotes, so they may not reflect only Indian sources of humor. But they do emanate from a double source, "the play of Yankee humor on racial mingling, and the Indian's own sense of wit and shrewdness."[26] Even when

A Seneca antler comb excavated in 1920 from the Boughton Hill site in western New York, which was occupied c. 1665–87. It depicts a Dutchman in a distinctive hat wearing a buttoned jacket and pantaloons edged with buttons. A small dog paws for attention from the musket-bearing man. From the *New York State Museum Bulletin,* nos. 227–28 (Albany, 1921).

the morphology of the tales resembles European precedents, they accurately convey Indian attitudes toward the intruders in their midst.

One such story describes how the early colonists asked their generous native hosts for a small parcel of land upon which to settle, the size merely of a cow's hide. Having seen a cow on board the settlers' ship, the Indians readily agreed. As soon as the bargain was concluded, however, the settlers killed a bull, their largest, cut the skin into a thin continuous strip, and measured out a huge piece of ground. In other versions the seat of a chair was uncaned for the same nefarious purpose.[27]

Another anecdote about sharp dealing featured a white trader who sold an Indian a packet of gunpowder, telling him that it contained the seeds of a fine, wheatlike grain. The gullible Indian planted and tended his new "seeds" carefully, but with no results. Some time later the trader demanded of the Indian the settlement of an overdue account, to which the Indian replied, "Me pay you when my powder grow."[28] That this kind of story once had a real grain of truth makes it no less effective. In 1622, after Opechancanough's warriors killed 347 Virginia colonists in a sudden uprising and confiscated many arms and ammunition, he ordered most of the gunpowder planted in expectation that he could "draw therefrom the like increase, as of his Maize or Corne, in Harvest next."[29]

As the natives increasingly were forced to conform to colonial expectations and institutions, they must have taken pleasure in the telling of anecdotes in which they outwitted white authorities. When one New England Indian was hailed before a justice of the peace for trespass and sabbath-breaking, he demanded a receipt for the fine he paid. The justice was somewhat surprised by the request but agreed to furnish the receipt if the culprit could show his need for it. The Indian explained in his humblest manner:

'Tis best to have things sure; for perhaps, by and by, you die;
an Indian being a little tougher, perhaps, I live a little
longer; then I die, and go up to God's house and knock. "Ah!
who comes there?" I must tell, it won't do to tell lies dere.
"Well, have you settled for cutting the tree on the sabbath
day?" Yes, sir. "Where is your receipt?" I haven't any.—Then
I must go away, along down from God's house, to HELL, to
get a receipt of you, sir; but if you will give me one now, sir,
it will save me all dat trouble.[30]

The Indians got an eyeful of European behavior in North
America, but many colonial officials felt that the colonists
who interacted with the natives most frequently were not out-
standing models of Western "civilization." So from time to
time they shipped carefully selected natives off to Europe
to view the white man at his best, with the expectation that
upon their return they would spread the gospel of European
superiority throughout their native villages. Among the earliest Indian tourists were three Tupinambas, who were taken
from their native Brazil to Rouen in 1562. Although they
were South Americans, their responses to Europe were remarkably similar to those of their northern brethren who followed. After talking with King Charles IX, the twelve-year-
old monarch, someone asked them what they found most
amazing about *la belle France*. Their first observation was
"they thought it very strange that so many grown men,
bearded, strong, and armed, who were around the king [his
Swiss guard] should submit to obey a child, and that one of
them was not chosen to command instead." And second,
"they had noticed that there were among us men full and
gorged with all sorts of good things, and that their other
halves were beggars at their doors, emaciated with hunger
and poverty; and they thought it strange that these needy
halves could endure such an injustice, and did not take the
others by the throat, or set fire to their houses."[31]

A half-century later, Savignon, an eighteen-year-old Huron

lad, made a similar trip to France with Champlain and had much the same reaction as did his Tupi predecessors. When he returned to Canada in 1611, he was deemed a liar by his tribesmen when he tried to describe the marvels he had seen, such as a "coach drawn by six or eight horses" and "a striking clock." Savignon "well remembered the good cheer he had enjoyed in France," particularly his presentation at the court of Louis XIII, and "boasted of it everywhere." Yet "he never had the wish to return" because of the social institutions and behavior he had seen. "Often when he saw two men quarrelling without coming to blows or killing one another, [he] would mock at them, saying that they were nought but women, and had no courage." He and his tribesmen deplored "the great number of needy and beggars" in France, attributing it to lack of charity, and blamed the French clergy, "saying that if [they] had some intelligence [they] would set some order in the matter, the remedies being simple." Even more alarming to Huron sensibilities was Savignon's report that "among the French, men were whipped, hanged and put to death without distinction of innocence or guilt." This persuaded the Hurons not to send their children to Quebec for schooling at the hands of the Recollects.[32]

Another visitor used some of his time in England to dispel one of his countrymen's dominant myths about the colonists. Uttamatomakkin, one of Powhatan's trusted councillors who accompanied Pocahontas to England in 1616, was amazed "at the sight of so much corn and trees in his journey from Plymouth to London." He, like many Indians, imagined that the dearth of these vital articles had brought the English to America.[33] When the Narragansetts asked Roger Williams why the English came to their country, they answered themselves, saying "It is because you want *firing:* for they," Williams explained, "having burnt up the *wood* in one place . . . are faine to follow the *wood;* and so to remove to a fresh new place for the woods sake."[34]

While the Indians were constantly making dismaying discoveries about the intruders, the Europeans were no less busy trying to lay open the secret springs of native behavior and culture. One of the rudest revelations the Europeans had was that the Indians—allegedly savage, poor, and unlettered—had a terrific superiority complex, not only at first contact but long after. When the French landed in Acadia in 1610, they were astounded to discover that the local Micmacs thought themselves "better, more valiant and more ingenious" than the French, and even "richer." After eighty years of contact with the French, the Micmacs had not changed their opinion. "There is no Indian," said a Micmac chief, "who does not consider himself infinitely more happy and more powerful than the French."[35] A New England sagamore, dressed in his finery with "six naked Indian spatterlashes at his heels for his guard," wrote one early observer, "thinks himself little inferior to the great Cham. He will not stick to say he is all one with King Charles. He thinks he can blow down castles with his breath and conquer kingdoms with his conceit."[36] The Iroquois were no different. According to an eighteenth-century Englishman who knew them well, "they seem always to have Lookd upon themselves as far Superiour to the rest of Mankind and accordingly Call themselves *Ongwehoenwe,* i.e. Men Surpassing all other men."[37]

Although the natives were quick to acknowledge the superiority of certain items of European technology, particularly metal implements and woven cloth, they were most reluctant to praise the life that the white men made from them. They simply preferred their own. To give but one example, the Micmacs could not understand the French fetish for large, permanent houses. Why, they asked, "do men of five to six feet in height need houses which are sixty to eighty?" They much preferred the sensibleness of Indians, "who carry their houses and their wigwams with them so that they may lodge wheresoever they please, independently of any seignior whatsoever." They were infinitely happier than the grasping strangers, they said, because "we are very content with the little we have."[38]

After considerable travel among the Indians of North Carolina, John Lawson knew it to be true. "There is one Vice very common every where, which I never found amongst them," he noted in 1709, "which is Envying other Mens Happiness. . . . Of this Sin I cannot say I ever saw an Example, though they are a People that set as great a Value upon themselves, as any sort of Men in the World." Because the Indians of North America valued "natural Vertues and Gifts" rather than material possessions, they did not envy the white men with their insatiable appetites for land, wealth, and power. Because, as Montaigne observed, "each man calls barbarism whatever is not his own practice," they clung to their own ways as long as possible, finding comfort as well as efficiency in the familiar.[39]

The mystery we should like to solve is how, in the face of inexplicable and uncontrollable diseases, admitted technological inferiority, demographic inundation, loss of land and power, and aggressive religious and cultural proselytizing, the Indians managed to sustain their magnificent, if disconcerting, self-regard. If we could solve that, we would possess the key to understanding the depth and range of their early feelings and attitudes toward the European intruders.

CHAPTER NINE

At the Water's Edge:
Trading in the
Sixteenth Century

AMERICAN HISTORIANS ARE JUST BEGINNING TO DISCOVER THAT North America had a full and important history in the sixteenth century.* In addition to perhaps four million Indians, the French, English, Spanish, and Portuguese were economically and, on occasion, politically preoccupied with the new continent. The Spanish penetrated deep into the Southeast and Southwest, establishing military posts and missionary centers wherever they went. When they chose not to settle, they did their utmost to ensure that European rivals did not outflank them. The zones of sharpest conflict were on the coasts of Florida, near the shipping lanes of the Spanish bullion fleets, and around Newfoundland, whose fish-laden waters drew fleets from all the major Western European ports. All of these ventures led to contact and sometimes conflict with the local natives.

With the major exception of David Quinn, the master of early exploration, historians have yet to examine the numerous and various interactions between Indians and European mariners in the sixteenth century. After the publication in 1979 of Quinn's five-volume *New American World: A Documentary History of North America to 1612*, they had little excuse. "At the Water's Edge" is my contribution to what I hope will be a burgeoning bibliography on the truly formative period of American history.

* James Axtell, "Europeans, Indians, and the Age of Discovery in American History Textbooks," *American Historical Review*, 92 (1987), 621–32.

As STRANGE AS IT MAY SEEM, A HOMELY FISH BROUGHT Western Europeans together with North Americans, perhaps even before Columbus bumped into the West Indies, and bound their two continents in an indissoluble union of fates. For once Europe's mariners were drawn to America's waters, they quickly discovered her native peoples and were drawn into commerce, competition, and conflict.

From the late fifteenth century, fishermen from the Atlantic ports of England, Spain, Portugal, and France headed each spring for the cold waters off Newfoundland in search of the meaty cod. In the form of lightly salted, sun-dried "poor john," this inexpensive "beef of the sea" was "inexhaustible manna" for Europe's peasants, armies, navies, and urban lower classes.[1] It was also welcome on the tables of Catholics who observed the Church's 57 fast days and 108 days of abstinence, a total of 165 days—five and a half months—in which meat could not be eaten.

The first fishermen to discover the cod-rich waters of the "new found world" may have sailed in the early 1480s from Bristol.[2] But it was an anglicized Venetian, John Cabot, who left the requisite documentary tracks of discovery in 1497. Cabot's reports that the northern seas so swarmed with fish that they could be taken in baskets kindled keen interest in America's offshore resources. By 1517 "an hundred sail" could be found in Newfoundland's summer harbors.[3] The discovery of the Grand Banks in the 1530s only increased the traffic between Europe and America. In the age of the Armada, fishing was definitely big business, the second largest in the European economy. While Spanish gold and silver lit the imaginations of sixteenth-century entrepreneurs, the number of men employed and the tonnage carried by the Newfoundland cod fleet was twice that of the great Spanish flotas. The Gulf of St. Lawrence was a pole of European activity in every way comparable to that of the Caribbean and the Gulf of Mexico.[4]

For forty or fifty years the northern gulf rivaled the southern even in the richness of its cargoes. After 1536 the cod fishermen were joined in America by Basque whalers, who followed Breton pilots to the narrow Strait of Belle Isle between Labrador and Newfoundland. There they chased bowhead and right whales with harpoons in fragile *chalupas,* as they had done for generations off their own Cantabrian coast. When it was shipped to Europe, refined "train oil" was as profitable as liquid gold. For whale oil lit the lamps of Europe, made soap and soup, lubricated everything from frying pans to clocks, and, since the whale was classified as a fish, served as *lard de carême*—Lenten fat—during holy days when meat products were prohibited.

At their peak, two thousand French and Spanish Basques worked out of ports on the northern shore of the Strait, through which the whales funneled each autumn. The twenty-to-thirty ships on which they came each year were not modest fishing barks but large Spanish galleons, heavily armed. In an age of cutthroat piracy, they had to be when even a small ship stowed 55,000 gallons of train oil worth $4-6 million in modern currency. At those rates, the Gulf of Mexico could not afford to look down its nose at its Laurentian cousin.[5]

Basque and other European ships sought to maximize profits by fishing for many markets in American waters. Whalers, the aristocrats of the trade, were not too proud to top their holds with cod. Fishermen would often stop at gulf islands to make train oil from walruses, whose tusks also sold as ivory and whose thick hides made excellent shields for archers and prevented ship's rigging from chafing. All sorts of watermen, even those who plied the banks, put into shore long enough to bargain for Indian furs. While fishing the Strait of Belle Isle in 1542, two Basque crews ate and drank with "very friendly" natives who understood "any language," French, English, Gascon or Basque. They then traded "deer," "wolf," and marten skins for "all kinds of ironware," particularly axes and knives.[6]

By the last quarter of the century, fishing ships often carried a pinnace for coasting in search of furs while the fishing proceeded. Contracts made in several French ports stipulated that vessels departing for "Canada" and the St. Lawrence were to engage in "the fishing of whales and other fish and traffic of merchandise with the Indians."[7] English interest in multipurpose voyages was greatly stimulated by two ships captured in 1591. The *Bonaventure* of Saint-Malo carried the oil, hides, and "teeth" of 1,500 walruses, valued conservatively at £1,430. Its train oil, five carcasses to a hogshead, was so sweet and unfishy that the soap-makers of Bristol, who supplied much of the English cloth industry, took quick notice. "The king of Spaine," declared the mayor of Bristol and the pirate ship's owner, "may burne some of his Olive trees." The French Basque *Catherine de St Vincent* was even more intriguing. Beneath her hatches was found "trayne oyle, Salmon & newland feshe And greate Store of Riche Fures," such as beaver, marten, and otter. On other voyages the ship had garnered black fox skins, "the rarest furres that are knowen."[8]

Long before the maritime fur trade began in earnest, the fishermen and whalers had been joined by hundreds of other European sailors on the east coast of North America. Some came to find a Northwest Passage through or around the new continent, hoping to beat European competitors to the known wealth of the East. Others sought to make a living in American waters by plundering the rich cargoes of national rivals, particularly those of Basque whalers and the Spanish bullion fleets that sailed annually through the narrow strait between Florida and the Bahamas. A few even came as tourists to gawk at the bruited wonders of the New World and its strange flora, fauna, and human inhabitants. Somewhat later, when it became known that America was as habitable as profitable, outposts and colonies were planted as factories for entrepreneurs, dumping grounds for convicts and paupers, havens for religious dissenters, and bastions for imperial contenders.[9]

All of these full- or part-time mariners and the American natives eventually met on the watery margin of their respective worlds, and, sometimes deliberately, often inadvertently, pulled each other into human and cultural experiences that were not merely novel but potentially revolutionary. Since the Europeans had initiated contact by thrusting themselves into the natives' world, the onus of change fell heavily on the Indians, who were often required to respond to unwonted and unwanted challenges from the strangers. But the natives were indispensable to most of the European projects on land, as they were not to the cod fishermen, and so they retained considerable cultural autonomy and room for maneuvering. At the same time, the Indians launched the Europeans who stayed in America on a centuries-long rite of passage. By 1600 the process had barely begun, but at the achievement of independence the cultural descendants of the cod fishers, pilgrims, and soldiers of fortune had been ineluctably molded into distinctive American shapes in large part by the impress of their native allies, trading partners, and nemeses.

The earliest explorers of North America were not interested in trade of any sort, at least not in America. Since they were new to the land, they were understandably preoccupied with charting its waters and cataloguing its floral, faunal, and mineral assets to interest investors and crowned heads in future extractive expeditions. They tended to see in the natives only slaves, future interpreters and guides, pawns in the imperial partition of the New World, or walking souvenirs. Columbus set a poor precedent on his first voyage by taking ten West Indians home to Spain, where six were baptized and presented at court as proof of his discovery and Spain's precedence. The following year, however, he took thirty prisoners of war from Hispaniola to sell as slaves in Seville. In the next three years, some 1,400 Indians were shipped to Spanish slave markets.[10]

Not to be outdone, Spain's Portuguese rivals soon got into the act. In 1501 Gaspar Corte-Real sent home to his sovereign about fifty Indian men and women from Newfoundland or the northern coasts. An Italian in Lisbon, after scrutinizing and fingering the human booty, noted that the men, despite their "terribly harsh" tattooed faces, "laugh considerably and manifest the greatest pleasure," probably to disguise their true feelings. "The women," he could not help but notice, "have small breasts and most beautiful bodies, and rather pleasant faces." The Venetian ambassador had his eye on other things. The gypsy-like men, he predicted, "will be excellent for labor and the best slaves that have hitherto been obtained," expressing a southerner's preference for hardy northern natives over the softer Arawaks purloined by Columbus.[11]

The unsavory Iberian appetite for slaves was fed again in 1525 when Estevão Gomes, a Portuguese pilot in the Spanish service, filled two ships with rich furs and fifty-eight Algonquians from New England, "all innocent and half-naked." For a time the port was all atwitter when it was reported that Gomes had returned from his search for a Northwest Passage with a shipload of cloves (*clavos*), presumably from the Spice Islands of the East, rather than a few dozen slaves (*esclavos*), which contravened the king's express orders not to use violence against any natives.[12]

By no means was the penchant for kidnapping confined to southern Europeans, although those taken by the French and the English were fewer and their treatment somewhat better. In 1502 John Amayne's cargo of salt fish included American hawks, an eagle, and three Indians, who were dressed in

"beasts' skins" and ate raw meat. Two years later, two of
them were seen in Westminster Palace, sartorially passing
as Englishmen. Normandy got its first look at "wild" Americans in 1509 when seven Indian men were captured in their
bark canoe and conveyed to Rouen. Six of them soon died,
but the survivor was carried to King Louis XII for exhibi-
tion. We would like to know the native's impression of people who, unlike his own, made a fetish of "bread, wine, [and]
money." The year before Gomes plundered New England,
Giovanni da Verrazzano, sailing for Francis I, captured an
eight-year-old Indian boy somewhere north of the Caro-
linas, but failed to pick up a feisty young woman who was
tall, very beautiful, and exceedingly shrill-voiced when man-
handled.[13]

Most of these early captives were taken as curiosities to
amuse or impress European officials and courtiers. A few
even reached more popular venues. A twenty-year-old Eskimo
woman and a seven-year-old child, taken by the French from
Labrador in 1566, were exhibited for money at the inns of
France, Germany, and the Low Countries. Their landlady
in The Hague attempted to introduce the woman to Christianity by showing her a statue of Christ, but the sealskin-
clad native could only shake her head, lift it up, and put her
hands on top of it. The good Dutch woman took this to
mean that she had some knowledge of the true Christian
God, but that was probably wishful thinking.[14]

The Eskimo man, woman, and baby boy lifted by Martin
Frobisher from Baffin Island in 1577 were subject to similar
though briefer celebrity in Bristol. Despite a broken rib
which eventually punctured a lung and led to his death, the
man Calichough entertained the mayor's dinner party by
paddling his kayak up and down the Avon and killing a
couple of ducks with his bird-dart. He may even have
mounted a horse, backwards, adding humor to the guests'
admiration. All three natives sat for portraits, as had their

A Nuremberg broadside advertising a twenty-year-old Eskimo mother and her seven-year-old daughter, who were kidnapped from Labrador and exhibited around Europe in 1566. Drawn from life, the woodcut accurately depicts the woman's facial tattoos and the cut of her sealskin parka, pants, and buskins. A similar broadside was published in Augsburg in the same year. From a copy of *Warhafftige Contrafey einer wilden Frawen . . . Novaterra gennant* (Nuremberg, 1566) in the Map Library of the British Library, London, by whose courtesy it is reproduced here.

brethren eleven years earlier, whose likenesses circulated from Germany in broadside.[15]

When European thoughts turned to settlement or the fur trade, the kidnapping of Indians took on new purpose. The goal then was to put native tongues to school in a "civilized" language to enable them to interpret for the Europeans when they returned to America. If the Indians were awed by the majesty and power of European cities, courts, and armies, so much the better, particularly if they conveyed that awe to their kinsmen. This is clearly what Jacques Cartier had in mind in 1534 when he kidnapped Taignoagny and Domagaya, sons of the headman of the St. Lawrence Iroquois at modern Quebec City. When he returned the following year, the boys acted as pilots up the tricky St. Lawrence and interpreted the words of Cartier and their father Donnacona. Cartier's motives were more mixed after his winter in Canada when he hoodwinked the chief, his sons, and three tribesmen into sailing to France with him. None of the natives returned to Canada on his final voyage in 1541, but one girl was said to have reached adulthood, and the group was supported at Saint-Malo for at least two years by the king. When the St. Lawrence was finally opened to sea-going fur traders in the 1580s, having been closed by Cartier's callous disregard for native freedom, the French again took two potential interpreters with them when they returned to Saint-Malo.[16] Thus the first extractive industry in colonial North America was kidnapping.

Fortunately, the first true trade with the natives was much less threatening and gave the new partners an opportunity to size each other up in relative safety. After several weeks at sea, virtually all European ships needed to be refurbished with firewood, fresh water, and provisions at early ports of call. Ships taking the southern route stopped in the Azores, Madeiras, Canaries, Cape Verdes, or West Indies en route, but those headed directly west from northern Europe saw only Irish ports before hitting Newfoundland or the coasts of Canada.

Wood and water were usually free for the taking, although Columbus paid the natives of Crooked Island hawk's bells and small glass beads to fill his water casks. Provisions, too, sometimes came at no expense if the natives extended their traditional hospitality to the bearded white strangers. But the mariners quickly learned that reciprocity was the social key to native America and began to reward their hosts with small presents. In 1542 Roberval swapped knives and other "trifles" for generous quantities of red shad with the Stada-conans around Quebec. Seven years later Spanish friars in southern Florida bought fresh fish with shirts because they had no beads, knives, or axes, which the Indians had learned to want. For shirts, knives, and fishhooks, French traders in the Chesapeake in 1560 purchased corn and pumpkins to supplant moldy ship's biscuits, as well as a thousand marten skins. A few years later in the same region, Spanish Jesuits attempting to found a mission on the York River were forced to "barter for maize with copper and tin" after initially refusing to pay for food as bad precedent.[17]

Just when the North American fur trade began is not documented, although the Vikings who spent three years in "Vinland," probably at L'Anse aux Meadows in northern Newfoundland, around 1010 A.D. have as firm a claim to priority as any. According to Norse sagas, they traded cow's milk and strips of red cloth for bales of sable and other furs with the Skraelings, who turned testy after they were refused metal weapons. In the early modern era, the taciturn New-foundland fishermen are always accorded first, if brief, respect, but not because they left written evidence of their enterprise. Archaeologists were the first to notice that six-teenth-century Seneca sites in western New York were strewn with ship's bolts, rigging rings, metal tips from belaying pins, and spiral brass earrings worn by Basque sailors. Only later, when they read Nicolas Denys's account of seventeenth-century Acadia, did they realize that fishing crews were notorious for practically selling their ships from under their captains, filling their sea chests with native furs exchanged for "biscuit, lead, quite new lines, sails, and many other things at the expense of the owners."[18]

By the time an Atlantic adventurer first mentions the fur trade, the trade is well under way. When Corte-Real sailed off with fifty natives in 1501, one of them had a piece of a gilt sword made in Italy and another wore a pair of Venetian silver rings in his ears; their heat-hardened javelins may have been tipped with steel.[19] By 1524 the coastal inhabitants of northern New England were so choosey about trade goods that they would accept only knives, fishhooks, and sharp metal. On a march inland Verrazzano saw many natives with what he believed to be " 'paternostri' beads of copper in their ears," though some or all of them may have been of native copper. Ten years later, Cartier found Micmacs inviting him to shore to trade by waving furs on sticks. By then, of course, the natives of the Gulf of St. Lawrence had trafficked with European fishermen for at least thirty years, perhaps half a century.[20]

The best evidence that the fur trade predates the earliest known records is that, by the advent of the first chroniclers, the natives had established regular trade protocols for dealing with the strangers, which were undoubtedly modifications of techniques for interacting with native neighbors and trading partners. These protocols consisted of several elements. Unlike native canoes or kayaks, European ships without experience in American waters had to be shown protective harbors and the best approaches to native trading sites or villages. This guidance the natives provided with animated sign or body language, just as the denizens of New York harbor showed Verrazzano's crew the safest place to beach their longboat. In Narragansett Bay natives in canoes guided

Most of the sixteenth-century trade with the Indians was conducted at seaside from European ships. When the ocean-going traders did not row their own longboats to shore, the Indians paddled their canoes out to the ships to commence trading. In this engraving, based on early written accounts rather than eye witness, Theodor de Bry depicts Englishmen trading knives and a broad-brimmed hat for furs, feathers, arrows, and shell necklaces (rendered incorrectly as whole shells rather than small wampum beads). From de Bry's *America Pars Decima*, Part XIII (Frankfurt-am-Main, 1634).

the *Dauphine* safely to port from a league out to sea.[21] By this time, apparently, the Indians no longer regarded the visitors as capricious and potentially dangerous "gods" or their ships as mysterious "floating islands," as they are often portrayed in retrospective native accounts of their first encounters. To some extent, the white man had already been desacralized by familiarity, and his technology reclassified from miraculous to mundane.[22]

When the Europeans landed safely, each partner sought to assure the other of his peaceful intentions. Occasionally, native suspicions were difficult to allay and the natives would lie concealed out of reach and sight; considering the European penchant for picking up human mementoes, their caution was not misplaced. The only way to win their trust was to leave gifts or trade goods in a conspicuous place. On Prince Edward Island, Cartier "placed a knife and a woollen girdle [sash] on a branch" to reassure a skittish native who had invited the French to land but then had run away. In 1577 Frobisher's desire to entice the natives of Frobisher's Straits into trade "caused knives, & other thinges, to be proferred unto them, whiche they would not take at our handes," wrote a gentleman chronicler, "but beeing layd on the ground, & the partie going away, they came and tooke up, leaving something of theirs to countervaile the same."[23]

Half a century earlier the natives of northern New England had been nearly as reticent. According to Verrazzano, "if we wanted to trade with them . . . they would come to the seashore on some rocks where the breakers were most violent, while we remained in the little boat, and they sent us what they wanted to give on a rope, continually shouting to us not to approach the land." After a quick and unceremonious exchange, the Indians "made all the signs of scorn and shame that any brute creature would make, such as showing their buttocks and laughing."[24]

Natives with less caution or fewer bad experiences with European visitors often performed striking ceremonies to celebrate the opening of peaceful relations with their new trading partners. To make an economic truce with John Davis's English crew in 1587, the Eskimos of Baffin Island pointed to the sun, cried *Iliaoute* in a loud voice, and struck their chests, which Davis learned to imitate. When Cartier made his way up the St. Lawrence toward Hochelaga on Montreal Island, the Iroquoian headman of Achelacy presented him with two of his children to signify a lasting alliance between his people and the bearers of awesome technological tidings. Since trade always meant peace in native America, socially important hostages were considered the best way to preserve it. The previous year the Micmacs of Chaleur Bay on the Gaspé peninsula had celebrated a successful trading session with Cartier by "dancing and going through many ceremonies, and throwing salt water over their heads with their hands." A large group of women had also danced and rubbed the arms and chests of the Frenchmen in welcome before joining hands and joyfully raising their arms to heaven.[25]

Festivities were effective on both sides. The English, at least, discovered that sales were enhanced by music. On his first voyage in search of a Northwest Passage, Davis opened friendly relations with a band of Eskimos by ordering the ship's musicians to play and the crew to dance on shore, which was soon followed by "friendly imbracings and signes of curtesie" all around. The next day the English did a brisk trade for five native kayaks, paddles, clothes, spears, and sealskins. When Bartholomew Gosnold's trading expedition left southern New England in 1602, the crew threw their caps into the air and made their native partners "the best farewell [they] could" with trumpet and cornet. The following year on Cape Cod, Martin Pring gathered two loads of sassafras from the woods of the local Nausets, who were diverted by the "homely Musicke" of a young man's guitar. After showering the musician with gifts, they danced around him "twentie in a Ring . . . using many Savage gestures, singing Io, Ia, Io, Ia, Ia, Io: him that first brake the ring, the rest would knocke and cry out upon." Small wonder that when Sir Humphrey Gilbert set out for the new-found land in 1578 he carried six musicians in addition to the usual martial complement of trumpeters and drummers.[26]

Another vital piece of protocol was the giving of gifts and special deference to native headmen, women, and children. The French particularly learned to deal with Algonquian and Iroquoian groups by going first to their leaders, who stood out by their appearance or the deference of their followers. When the leaders gave their blessing to an exchange, the French gave other small gifts to the women and children present, assuming that the way to a man's heart—and fur cache—was through his family. In the seventeenth century and beyond, Indian women themselves were known to peddle the furs they had so carefully processed after their menfolk had killed the animals. But in the sixteenth century either the women did not get personally involved in the trade, which took place, after all, outside the villages which were their domain, or the male European observers were blind to their role, for no notice was taken of female traders of furs. Presumably, women bartered the produce of their own gardens to sailors seeking relief from weevilly biscuits.

Perhaps because of his previous experiences with the Tupinamba in Brazil, Jacques Cartier seemed to know instinctively that the male hunters he met in Canada had to be courted through their headmen and families. When he arrived in Chaleur Bay in 1534, he sent two crewmen ashore to mollify a band of fur-bearing Micmacs with gifts of knives and iron goods and "a red cap to give to their chief." Shortly, he met three hundred down-at-the-heel Iroquoians from upriver fishing in the Gaspé basin. All the women scattered into the woods, save two or three stalwarts "to whom," Cartier says, "we gave each a comb and a little tin bell." This generosity prompted the men to allow the other twenty women to emerge for gifts; each received a tin ring. When Chief Donnacona and his sons canoed out to the flagship to protest the French erection of a thirty-foot cross at the mouth of the harbor, allegedly as a landmark for future trading ships, Cartier made them come aboard, plied them with food, drink, and "good cheer," and festooned two sons in "shirts and ribbons and in red caps, and put a little brass chain around the neck of each." Thus were Taignoagny and Domagaya selected to spend a junior year abroad learning the words and ways of the French.[27]

When Cartier visited Hochelaga the following year, he was royally greeted with gifts of fish and cornbread. To recompense the natives for their kindness and to seal his status as a generous dignitary, he had the women "all sit down in a row and gave them some tin beads and other trifles; and to some of the men he gave knives." The next day Cartier presented the village headman with two hatchets, two knives, a cross, and a crucifix, "which he made him kiss and then hung it about his neck." After an imposing ceremony of gospel-reading and faith-healing, the captain lined up all the men, women, and children in separate rows. To the other headmen he gave hatchets, to the men knives. The women got beads and other small "trinkets," and the children had to scramble for "little rings and tin *agnus Dei,* which afforded them great amusement." The finale was a blast of trumpets and other musical instruments, "whereat the Indians were much delighted." Cartier's *savoir faire* was rewarded by the headman, who took the crown from his own head and placed it on the captain's. If trade had been the goal of this voyage, Cartier would have become a rich man. But the publication of his *Brief Recit* in 1545 enabled his successors to prosper by showing them the established protocol of American trade and diplomacy.[28]

The last lesson in native protocol the Europeans had to learn was not to haggle over exchange values (in a barter economy, "prices" technically do not exist). There was room for polite negotiation, but only within the bounds of native etiquette. David Ingram, an English mariner who had allegedly walked from the Gulf of Mexico to Cape Breton, advised the America-bound expedition of Sir Humphrey Gilbert in 1572 that "if you will barter wares with [the Indians], then leave the thinge you will sell, on the grounde, and goe from it a prety waye. Then they come and take it, and sett doune such wares as they will [give] for it in the place. If you thinke it not sufficient, then leave their wares with signes that you like it not. And then they will bringe more untill either they or you be satisfied or will give no more. Or else," he continued, "you may hange your wares on a longe pike or pooles [pole's] end and so putt more or lesse on it till you have agreed on the bargaine and they will hange out their wares on a pooles end in like maner."[29]

In most instances, the natives literally "sold" the clothes off their backs and the boats from under them, expecting only that their European partners would return fair value. If they were disappointed, with one exception they never said so, at least in words or gestures the strangers could understand. Only Cartier's worldly-wise interpreters, Taignoagny and Domagaya, knew enough of European economic values to suspect the fairness of the exchange their tribesmen made with the French. When Cartier swapped various "trinkets" (*menues choses*) for eels and fish during the winter at Stadacona, the French were annoyed to find the interpreters informing the villagers that "what we bartered to them was of no value, and that for what they brought us, they could as easily get hatchets as knives."[30]

Because nearly everything the Europeans had to offer was made of material new to the natives, the natives accepted or expected the same kinds of trade goods for cheap (in European eyes) provisions as for the rarest and richest furs. This sometimes confounded the Europeans' sense of values but more often led them to think that they had taken keen advantage of the gullible natives. High demand at the end of a long, salty voyage made the exchange for fresh food and water seem at least equitable. But in return for pricey furs the mariners gave only what they considered "trifles," because they took for granted the complex processes of manufacture and transportation that underlay their relatively low cost. Étienne Bellenger boasted to an English diplomat that in 1583 he had sowed 40 crowns' worth of "trifles" on the coasts of Acadia and reaped furs that sold in Paris for 440 crowns.[31]

By the same token, the Indians believed themselves the shrewder party because they bartered their own common "trash" for exotic, colorful, and labor-saving items. Since values are always culturally relative, neither partner was wrong. And since the maritime trade was so irregular and haphazard, the trade items on both sides retained their novelty and relative value throughout the sixteenth century. Thus both partners were glad to get what they could and both thought they made out like bandits.

What specifically were these "trifles" and "trash" that seemed so valuable to the other partner? It is customary to think of the North American fur trade largely as a beaver trade, but throughout most of the sixteenth century other furs were more prominent. By the last two decades of the century the beaver hat was gaining popularity in aristocratic circles, but the middling classes had not yet caught the full fever of furry fashion. And until European demand persuaded them to do otherwise, the Indians of the Northeast showed little interest in hunting the elusive beaver. Archaeologists who tally the animal remains on pre-contact Iroquois sites, for example, typically find the bones of only one beaver but numerous whitetail deer, black bears, woodchucks, raccoons, and porcupines.[32] By 1581, when the St. Lawrence was reopened to the French, European hatters were requesting more beavers. In Paris two years later, Richard Hakluyt (the son of a skinner) saw 20,000 crowns' worth of Canadian furs in the shop of the king's skinner, including enough beaver from a recent voyage for six hundred felt hats.[33]

Rather than new fashions in headware, the sixteenth-century fur market revolved around plush pelts of decorative value. Furs were not made into full-bodied winter coats, as in native America, but used only to make muffs for hands and feet and to trim the rich silks and velvets of the upper classes. For ostentatious ruffs, borders, and collars, European gentlefolk preferred a variety of precious "small furs," which could no longer be gotten in sufficient quantity from the Baltic or Russia. While kings and queens affected ermine and sable, nobles and courtiers of other stripes favored fox, otter, lynx, fisher, and particularly marten, the preferred substitute for Siberian sable.[34]

In the 1540s the French sent ships annually down the coast from Chesapeake Bay to South Carolina to trade for martens. On one trip, which excited Spanish jealousy, they picked up 2,000 skins in two days from canoe-borne natives. When Thomas Harriot advertised the "Merchantable commodities" of Virginia forty years later, he promised that the English could harvest "store" of marten furs by the Roanoke natives, although they had produced only two skins while he was there. Monsieur Bellenger had done much better. In his Acadian trove were numerous "Martens enclyning unto Sables," the ultimate compliment.[35]

The French appetite for marten must have been whetted by reports from America. Jean Alphonse, the crack Rochellais pilot who commanded Roberval's fleet to Canada in 1542, let it be known that the natives as far as coastal Maine wore mantles of marten. And one of the *Singularitez de la France antarctique,* wrote André Thevet, the king's cosmographer, was that in winter the Laurentian Indians not only wore large marten coats but wrapped their greasy heads and their unhousebroken babies in "sable martens." "These we esteem here for their rarity," he noted with some chagrin, "and thus

In late medieval Europe, "small furs" from Russia and the Baltic decorated the elegant clothing of the aristocracy and well-to-do, and beaver
had not yet replaced wool and velvet in the making of hats. Jan Van
Eyck's 1434 portrait of Giovanni Arnolfini and his wife, Italians living
in the merchant community of Bruges, captures the sumptuary importance of furs before the discovery of North America produced a vast
new supply and fed a new fashion in headwear. From Robert Delort,
Life in the Middle Ages (New York, 1972).

such furs are reserved for the ornaments of princes and great lords."[36]

Even more desirable were black foxes, which were "of such excellent beauty that they seem to shame the marten." A rare variation on the common red or gray fox, they were found primarily in Canada, the Maritimes, and Newfoundland, when they could be found at all. Their shimmering jet-black fur caught the fancy of Europe's lords and ladies no less than the eye of the Hurons, who accounted them "the rarest and most valuable of the three species" of fox in their country. The trick was to afford it: in 1584 one skin brought £100 in London. When French Basques seized an English privateer in Newfoundland in that year, they garnered a sizable fortune in black fox alone; the captain unsuccessfully sued for the return of £1,500 worth, which far outweighed his losses in Caribbean spices and pearls. Well into the next century, even with a burgeoning supply of furs from America, an all-black pelt commanded "several hundred crowns." Those suffering from the courtier's disease may have been willing to pay the price; as Lord Burghley was assured, there was "no soche thinge to Ease a man of the payne of the gowte as thes blacke Foxe Skynes."[37]

Luxury furs were all well and good for the rich, but Europe's poor and middling classes also needed leather of a common sort, which continental cattle-raisers could not fully supply. Workingmen's pants and aprons, shoes for all stations, saddles, saddlebags, tackle, and harness, bookbindings, covered seats and luggage were all made of leather. So the coastal traders of the sixteenth century did not disdain the unfurry skins of larger American animals. King Francis I was pleased to learn that Canada bred "certain animals whose hides as leather are worth ten cruzados each, and for this sum they are sold in France." When John Walker, an English seaman, visited Penobscot Bay in 1580, he discovered in an unattended Etchemin lodge 240 hides of "a kinde of Beaste, much bigger than an Oxe," probably the moose. Each hide was eighteen feet square and sold in France for £2. In Acadia, Étienne Bellenger picked up several of the same "Buff hides reddie dressed [tanned] upon both sides," as well as "Deere skynes dressed well on the inner side, with the hayre on the outside"; both sorts were painted on the skin side with "divers excellent colours, as redd, tawnye, yellowe, and vermillyon." With just a hint of ecological concern, Harriot assured his English readers that "Deers skinnes dressed after the maner of Chamoes, or undressed, are to be had of the natural inhabitants [of Virginia] thousands yerely by way of traffike for trifles, and no more waste or spoile of Deere then is and hath bene ordinarily in time before."[38]

Small or large, rare or common, the best furs from the European standpoint were those that had been worn by the natives for a year or two as "matchcoats" or robes. In the winter the Indians wore these garments fur side in, next to their bodies which customarily were rubbed with seal, bear, or raccoon grease as further protection against the cold. The grease and everyday sweat worked their way into the leather, softening it and in effect completing the tanning process begun by the Indian women who fashioned the garments. Beaver pelts especially benefited from this treatment because it wore off the long, lighter-hued "guard hairs" for the European hatters, who wanted only the soft, darker underdown with its microscopically barbed hairs for making felt. Accordingly, the Indians who sold the used beaver coats from their backs commanded the best bargains from traders eager for *castor gras d'hiver,* "greasy winter beaver." Less valuable was *castor sec,* unworn "dry beaver" with thinner, warmweather fur, extraneous guard hairs, and a stiff, parchmentlike hide.

To Europe's sea-going traders, native furs were well worth a cold, dangerous voyage across the Atlantic. But Indian hunters and trappers put little value on the skins which "cost

According to Samuel Champlain, in the early seventeenth century the Canadian Indians in winter wore robes of deer, bear, or beaver "shaped like a cloak, which they wear in the Irish or Egyptian fashion, and sleeves which are tied behind by a cord." Beaver "matchcoats" of this type were especially valued by European fur traders because the skins were supple with grease and smoke and the long guard hairs were worn off, leaving the soft *duvet* used in felting. From Champlain's *Voyages* (Paris, 1620).

them almost nothing," except in time (which they had in abundance) and effort (which they knew how to minimize with astute woodlore). Sixteenth-century Canadians undoubtedly felt the same way their early seventeenth-century descendants did as they were courted by European traders of many nations and countless commercial interests. "The Beaver does everything perfectly well," a Montagnais man told a French missionary, "it makes kettles, hatchets, swords, knives, bread: . . . in short, it makes everything." The missionary felt obliged to explain to his French readers that the Indian was "making sport of us Europeans, who have such a fondness for the skin of this animal and who fight to see who will give the most to these Barbarians to get it." France's competitors were seen in no better light. Showing a beautiful knife to the priest, the Indian exclaimed, "The English have no sense; they give us twenty knives like this for one Beaver skin." But even an Englishman had the sense to realize the sharp irony in a cultural situation where "foule hands (in smoakie houses) [had] the first handling of those Furres which are after worne upon the hands of Queens and heads of Princes."[39]

In return for these profitable—if odoriferous—furs, the Europeans gave largely what they considered "trinkets," "baubles," or "toys." But the natives saw particularly in metal and cloth goods miracles of technology and spiritual power, for anyone who could make large, unusual, or ingenious objects was regarded as possessing *manitou* (in Algonquian) or an exceptional soul. Unlike the Aztecs and Incas of Latin America, the Woodland Indians had no metallurgy, only hand-hammered native copper, and no woven cloth save netlike hemp or grass mantles for summer wear. Accordingly, in tribe after tribe, they dubbed the first Europeans they met "Iron-workers" or "Cloth makers."[40]

The metal goods the natives obtained were of two kinds. The first was traditional or instantly recognizable tools,

though made of superior materials, to shorten or improve
their work: fishhooks and spears, knives, machetes, and cutting hooks to hack away the semi-tropical undergrowth of the
Southeast, spades and hoes for farming, axes, celts, and
wedges for cutting firewood and building palisades, scissors,
needles, and awls for making leather clothing and moccasins.
Rarely found on sixteenth-century native sites or on European lists of trade goods are guns, which quickly would have
become useless without European smiths to repair them and
residential traders to supply powder and shot. Understandably, before the natives saw them in action, European weapons
were not particularly attractive. On Columbus's "San Salvador" the Arawaks cut themselves by grasping Spanish swords
by the blades. And according to Verrazzano, the Indians of
Narragansett Bay in 1524 did not yet appreciate metals like
iron and steel, "for many times when we showed them some
of our arms, they did not admire them, nor ask for them, but
merely examined the workmanship."[41]

It was only a matter of time, however, before metal points
and blades of all kinds were in great demand. After his first
voyage to Canada in 1534, Cartier knew the Iroquoian words
for *hatchet, knife,* and *sword;* by the second voyage he had
learned a phrase he must have heard often, "Give me a
knife." Most eastern tribes loved copper and brass kettles—
handles or bodies—for making arrow points and ornaments,
not for cooking. The natives around the French Fort Caroline in Florida even broke new knife blades and used the
points to tip their arrows. The Eskimos near Baffin Island
become incontinent thieves in the sight of ordinary nails.
In 1587 they purloined two strakes from a new pinnace
"onely for the love of the yron in the boords." Like the
Beothuks of seventeenth-century Newfoundland, they hammered the nails into durable spear and arrow points.[42]

The Indians' second and major use of metal was decorative. Most tools brought by the Europeans were already in

the native workshop; what was new was shiny metal objects that could be used directly or modified as personal ornaments. Buttons were worn, not to fasten clothing, but as jewelry; Frobisher met Eskimos who wore copper buttons as decorative headware, which shone against their oily black hair. A major item in the Spanish trade kit was bells of various sizes but primarily "hawk's bells," which in Europe were tied to the legs of pet hawks and falcons. One Florida village even got its hands on a set of English sleigh bells. The inventory for Gilbert's 1583 voyage to Newfoundland included a firkin of Morris bells, largely "to delight the Savage people," wrote a crewman, "whom we intended to winne by all faire meanes possible."[43]

Sheet brass and copper and kettles, old and new, were highly prized because they could be cut and made into traditional objects but would last longer than shell, wood, or bone. Favorite pieces were bracelets, finger rings, gorgets or small breastplates, tubular beads and bangles to sew on clothing or wear as earrings, and incised pendants. One Floridian wore at his ear a small copper plate, "wherwithe they use to scrape and take awaye the sweat from their bodies." Before being buried with it, another made an elongated gorget from an incised copper plate featuring a European man in pantaloons opposite a stag or bull with a prominent penis. Since he was interested in the metal to fashion a traditional ornament, he cut the piece right across both figures, drilled two holes at the top for a thong, and embossed the margin with a punch.[44]

The strong native preference for their own cultural values was also shown by their treatment of Spanish coins, gold, and silver picked up from shipwrecks along the Florida and Georgia coasts. Before drooling Europeans taught them otherwise, the natives put no inordinate value on the "precious" metals, anymore than they did on "precious" furs, and traded them away "for little or nothing" to bauble-bearing French

An incised copper plate shows evidence of Indian traditionalism in using novel European trade goods. The plate originally depicted a Spaniard wearing pantaloons facing a stag or bull. Its Indian owner, however, cut it into a traditional gorget, punched two holes from which to suspend it, and embossed it with dots. The item was excavated from a sixteenth-century cemetery in St. Mark's Wildlife Refuge near the Gulf coast of the Florida panhandle. From Hale G. Smith, *The European and the Indian* (Gainesville, 1956), reproduced by courtesy of the Florida Anthropological Society.

and Spanish soldiers, who sought to gain their friendship while fortifying the coast for their respective sovereigns. John Sparke, an English seaman who visited Fort Caroline in 1565, thought the Indians "had estimation of their golde & silver." But he mistook acquired for traditional values, for the natives habitually flattened, cut, drilled, and incised gold and silver bars, coins, and jewelry to make their own kinds of ornaments. Silver coins were flattened and rolled into heavy tubular beads. Gold coins and discs were beaten into concavo-convex shapes, perforated, and punched around the margin, as were nine copper maravedies bearing the likeness of Charles I of Spain.[45]

While the Indians were understandably drawn to exotic new metals, they were also grateful for more mundane cloth and clothing. In the sixteenth century, wool blankets had not made their conspicuous appearance in trade inventories; the famous striped Hudson's Bay blanket was more than a century in the future. But other types of woven fabrics were major trade items from an early date. When John Cabot set off on his fatal third voyage in 1498, he was accompanied by three or four small Bristol ships freighted with "slight & gross merchandises [such] as coarse cloth, caps, laces, points & other trifles." In 1517 John Rastell, Sir Thomas More's brother-in-law, set out to plant a colony in the New World, armed with "packs of friezes and canvas and coffers of silk and tukes and other mercery ware." One of the first words Cartier learned from the Stadaconans was *Cahoneta*, "Red cloth." By 1584 it was well known in English trading circles that the Indians all around the Gulf of St. Lawrence, because of the sharp cold there, were "greately delighted with any cappe or garment made of course wollen clothe." Accordingly, Richard Hakluyt predicted that the English would find "greate utteraunce of our clothes, especially of our coursest and basest northerne doosens [dozens] and our Irishe and Welshe fri[e]zes, and rugges."[46]

While the natives of southern New England preferred "red and blue above all colors," as of 1524 they atypically had no interest in cloth of any kind. Within a century Dutch traders from New Netherland had given the Narragansetts a taste for cloth, which the undersupplied pilgrims at Plymouth were not able to capitalize on. Even when Plymouth officials established a trading post on the Kennebec in Maine, they were forced to buy "coats, shirts, rugs, and blankets" from French and English fishermen who carried generous amounts of such items, much as their sixteenth-century predecessors had.[47]

In the warm Southeast, shirts were big sellers because they were colorful, lighter than buckskin, and dried more quickly without losing their softness. In 1549 Spanish friars made several material and spiritual inroads upon native Florida on the strength of a supply of extra shirts. By 1565 René de Laudonnière's starving colonists at Fort Caroline were forced, in a move reminiscent of the Micmacs who doffed their fur mantles for Cartier, "to give away the very shirts from their backs to get one fish" from the local Timucuas. More commonly, the French and the Spanish used clothing to get local chiefs into the habit of alliance or submission. When the French first came to reconnoiter the area around the St. John's River in 1562, they bestowed on the "kings" of both sides of the river and their councillors beautiful "gownes of blewe clothe garnished with yellowe flowers de luce." Two years later, when Fort Caroline was built, Laudonnière sent to remote chiefs who desired the friendship of the French some metal tools and "two whole sutes of apparell." Once the French were eradicated by Spanish arms the following year, Captain Juan Pardo was sent inland from the South Carolina coast to establish a line of six forts on New Spain's northeastern flank. In addition to a variety of metal tools and ornaments, he distributed among friendly headmen fifty pieces of red, green, and "colored" taffeta, "London cloth," satin, silk, and linen.[48]

Measured against valuable furs or invaluable alliances, metal tools and cloth seemed "trifling" expenses to the Europeans, because they counted only the wholesale cost of such items and conveniently forgot the complex operations that produced them. Unlike an Indian trader, who killed his own game, had its fur processed by his wife, and perhaps wore it for a year or two, the European trader handled only the final product of a long skein of economic transactions, whose division of labor, high volume, and efficient distribution ensured him a fairly low price. Like most urban consumers, the sea-going traders of the sixteenth century had no acquaintance with the dirty miners who hacked iron ore from the stubborn bowels of the earth, the carters who carried it to a smelting house, the sooty smelters who refined it in their roaring furnaces, or the blacksmiths who hand-forged the pig iron into standardized axe heads, knife blades, and celts. For the same reason, the traders were equally unaware of the Cotswold farmers, shearers, carders, spinners, and weavers who transformed sheep's wool into warm Witney blankets or of the poor Irish cottagers whose cold, stiff fingers shuttled gray napped friezes into existence.[49]

Although substantial woven and metal goods were most popular in Indian country, European traders also tried to interest their American partners in smaller and lighter objects of some utilitarian but mostly exotic value. Written and archaeological records of sixteenth-century trade goods contain a number of surprising additions to and omissions from the standard inventories of the next century. We are not particularly surprised to learn that Indians accepted blue and white glass beads (which resembled their own shell beads), ivory or bone combs (like their own bone combs), looking glasses (a novel way to apply one's own face paint or to fix one's hair), or even broken bottles (from which arrowheads could be flaked). But we might wonder how highly they valued the handle of a pewter demitasse spoon, twangy jew's harps, "tablets of glasse, wherein the image of King Charles the ninth was drawen very lively," pieces of paper, or playing cards (a Calusa man gave a Spanish soldier 70 ducats of gold for an ace of diamonds, but he also let half a bar of silver worth 100 ducats go for a pair of scissors).[50]

Upon leaving Kodlunarn Island in 1578, Martin Frobisher built a small house and "garnished it with many kindes of trifles . . . thereby to allure & entice the people to some familiaritie against other yeares"—a kind of new world Harrods. The Eskimos undoubtedly appreciated the free "Pinnes, Pointes, Laces, [looking] Glasses, [and] Kombes," but whether they regarded "Babes on horsebacke and on foote" and "innumerable other such fansies & toyes" with the childlike awe that was expected of them is unknown, but not likely.[51]

Besides firearms, a few key items did not make a conspicuous appearance until the seventeenth century. No notice is taken of liquor and little notice of clay pipes (whose stems later made good discoidal beads). We do not hear of tobacco until 1597, when a crew of French Basques brought home from Newfoundland, in addition to a load of fish and train oil, "fifty buckskynnes, forty bever skinnes, [and] twenty martins" which they obtained "of the Savadges in trucke for tobacco." Eight years later the *Castor and Pollux* with an Anglo-French crew stopped in the West Indies to pick up tobacco and maize before proceeding up the Atlantic coast to barter for sassafras and ginseng.[52]

Although maritime traders and garrison soldiers conveyed the bulk of European goods to the Indians, many items, particularly metal, reached native users directly when colonial forts and settlements were abandoned or when ships broke up in the relentless surf or on the rocky ledges of the eastern seaboard. It would be difficult to overestimate the number of points, blades, and scrapers that were made from just the nails and hinges left behind at Cartier's fort on the St. Charles, Roberval's miniature city at Cap Rouge, and Roanoke. Cartier specifically gave the Stadaconans the hull of an old ship when he returned to France in 1536 so they could extract and make use of the nails. Roberval left behind three towers and four courts of buildings.[53]

Europeans in Florida were equally generous. When Laudonnière's troops left Florida for the first time in 1563, they bequeathed to the Indians around Charlesfort "all the marchandise that remained," including cutting hooks and shirts. When they pulled out for the last time two years later, Laudonnière planned to fire the fort and all its contents. But he acceded to the wishes of the local chiefs who, he said, "prayed me that I would leave them my house, [and] that I would forbid my souldiers to beate downe the Fort and their lodgings." Within three years the Spanish similarly jettisoned all six of the forts they had built in modern-day North Carolina, South Carolina, and Tennessee, complete with substantial numbers of nails, chisels, knives, and other tools. The nearly 800 pounds of abandoned lead balls, match cord, and powder must have done the natives little good without firearms, and maybe even considerable harm if used carelessly.[54]

As the Pardo expedition suggests, European trade and its cultural effects were not confined to native settlements along the Atlantic coast. Water linkages and long-established trade routes enabled goods obtained on the coast to travel far inland without skipping a paddle beat. In the Southeast, Spanish entradas like Hernando de Soto's (1539–43) left vast quantities of European metal, glass, and cloth in their bloody wakes, as well as fast-breeding hogs, deadly microbes, and psychological havoc. Chains and manacles to enslave Indian porters were probably the least attractive artifacts introduced by de Soto, but weapons, clothing, and ornaments stripped from Spanish victims may have served as some compensation.[55]

The largest routes to the interior were Chesapeake Bay and the St. Lawrence River. From French, Spanish, and English ships rolling in the mouth of the bay, trade goods traveled in native canoes up its indented reaches to the Susquehanna River, then up that broad river and its East Branch into the heart of Oneida Iroquois country or over small connecting creeks and rivers into the other Iroquois homelands. From there the goods were bartered along traditional trading paths to the Iroquoian-speaking Eries, Neutrals, Petuns, and even Hurons in southern Ontario. But the Hurons and Petuns could more easily obtain European treasure via the "Great Circle Route," which linked Georgian Bay, Lake Nipissing, and Lac St. Jean with the Saguenay, St. Lawrence, and Ottawa rivers in a sweeping clockwise movement of goods.[56]

Within twenty-five years on either side of 1550, each of the Iroquoian nations, from the Susquehannocks on the Susquehanna to the Hurons on Lake Huron, had begun to receive their first European goods indirectly from the traders and fishermen on the Atlantic coast, usually small pieces of copper and brass, nails, awls, knives, axes, and beads. Oddly, the groups one would expect to have received the most obtained almost nothing, if the archaeological record does not deceive. More than 125 sites belonging to the St. Lawrence Iroquois have yielded hundreds of thousands of artifacts, but only nine small items of European origin, and none resembling the gifts Cartier presented to the natives in his two voyages up the river. This suggests that in the sixteenth century the Chesapeake-Susquehanna route was more important than the more obvious St. Lawrence for spreading European material culture into the native Northeast. Metal and cloth (which seldom survives archaeologically) were simply shunted along watery paths traditionally used to transport mid-Atlantic marine shell, particularly *Busycon,* to Iroquoian necklace- and bead-makers all across central New York.[57]

In another part of the Northeast, Etchemin and Micmac middlemen, sailing Basque shallops, wearing various items of European clothing, and speaking a half-Basque, half-Indian trade jargon, bartered furs from the coast of Maine for European trade goods in the Gulf of St. Lawrence and at Tadoussac, a major rendezvous for French and Basque traders. When returned to Maine, the goods traveled up the Saco, Androscoggin, Kennebec, and Penobscot rivers to interior tribes, mostly Abenakis, or along the coast to the "Armouchiquois" of Massachusetts, who supplied corn, beans, pumpkins, tobacco, and shell beads to the northern groups who had little or none of their own. Until the seventeenth century, few fishermen or traders seem to have bothered or needed to cruise beyond Nova Scotia and the Bay of Fundy for furs or cod. So enterprising natives turned their familiarity with the sea to account by mediating the coastal trade. The stack of moose hides lifted by John Walker in 1580 from a native hut on Penobscot Bay was undoubtedly awaiting shipment to the gulf by its Etchemin owners.[58]

The sixteenth century in North America was a period of cultural as well as geographical exploration, a time for American natives and European newcomers to feel each other out. Complicating the process was the irregularity of contact. Small garrisons of Spanish soldiers came to Florida to stay and Basque whalers consistently plied the Strait of Belle Isle, but most fishermen came and went, seldom returning to the same spot. Sea-going traders, out to make a quick profit, were even more unreliable. Like the sea itself, the maritime trade was unpredictable and often unruly.

The use of native protocol helped to stabilize sensitive and potentially explosive encounters. Among the Inuit phrases

John Davis's crew quickly learned to use were "I mean no harme," "Come hither," "Eate some," and "Wil you have this?" At the same time, the natives, although they were on home soil, learned to respect European preferences, persons, and property, and not only because of the strangers' superior firepower. As a French captain put it, "in the end they were constrained to forget their superstitions, and to apply themselves to our nature, which was somewhat strange unto them at the first." Attracted by European trade goods, they made an effort to ensure a steady flow of them their way. They volunteered to work for the landed immigrants, flensing whales, hunting or growing food, diving for pearls, and digging sassafras. They imitated European words, phrases, and even tunes, as the Eskimos on Baffin Island did for Frobisher in 1578. They drew maps for the strangers and whetted their appetites by filling their ears with rich stories about rich kingdoms just over the horizon. Algonquians on Cape Cod even persuaded an English crew that they made butter and cheese from the milk of tame fallow deer and caribou.[59]

Mutual trust, effort, and necessity often produced not only satisfactory economic exchanges but delightful personal encounters. Indians and Europeans made music and danced together. They shot off their respective weapons, showed off their respective ingenuity, and played their national games. John Davis's crew had leaping contests with the denizens of Baffin Island, which the English mostly won, but mostly lost at wrestling, even though they had some reputed wrestlers aboard. Later several parties of natives waved the crew ashore to play football, but the English, inured to rough Sunday sport on village greens, "did cast them downe as soone as they did come to strike the ball," which the "strong and nimble" Eskimos did not seem to mind.[60] And as might be predicted of men who had just come off a long, cold voyage, homesick mariners made love with native women, sometimes—to judge from the native protectiveness of their women—with more force than finesse. European crewmen quickly acquired enough fluency to whisper "Kiss me" and "Let us go to bed," as well as the words for *phallus, testicles, vagina,* and *pubic hair.*[61]

Too frequently, however, the cultural interface wore a scowl, largely because European ships carried not only fish hooks and trade goods but large ladings of cultural arrogance. Because they were poselytizing Christians, technologically advanced, and citizens of large nation-states, most European mariners felt they had a right to usurp native territory with a wooden cross or piece of parchment and to steal native people and property. The thirty English gentlemen who left the Inns of Court and Chancery in 1536 to sightsee in Newfoundland certainly carried no brief for America's natives. As soon as one of them spied a boatload of Beothuks approaching, he called the rest above decks to man a longboat "to meete them and to take them." When the natives fled, the tourists went to their campsite and liberated a "bravely" decorated moccasin and a "great warme mitten." Apparently, a side of roast bear on the spit was not to their taste. When native people could not be snatched as souvenirs, Frobisher's men fell back on their vital sled dogs.[62]

Europeans also felt free to contemn native customs not involved with trade. Religious totems they dismissed as "superstitious toyes." Because the Eskimos ate raw meat, Frobisher's chronicler thought them "Anthropophagi, or devourers of mans fleshe." When Frobisher kidnapped an old woman, some of his sailors suspected her of being a devil or a witch, so they "plucked off her buskins, to see if she were cloven footed." When she proved to have ten normal toes, they released her, glad not to have to endure her "oughly hewe and deformitie" all the way home. After a happy bartering session, John Davis was urged by his Eskimo partners to stand in the smoke of a "sacrificial" fire, which was used throughout eastern America to bless sacred and revered objects. Suspicious of its purpose, he thrust one of the natives into the smoke and ordered his men to "tread out the fire, & to spurne it into the sea . . . to shew them that we did contemne their sorcery." When missionaries came to the New World in the next century, they were no more iconoclastic or contemptuous of native custom.[63]

As provocations like these mounted, the natives "inexplicably" ambushed and killed seamen and stole their property with utter contempt for "civilized" law. Often without knowing the antecedent affront, European crews found themselves being taunted or shot at. Étienne Bellenger lost a pinnace and two crewmen on the coast of Acadia when the crew trusted a party of Micmacs too far. Having kidnapped a man, woman, and child, Frobisher and his men were still incensed by elaborate efforts to lure them to shore. While several of their fellows lay hidden behind rocks, one or two natives alternately waved a white fur, clapped their unarmed hands, laid out food on a rock, and pretended to be disabled. The English finally rang the curtain down on this "counterfeite pageant" by firing a volley at the avengers. These targets just ran away, but by 1564 in Florida and 1593 on Cape Breton, natives had learned to drop to the ground "assoone as ever they saw the harquebuze laide to the cheeke" of a European warrior.[64]

The rising tide of contact, competition, and conflict in the sixteenth century also pitted native against native for access to the Europeans' technology and its attendant spiritual power. Inland tribes sought reliable sources of trade goods, preferably without the undue intervention of coastal tribes. Those groups who were especially well situated on converging watersheds or traditional trade routes may have wished to take advantage of their geographical fortune by supplying tribes even farther from the coast. And many groups worried about the advantages their rivals and neighbors would gain from superior supplies of metal weapons and prestigious goods. For reasons such as these, and undoubtedly others hidden from the prying eyes of historians and archaeologists, three major confederacies sprang up at the end of the sixteenth century. In tidewater Virginia, Powhatan, a keen student of power politics, strong-armed his way from six inherited tribes to an awesome confederacy of thirty tribes. Five Iroquois "nations" in present-day New York fashioned America's most famous and most powerful confederacy in the interests of legislated peace between members and imposed peace upon neighbors. Perhaps in defensive retaliation, five Huron tribes formed a league in southern Ontario which, like the Powhatan confederacy, was only completed on the eve of sustained contact with the Europeans in the early seventeenth century. In a very short time, each of these confederations muscled or palavered their way to the center of European attention.[65]

The inital meeting of Indians and Europeans left rich intellectual legacies as well. One was the expansion of known worlds. While the Europeans discovered for themselves a whole "new world," a continent that was not on any of their maps, the Indians were forced to acknowledge the existence of lands beyond the waters surrounding their hemispheric "island on a turtle's back," as their homeland was called in many of their creation myths. Perhaps equally astonishing to both parties was the sudden expansion of humankind. On one fateful day in 1492, Europeans, who believed that yellow Asians and black Africans with themselves comprised the human family of Noah, encountered a race of brown people who were given no space in any of the bibles or encyclopedias of the day. At the same moment, native Americans must have suddenly realized that they, too, stood at the watery edge of a vast, unknown world, only dimly perceived and portentous for being so. Each came face-to-face with a new, ineluctable "other," and the early histories of three continents would be written in large measure by how much of themselves they came to recognize.

CHAPTER TEN

The Rise and Fall
of the Powhatan Empire

SCHOLAR-TEACHERS HAVE AN OPPORTUNITY, IF NOT AN OBLIGATION, to advance knowledge by writing for audiences much larger than their own classes and cliques of fellow specialists. If history is to exert any influence on society-at-large, historians who practice on the fore-edge of scholarship must diffuse their discoveries as widely as possible. I was therefore delighted when the Colonial Williamsburg Foundation asked me to contribute a booklet on Virginia's Indians to their new "Foundations of America" series, which is aimed primarily at advanced high school students.

In recent years, the ethnohistory of the Chesapeake has grown tremendously in the hands of Philip Barbour, Edmund Morgan, Alden Vaughan, Fred Fausz, and Christian Feest. But rather than provide readers with a pastiche of their writings, I decided to re-read the primary documents and come to my own conclusions. It took little time to arrive at the essay's interpretive focus, which is reflected in the title. Powhatan's unusual Indian empire was just being completed in 1607 when the English arrived in the James River, and it was finally destroyed shortly after its final uprising in 1644.

I am grateful to Colonial Williamsburg for the opportunity to reach a larger audience for ethnohistory and for permitting me to publish the essay here. I have added footnotes to serve the curious and the scholarly.

Today, "empire" is not a word most Americans associate with their nation or its past. Because we do not wish to see ourselves or our ancestors as "imperialists," we have, from the very beginning, regarded America as a "virgin land," a wide-open continent largely devoid of human inhabitants and free for the taking. In doing so, we have seriously misread our history.

For in the first decade of the seventeenth century, what became the United States began in Virginia as a fierce clash of empires. The invaders were English, a mixture of experienced soldiers, desperate servants, and hopeful settlers, all unwitting makers of the first British Empire. The American empire they sought to conquer was not Spanish, Dutch, or French, as we might expect, but an unusual Indian mini-state headed by a powerful "emperor."

By mid-century the English were firmly planted in Virginia, but only at a tremendous cost in human life, both English and native. The Powhatan empire (as it is called after its native leader) lay in ruins as royal Virginia began her steady rise to become the largest and wealthiest English colony on the continent and, in due course, the political birthplace of the nation.

Tsenacommacoh: Seat of Empire

Powhatan's empire lay in the tidewater region of Virginia, bounded on the north by the Potomac River, on the south by the Great Dismal Swamp, and on the west by the falls of the major tidal rivers that sliced the area into long peninsulas. It was also defined by its native enemies: Iroquoian-speakers on its northern and southern flanks, Siouan-speakers in the hills to the west.

Powhatan's empire-building began on modest foundations sometime in the last quarter of the sixteenth century, when he inherited six tribes on the upper James and middle York rivers. In 1597 he conquered the Kecoughtans, a large and prosperous tribe at the mouth of the James. By 1608 he had forged some thirty tribes into a monarchy with himself as paramount chief or *werowance*. With the exception of the Chesapeakes at Cape Henry and the semi-independent Chickahominies on the river to which they gave their name, all of the tribes between the James and Piankatank rivers were under Powhatan's thumb, obedient to the relatives and trusted councillors he intruded as local chiefs. Even tribes on the Eastern Shore across Chesapeake Bay and on the Potomac paid him tribute to remain free from his imperial embrace.[1]

A native monarchy such as Powhatan's was highly unusual north of the Aztecs in Mexico. Eastern Woodland tribes were known to confederate loosely to reduce conflict between themselves and for defense against common enemies; the five-nation Huron and Iroquois confederacies in southern Ontario and New York are the best known. But most Indians on the Atlantic coast were notorious individualists, who tolerated only minimal interference in their lives. Villages of a few hundred people were the largest polities they recognized, and the authority of their elected or hereditary chiefs depended solely on their powers of persuasion. Coercion was out of the question where jails, police, and standing armies were absent and personal revenge was the guiding principle of native law.

How Powhatan (pronounced Pō'-ĕ-tan) managed to fashion a monarchy from such unlikely material we do not know. His ruthless use of armed might, "subtle understanding," and "politique carriage" obviously had much to do with his success.[2] And we can only guess at his reasons for doing so. The most plausible reason is that he feared the loss of his exposed inheritance. His own birthplace and two-thirds of his tribal patrimony lay near the falls of the upper James, a short pad-

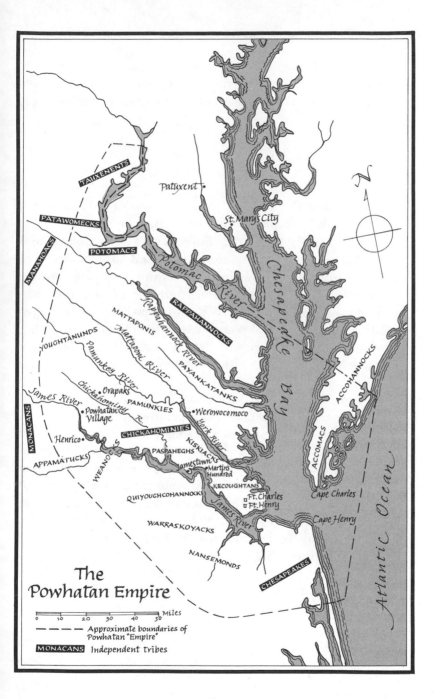

The
Powhatan Empire

```
0    10   20   30   40   50  Miles
```
——— Approximate boundaries of
Powhatan "Empire"

MONACANS Independent tribes

dle from traditional Monacan and Manahoacan enemies to the west. His York River tribes lay exposed to a new and even more dangerous threat, as events in his young manhood had shown.

Threat from the East

Throughout the sixteenth century, Spanish, French, and English ships put into Chesapeake Bay in search of fresh water, firewood, and trade. Three kinds of exchange took place between the sailors and the coastal inhabitants. The first was inadvertent—the introduction of European diseases to native populations without experience of or immunities to them. Epidemics of smallpox, influenza, plague, and even relatively benign childhood diseases such as measles scythed through Indian villages with lethal efficiency. In 1608 Powhatan told the English, with some exaggeration, that he had seen "the death of all my people thrice, and not one living of those 3 generations, but my selfe."[3]

The first epidemic may have resulted from another exchange made in 1561, when a young York River Indian, the nephew of the local chief and probably a relative of Powhatan, was kidnapped by a Spanish crew. (European explorers had an incurable itch for human souvenirs.) After education in Hispanic ways and Catholic religion in Spain and Havana, he was baptized Don Luis de Velasco. Nine years later he led a small party of Jesuit missionaries back to the York, which he had advertised in his new tongue as a land of milk and honey. But the priests found only "famine and death," which had ravaged the population for six years. Don Luis soon ran off to his own people, took several wives native-style, and led an attack on the mission. With hatchets the priests had traded for corn, the "renegade" and his tribesman killed all of the Spaniards but a boy. The following year, 1572, a Spanish fleet exacted terrible revenge by killing many natives and hanging the chief from the yardarm of their flagship.[4]

The third kind of exchange was more benign in the transaction but equally alarming in its implications for the inland tribes. The Europeans traded metal tools, cloth, and small luxuries they regarded as "toys" or "baubles" for native furs, pearls, and food. The land-bound Powhatans envied their coastal neighbors who were given shiny copper pieces for mere corn, and feared those who obtained iron tools which could be cut and hammered into deadly weapons.[5]

For any or all of these reasons—to build a viable population, to protect it from European invaders, and to monopolize access to the seaborne trade—Powhatan may have dared to dream of empire. Although his inherited tribes were too far and too weak to have wiped out Sir Walter Ralegh's colony at Roanoke in the 1580s, the last two reasons undoubtedly prompted him in 1606 or 1607 to assassinate the Roanoke survivors who were sheltered by tribes south of the James. That the Englishmen had taught his native rivals how to beat copper from local mines and to build two-story stone houses gave Powhatan only more cause for envy.[6]

The Emperor

We know very little about the young man who built this novel empire, but from English descriptions of the aging ruler we begin to understand the measure and secret of his success. When the English first met him in 1607, he was in his sixties. Despite his age and the hard times he had seen, he was a tall, well-proportioned man, sinewy, active, and hardy. Lank gray hair hung to his broad shoulders, framing a round face, somewhat sad and "sower." Wisps of gray beard—usually plucked by the Indians—protruded from his upper lip and chin. Unlike the monarchs of Europe, Powhatan dressed like

POWHATAN

H. eld this ſtate & faſhion when Capt. Smith
was deliuered to him priſoner
1607

Appamatuck

When Captain John Smith first saw the "Emperor" Powhatan in the
winter of 1607, the Indian's regal bearing was cause for special note.
After his military experiences in eastern and western Europe, Smith was
not easily impressed; but Powhatan, seated on his raised "throne" in a
longhouse, drew Smith's admiration for his dignified demeanor and his
astute statecraft. From an engraved map of Virginia by Smith and
William Hole in Smith's *Generall Historie of Virginia* (London, 1624).

a commoner, in deerskin breechclout, moccasins, and raccoon cape or mantle, which he made himself. Met in the woods alone, he would not have struck the English as extraordinary.

When the English met him, however, he was never alone and never ordinary. For he never deigned to visit the English in their settlements; the colonists always paid court to him at his native capital. There, surrounded by his bodyguard of forty tall bowmen, the finest of his hundred wives, and his chief councillors, priests, and orators, he sat on an elevated throne "with such a Majestie as I cannot expresse," marveled Captain John Smith, who was not easily impressed, "nor yet have often seene, either in Pagan or Christian."[7] From that fur-lined eminence he dispensed orders to his thirty-three "kings" and two "queens" and summary justice to his people.

While Indian law was custom, Powhatan's will was also law. Out of fear and respect, his people esteemed him "not only as a king but as halfe a God."[8] His werowances knew accurately their respective territories, but they held them all from Powhatan, to whom they paid tribute amounting to 80 percent of all furs, copper, pearls, game, and corn. The valuables he promptly stored in a treasure house half as long as a football field, attended only by priests and guarded at its four corners by fierce carved images.[9] By redistributing most of the food to the taxpayers, the emperor, like the federal government, earned their gratitude and allegiance. By the same token, his justice was terrible and swift. Petty offenders were beaten bloody with cudgels; serious offenders were thrown into pits of hot coals, brained on altar stones, or tortured and butchered with razor-sharp shells and reeds. Understandably, subjects went out of their way to avoid his displeasure.

Tassantasses: The English Strangers

When the first three English ships tacked into the James in April 1607, of course, their hundred and four passengers had no knowledge of Powhatan or his empire. Blissfully unaware of his 14,000 subjects and 3,200 warriors, they were unafraid of his terrible majesty. Their minds were on other things. They, too, had dreamed of empire, and in Virginia they sought to make their dreams come true.

All through the reign of Queen Elizabeth, the "Virgin Queen" for whom Ralegh had named the region, the Protestant English had coveted the fabulous wealth extracted from the New World by the Spanish, their Catholic archrivals in Europe. Surely, gold and silver like that of the Incas and Aztecs could be found in the temperate zones of North America. If not, English privateers could lie on the southern coast to pounce on the Spanish bullion fleets as they navigated the narrow Strait of Florida and the Bahama Channel.

Gold-digging and piracy were incentives for some, but most investors in colonial enterprise had other, equally quixotic, goals. One was to discover, at long last, a Northwest Passage through the inconvenient American continent to the legendary riches of the Orient and East Indies. Chesapeake Bay and its large rivers flowing from the northwest fired many imaginations.

Another goal was to convert the American "savages" to Christianity and a European brand of "civility." The best way to do this, it was thought, was to establish faithful replicas of Old World society in the New and a "good and sociable traffique" with the natives. The godly lives of the settlers and the goodly lines of their wares would quickly seduce the natives from their "anarchy" and "Devil-worship" to "the true knowledge of God, and the Obedience to us."[10] In that day, politics and religion were old bedfellows.

Since full-scale colonies were expensive and long-term projects, Virginia's initial investors thought more of planting a commercial outpost in the midst of the native population. From a secure base on a major route to the interior, company employees could trade English cloth and iron goods for American minerals, furs, and rare natural products. In time, they could even expect to export citrus, olives, wines, and silk, which normally came from hostile Spain and Portugal.

The Virginia Company

For the first seventeen years in Virginia, most of the English colonists were governed by and worked for the Virginia Company of London, a joint-stock enterprise of gentry and merchant investors. While King James I gave them a royal charter and a royally appointed council oversaw their affairs for the first three years, the company was a private venture whose commercial goals took precedence over national concerns. The main object of the colony was to produce a return on the stockholders' investments; it not only had to pay its own way but to turn a profit. If it could not do so in a reasonable time, the colony would have to be abandoned as a business venture or, as eventually happened, taken over by the crown.

The corporate search for profits molded the early character of the colony and deeply affected its relations with the Powhatans. As the first ships left England, the London Council instructed its colonial officers to "have Great Care not to Offend the naturals" (the Indians) as the colonists moved over the countryside in search of rich minerals and the passage to the "East India Sea." They were also ordered to trade with the Indians for corn before the natives realized the English meant to settle among them, in the event that the English seed corn did not prosper in the first year.[11] But what was intended as a temporary measure quickly became a way of life, because the food supplies sent from England were never adequate and the majority of colonists were singularly ill-suited for the task of colonization.

In the first flush of commercial zeal, the company recruited too many "big wigs" and too few "horny hands." Of the initial 295 settlers, 92 were tender-fingered gentlemen, accompanied by seven tailors, two goldsmiths, two refiners, a jeweler, a perfumer, and a pipe-maker; only two blacksmiths, three masons, four carpenters, and forty-four ordinary laborers were sent to build and sustain the colony.[12] Conspicuously underrepresented were husbandmen to feed the adventurers, and soldiers equally handy with pickaxe and musket. When supplies sent from London spoiled in transit, were eaten by rats in storage, or were wasted by ships' crews that dallied too long in Virginia ports, the colonists were forced to beg, borrow, or steal food from the Powhatans, who often had little enough for winter consumption and spring seed.

First Encounters

Food was not yet a problem in May 1607 when the English moored their three ships to the trees on Jamestown Island and began to build a triangular fort and living quarters. While the fort was under construction, Captain Christopher Newport, a one-armed former privateer, took two dozen men to explore the river and its native habitations.[13] Armed with a map drawn by an Indian guide, the party sailed upriver as far as the falls near modern-day Richmond. Along the way they exchanged gifts and courtesies with Powhatan's local werowances, who were easily identified by their red-dyed deer hair "crowns." Near the falls they met Powhatan himself for the first time, who warned the English not to proceed any farther lest they be set upon by his enemies, the Monacans. (In fact, he was probably more worried that the gun-toting strangers would be drawn into alliance with the Monacans.) The two leaders then concluded a military pact against the Monacans and a revenge pact against the Chesapeakes, who had attacked the English when they first landed in late April. To seal their new league of friendship, Powhatan gave his own fur mantle to Newport, who reciprocated with glass beads, hawk's bells, pocket knives, and scissors. Then the parties toasted their union with draughts of English beer, brandy, and sack, which gave more than one Indian leader a powerful bellyache.

The Englishmen's "hot drinks" were to prove less painful to the Powhatans than two other foreign introductions. The first was the surreptitious English claim to the whole "River of Powhatan," which they promptly renamed the James in honor of their own king. This was done in the presence of only one Indian on an island at the falls by planting a wooden cross inscribed "Jacobus Rex. 1607" and giving a "great shout." When their native guide Nauirans looked suspicious, Newport explained with a straight face that the two arms of the cross signified Powhatan and himself, the joint where they met was their league of amity, and the shout the reverence they paid to Powhatan. When Nauirans later conveyed the English version of this presumptuous ceremony to Powhatan, he too was taken in, at least temporarily.[14]

The English were not totally disingenuous with the Indians because they thought their "discovery" of the river gave their sovereign "the most right unto it" against the competing claims of other *Christian* kings, particularly the Spanish.[15] When they thought at all of native rights to Virginia, they saw them as temporary "natural" impediments to the superior "civil" claims of "civilized" people. The waters of the James, of course, belonged to the society whose naval technology could dominate its course.

Although the English were badly outnumbered, they lost no time in trying to persuade the Powhatans that, even if the

European version of "international" law did not support their American claims, might made right. Perhaps the tribe that needed the most persuasion was the Paspahegh, in whose territory Jamestown was located. Although the intruders understood no Algonquian dialect, they claimed that the Paspahegh werowance had *by signs* given them as much land as they desired. But the chief and a hundred bowmen had left the negotiations "in great anger" and thereafter did their best to rid the land of the interlopers by hook or crook. When forty bowmen appeared at the fort two days later, the English sought to impress them with shows of military power. The plan literally misfired when a soldier asked an Indian to shoot an arrow at a wooden English shield, which a pistol could not pierce. When the bowman sent his shaft a foot through the shield, the English hurried to cover their chagrin by putting up a steel shield. The second arrow shattered on impact, causing the bowman to bite another arrow in rage and stomp off.[16]

Body armor—mail, breast-plate, and morion—was even more daunting to lightly-clad warriors wielding hand-held weapons. With or without armor, however, the English sought to impose their will in Virginia largely with firearms. As they returned from the falls, Newport's party was eager to demonstrate their guns to the local natives, who through pantomime had made them realize the cruel ferocity and speed of native warfare. The "thunder" and smoke of English matchlocks was, of course, terrifying; several Indians who were visiting the English shallop leaped overboard when a soldier discharged his weapon.[17] Time would soon show how lethal lead balls were and how horribly they shattered bones and tore tissue even when they were not, quite unlike stone-tipped arrows. Until the Powhatans could obtain their own guns, their only recourse was to stay well hidden behind trees, to drop flat at the report or flash of a musket, or to have their shamans conjure rain, with which to extinguish English matches and soak their powder.

Testing Time

Newport's party returned from their peaceful river mission to find the Jamestown fort recovering from a hot attack by several hundred Paspaheghs, who were driven off largely by bar shot fired from the ships' guns. The honeymoon was clearly over. For the next two years the English and the Powhatans felt each other out, probing for weaknesses and ways to use the other without provoking a final break. Force and fear would play key roles in the drama of contact, but so would economic necessity, social compromise, and political accommodation.

Powhatan's policy toward the intruders was double-edged. On the one hand, he had as best he could to limit their land acquisitions, constrict their military movements, and persuade them to keep their noses out of his political tents, tasks which carried the risk of confrontation and warfare. On the other hand, he needed to cultivate their friendship in order to maintain a steady supply of desirable trade goods and to secure their armed services against his traditional enemies west of the fall line and reluctant members of his confederacy who might try to bolt. This meant that enough Englishmen would have to be kept alive to ensure the continued arrival of the company ships but not enough to overrun his lands and seduce his subjects. The result was a policy that vacillated between killing and kindness, depending on the moods and needs of Powhatan and his local werowances as well as those of the English settlers and their London sponsors.

Because the tribes nearest Jamestown were pressed the hardest by the hungry English presence, their responses were understandably the least friendly. They sent a steady stream of armed spies to keep an eye on the fort, to steal metal tools and weapons, and to kill any English stragglers they could find. Despite their apparent ferocity, they also received English runaways who fled to them for food, freedom, or shelter. The English were initially surprised when these renegades were returned unharmed during interludes of peace, grateful at least that their neighbors were "no Canyballs."[18]

But other tribes and these tribes at other times pursued a policy of wary welcome. When several of his confederates murmured at the first English planting in their country, the werowance of Powhatan's town near the falls asked, "Why should you bee offended with them as long as they hurt you not, nor take any thing away by force? They take but a little waste ground"—an apt description of Jamestown Island—"which doth you nor any of us any good."[19] Out of kindness or cunning, other tribes supplied the inept settlers with corn, bread, fish, and meat, sometimes gratis, often for copper, hatchets, and precious blue glass beads. They also taught them how to plant corn and other vegetables Indian-style, by hilling rather than wholesale plowing, and to build fish weirs and tackle. When English food was in extremely short supply one summer, the natives even took several groups of colonists into their scattered settlements, where fastidious stomachs quickly learned to relish "Salvage trash."[20]

The proud Powhatans did not fail to detect the least trace of contempt in English attitudes such as this, nor did they disguise their own scorn for people who could not feed themselves. Powhatan reminded an English trading party that strong-arm tactics would only cause the productive natives to "hide our provisions and flie to the woodes, whereby you must famish." When seventeen colonists deserted to the Kecoughtans in search of food, they were all killed and their mouths stuffed with bread, to symbolize the natives' contempt for such weakness.[21]

For Powhatan's own part, that "subtell owlde foxe" played a deft game of keeping the English off balance and dependent on his good will.[22] At times the English believed that he had ordered his confederates to starve them out by refusing to trade food or by secretly moving their settlements out of reach. On another occasion he invited the English to move their settlement from Paspahegh country to his own, where he said he could guarantee their "safety" and feed them generously. Whenever English parties visited his towns, he tried to persuade them as friends and allies to lay down their arms, saying that their guns frightened his women and children or that the burning matches for the muskets made them sick. More than once he tried to ambush the visitors, with no little success. As we all know, he captured Captain John Smith, but he also inveigled thirty-four traders into his people's lodges in twos and threes before they were captured, tortured, and killed.

Yet at other times the "Emperor" appeared to be the colonists' firm friend. He ordered the Paspaheghs to cease their harassment of the fort and to provide it with food. He treated his captive John Smith well and sent him home with guides, servants, and a load of bread. In exchange for an English student-interpreter, he sent Namontack, his symbolic "son," with Captain Newport to England to celebrate the alliance of the two empires (and perhaps, as Smith suggested, "to know our strength and Countries condition").[23] He sent his real and favorite daughter Pocahontas to Jamestown to heal a temporary breach and to ask for the return of Indian prisoners. In an apparent gesture toward "civility," he asked the English to build him an English-style frame house and to provide him with a grindstone, a cock, and a hen. He may even have promised that he and his sons would "abandon their religion and believe in the God of the English," which led a credulous Irish visitor to boast that "it seems easy to convert them because they are so friendly."[24]

English Policy toward the Powhatans

By the same token, English policy toward the Powhatans was framed in unequal measure by colonial ideology, native unpredictability, and cruel necessity. The colonists were presented with two imperatives. The first was the company's order not to offend the natives while discovering commodities for profitable export. The second was the more serious need to survive in the face of inadequate supplies and an inscrutable and often hostile native population. Local conditions in Virginia only exaggerated the incompatibility of these demands. Not only did Jamestown have too few farmers, but those it might have had were diverted from timely labor by a feverish search for nonexistent gold. Infected by "gilded refiners with their golden promises," the colonists could talk, dream, or work at nothing but "dig gold, wash gold, refine gold, load gold."[25] Weak, self-aggrandizing, factionalized leadership allowed fields to go unplanted, fish uncaught, and shelter unbuilt as company ships dumped more people into the colony. Some of the newcomers' carelessness led to the burning of the whole town and much of its palisade in the winter of 1608.

But the worst problem was the frightful mortality of the colonists, who arrived weakened by long voyages only to find little or no housing, pitiful food allowances, and a pestilential location. Despite the company warning not to settle in any "low and moist place," the colonists had chosen Jamestown Island, an unprepossessing tangle of bogs and marshes. It was located half-way up the James where the fresh water from upriver met the salt water tides of Chesapeake Bay, producing a stagnant zone that was seldom flushed of impurities. This water not only rolled by the doors of the fort but seeped into the island's water table, where it was drunk from shallow wells. Consequently, Jamestown became a giant morgue for

Virginia adventurers, particularly in the summer, because the turbid water harbored the organisms that cause dysentery and typhoid as well as enough salt to cause salt poisoning. Wracked by "Swellings, Fluxes, [and] Burning Fevers," plagued by the constant threat of starvation, and confined to close quarters by aggressive Indians, the colonists lapsed into apathy and listlessness and perished in alarming numbers. When the first supply ship arrived in January 1608, just thirty-eight of the initial 104 colonists were barely alive. Hundreds more died in the ensuing years, far fewer from Powhatan arrows than from their own heedlessness.[26]

For all these reasons the English needed to befriend and make peace with Powhatan. So they went out of their way to please him with gifts, follow his trading protocol, and assist him in his feuds with the Monacans. Upon his release from captivity, John Smith with Captain Newport presented the old chief "a sute of red cloath, a white Greyhound, and a Hatte." In acceding to his wish for a "great Gunne," they even offered to send him four demi-culverins by his servants, "being sure that none could carrie them" or procure the requisite powder and shot.[27] On a sincerer note, Newport bent to Powhatan's demand that trade be conducted not in a "pedling manner," item for item, but after seeing "all our Hatchets and Copper together, for which he would give us corne."[28] Not until Smith saw that Powhatan had developed a sudden craving for blue glass beads did the English get what they considered a square deal. The following September, Newport and 120 soldiers made good on his promise to visit the Monacans, but the trip proved an empty gesture. Newport returned with none of the women and children captives Powhatan had wanted to adopt, nor had he slain any men, probably because his eyes were firmly fixed on gold mines, Lost Colonists, and the South Sea.

The desire of the English to gratify the "Emperor" and to enlist him more fully in their own imperial cause is perfectly

symbolized by Newport's attempt to "crown" him as a tributary to King James in September 1608. At Werowocomoco,
Powhatan's capital on the north bank of the York, Newport
presented the chief an English basin, ewer, and bed (which
he proudly stored in his treasure house) and draped him in a
scarlet cloak. "But a fowle trouble there was to make him
kneele to receave his [copper] crowne," Smith reported, "he
neither knowing the majestie, nor meaning of a Crowne, nor
bending of the knee . . . At last by leaning hard on his
shoulders, he a little stooped, and Newport put the Crowne
on his head." Then the boats fired a volley in his honor,
which startled the old man into "a horrible fear." To conclude this comic scene, Powhatan gave his old moccasins and
mantle to Newport to repay his kindness.[29]

The Reign of Captain Smith

John Smith was not amused. Having dealt with the Powhatans at close range while Newport was scuttling back and
forth across the Atlantic, he was certain that "this stately
kinde of soliciting made [Powhatan] so much overvalue himself" that he was contemptuous of the English rather than
impressed or grateful. Smith also put no faith in the Indians'
word, believing them to be "inconstant in everie thing, but
what feare constraineth them to keepe."[30] Accordingly, after
he was elected president of the colony in the fall of 1608, he
instituted a "get-tough" policy with both the mismanaged
colonists and the natives. To begin to solve the food crisis at
home, he put everyone to work, some to fish, some to plant,
others to cut cedar clapboards for export. Palisades were repaired and houses built. Perhaps most important, he built a
blockhouse to stymie the illegal Indian trade, which the settlers were underwriting to their private advantage rather than

the company's with tools, swords, pikes, and even guns stolen from the company store.

To "suppresse the insolencie of those proud Savages," Smith trained nearly a hundred soldiers in the language, customs, and fighting-style of the Powhatans.[31] With these commandoes he proceeded to serve notice on the natives that he would not be trifled with. When the Paspaheghs and Chickahominies sent their warriors against him or refused to trade, he pursued them with such vehemence and did such damage to their houses, boats, and weirs that they quickly sued for peace and loaded his barges with corn. To secure the return of stolen weapons and tools he did not scruple to torture Indian prisoners or, worse yet from their standpoint, shackle them in a dungeon.

His field commanders were equally ruthless. When two English emissaries sent to purchase an island from the Nansemonds were tortured and killed, troops under Captains John Martin and George Percy "Beate the Salvages outt of the Island, burned their howses, Ransaked their Temples, Tooke downe the Corp[s]es of the deade kings from of[f] their Toambes, and caryed away their pearles, Copper and braceletts, wherewith they doe decor[at]e their kings funeralles." When Captain Francis West and three dozen men were sent to the Potomac to trade for corn, they loaded their pinnace but "used some harshe and Crewell dealinge by cutteinge of[f] towe of the Salvages heads and other extremetyes."[32]

Smith saved Powhatan and his younger brother and successor Opechancanough (pronounced Ō-pĕ-chań-că-nō) for himself. In the winter of 1608–9 he and thirty-eight men visited the Pamunkeys on the York in search of corn. At Werowocomoco Powhatan and Smith engaged in some spirited verbal sparring before the English, with cocked matches, forced a phalanx of warriors to drop their weapons and load the boats with corn. Before Smith left, Powhatan scolded him for his pugnacious approach but confessed that "it is better to eate good meate, lie well, and sleep quietly with my women & children, laugh and be merrie with you, have copper, hatchets, or what I want, being your friend: then bee forced to flie from al[l], to lie cold in the woods, feed upon acorns, roots, and such trash, and be so hunted by you, that I can neither rest, eat, nor sleepe."[33]

That Smith's new policy was practical if not pretty was shown two days later when the English party reached Opechancanough's town of Pamunkey. After trading for a partial load, Smith and fifteen soldiers suddenly found themselves surrounded by several hundred warriors. In the course of challenging Opechancanough to hand-to-hand combat, "conquerer take all," Smith grabbed the taller Indian by his scalplock and held a cocked pistol to his "trembling" breast. With customary bravado, Smith warned the surprised Pamunkeys that if they shed "one drop of blood" of any of his men, he would not cease revenge until he had eradicated the whole nation. Reminding them that it was they and their chief who had captured him the year before, he concluded, "You promised to fraught my ship ere I departed, and so you shall, or I meane to load her with your dead carkases." The rest of the day went swimmingly, but Opechancanough never forgot his rough handling at the hands of the brash invaders. As Smith well knew, "they seldome forget an injury."[34]

When Smith returned to England in the fall of 1609, having been seriously burned by an exploding powder bag, the colonists reverted to their old tricks and entered a horrible winter of famine and death. While Smith was no saint, the colony had prospered briefly under his forceful command. It was he, for example, who had the good sense to send many colonists away from the lethal waters of Jamestown to live with the natives in the summer of 1609. Perhaps his greatest legacy was an Indian policy that respected the natives' military audacity and economic shrewdness while meeting them

C. Smith taketh the King of Pamavkee prisoner 1608

His men badly outnumbered by Pamunkey warriors, Captain John Smith grabs Opechancanough by his scalplock (the physical manifestation of the soul and considered sacred), holds a pistol to his chest, and threatens to load a barge with carcasses if the Indians do not produce the corn they had promised to trade. An engraving by Robert Vaughan from Smith's *Generall Historie of Virginia* (London, 1624).

head-on with daring and determination. As he had once told Powhatan, "I have but one God, I honour but one king; and I live not here as your subject, but as your friend."[35] Like this little captain with the Napoleonic personality, the imperial representatives who succeeded him would not be bullied by Powhatan or his empire.

The Starving Time

The shuffle of officers that followed Smith's departure left the colony bereft of strong leadership as it entered an infamous half-year known as "the starving time." With his chief nemesis gone, Powhatan again sent his warriors against the intruders and sought to starve them out. In the night he "cut off some of our boats; he drave away all the deer into the farther part of the country; he and his people destroyed our hogs (to the number of about six hundred); he sent none of his Indians to trade with us but laid secret ambushes in the woods." "Now for corne, provision, and contribution from the Salvages," the colonists had "nothing but mortal wounds with clubs and arrowes." Even with foreknowledge of the bloody uses to which they would be put, the settlers scrambled to sell the Indians "swords, arrowes, peeces [guns], or anything" to obtain a little corn or fish. After six months, only sixty cadaverous survivors remained from the nearly five hundred souls left by Smith. The rest had perished for "want of providence, industrie, and governement." Driven to extremes by the "sharpe pricke of hunger," they fed upon anything that moved and several things that did not—horses, dogs, cats, rats, snakes, roots, old shoe leather, and even corpses. Some of the poorer sort excavated recent Indian graves and stewed up the remains with roots and herbs. Another man "murdered his wyfe, Ripped the childe outt of her woambe and threw itt into the River, and after chopped the

Mother in pieces and salted her for his foode." He managed to digest part of his grisly fare before the better-fed authorities discovered his crime and executed him.[36]

The English threat to the Powhatan empire nearly extinguished itself in that desperate winter of 1609–10. Many of those who did not die from disease or starvation ran away to the Indians, feeling that a slim chance of survival was better than none at all. By the time two small pinnaces arrived in May bearing reinforcements under Sir Thomas Gates, the new governor whose supply ship had been wrecked on Bermuda, the colony's will to persevere was gone. So in early June the whole colony tumbled into four pinnaces and turned tail for home. Fortunately, they did not put torch to the fort as they left, because before they could get out of the James they met three well-furnished ships under Lord de la Warr, the newly appointed captain-general, with three hundred men. Much to Powhatan's chagrin, Jamestown was not only repopulated and enlarged but the colony was placed under tough military discipline and began to send out permanent tentacles of fortified settlement up and down the James. In leaders like Gates and Sir Thomas Dale, soldiers cut from John Smith's cloth and fresh from command experience in Ireland and the Netherlands, Powhatan met his match for the second time.

The Military Regime

In issuing orders to its colonial officers under the new charter of 1609, the Virginia Company had already foreseen the necessity of striking a more bellicose pose to ensure the colony's survival and prosperity. The Indians were now considered critical not only to survival but to prosperity as well. The first order of external business was thus to reduce the Powhatan empire from independent to tributary status. Since Pow-

hatan obviously "loved not our neighbourhood" and could
not be trusted, the company deemed it essential, if he could
not be made prisoner, to make his werowances "acknowledge
no other lord but Kinge James" and to free them all from his
"tirrany." Rather than the 80 percent duties levied by the emperor, each chief would deliver to the English "so many mea-
sures of corne at every harvest, soe many basketts of dye, so
many dozens of skins, [and] so many of his people to worke
weekely" in clearing ground for planting, in return for protection from their enemies. If they refused to cooperate and
fled into the woods, the colonists were to seize half their har-
vests and their leading families, the young males of which they
would educate in Christian civility for future leadership roles
in the brave new English world. To speed the conversion of
the whole empire, which was considered "the most pious and
noble end of this plantation," the native priests and shamans
were to be surprised, imprisoned, and perhaps put to death,
so great was their "continuall tirrany" over the credulous
laity. If the colonists needed any help in these tasks, they were
to make alliances with Powhatan's traditional enemies.[37]

After organizing the colonists into work-train bands of fifty
men each and laying down the martial law to govern them,
the officers bent to their initial military task—revenge. Not
unlike their native adversaries, they pursued it with all the
callous cruelty that war can breed. Spies caught around the
fort were either executed as "a Terrour to the Reste" or had a
hand cut off and were sent home with it as a warning. To revenge the deaths of the seventeen food-seeking runaways at
the hands of the Kecoughtans the previous year, Gates sent a
taborer ashore to lure the Indians with his playing and dancing. When they assembled around the entertainer, Gates and
his troops ambushed them and seized their village and fertile
fields. Two forts were erected to command the area and to
serve as healthy points of disembarkation for new settlers.[38]

In August seventy men under Captain Percy, led by an Indian prisoner in a hand-lock, assaulted the Paspahegh town, killing sixteen and capturing the chief's wife and children. After burning the natives' houses and cutting down their corn (which was not unneeded in Jamestown), the soldiers groused that any natives were spared. So a military council met and decided to put the children to death, "which was effected by Throweinge them overboard and shoteinge owtt their Braynes in the water." With great difficulty Percy managed to prevent his men from burning the "Queen" at the stake until she could more humanely be put to the sword. On the way home the expedition stopped at Chickahominy to cut down the inhabitants' corn and burn their houses, temples, and religious "idols."[39]

Such scenes were repeated up and down the river all fall and the following summer after the arrival of nearly six hundred men and "a great store of Armour," munitions, cattle, and provisions. The Nansemonds were Sir Thomas Dale's first target. The Indians were nonplussed by his hundred men in armor, who did not fall as they had in other conflicts. So their conjurers began a series of "exorcismes, conjuracyons and charmes, throweinge fyer upp into the skyes, Runneinge up and downe with Rattles, and makeinge many dyabolicall gestures" in hopes of producing a rainstorm to extinguish the English matches. (They did not yet know the power of rust.) The English destroyed their village and crops, killed many, and captured some anyway.[40] In the late summer Dale took three hundred men to fortify and inhabit the falls on a permanent basis. They built Henrico on a defensible neck of land and paled it like an English town in colonial Ireland. Several other paled plantations were laid out nearby, including some five miles away on a large neck of land taken from the Appamatucks the following winter. When some of Dale's lazy men ran off to the Indians, those he captured felt the full force of martial law "to terrefy the reste." "Some he apointed to be hanged, Some burned, Some to be broken upon wheles, others to be staked, and some to be shott."[41]

Powhatan dealt with these and other invasions of his territory in two ways. First, in the interest of safety, he moved his capital from Werowocomoco, only twelve or fifteen miles overland from Jamestown, to Orapaks at the head of the Chickahominy River. Second, from his new seat he dispatched war parties to harass the English at the falls. Their arrows claimed a few soldiers, including Lord de la Warr's nephew, and they captured at least two prisoners, but the colonial juggernaut could not be stopped. So the warriors resorted to flinging "a kind of angry song" at the English, which concluded with a petition to their *Okis* or deities to plague the English and their posterity.[42] The leader of these forces was Nemattanow, whom the colonists called "Jack-of-the-Feathers" because he appeared in the field "all covered over with feathers and Swans wings fastened unto his showlders as thowghte he meante to flye." For the next eleven years this clever and courageous war captain would persuade his followers that he was impervious to English shot and secretly led the Powhatans in a revitalization movement to rid themselves and their lands of the proliferating Tassantasses.[43]

Virginia's Nonpareil

The English and the Powhatans continued to skirmish until 1614, when an uneasy peace settled over the tidewater for the first time in seven years. The unwitting though not unwilling agent of this cease-fire was Pocahontas, the "Little Wanton" who as an eleven-year-old used to cartwheel naked through the fort with the ships' boys. In April 1613, while visiting the Potomacs, she was enticed on board Captain Samuel Argall's trading ship and detained as a hostage for her father's return of English weapons, tools, and runaways. Powhatan sent no reply for three months, and then returned only seven men with seven broken muskets. The English felt that he could do much better, so they sent his daughter to Henrico for instruction from the Reverend Alexander Whitaker. Pocahontas took so well to the English way of life that she renounced her native "idolatry," converted to Christianity, and was baptized Rebecca. As everyone knows, she also took to John Rolfe, a twenty-eight-year-old widower who had just begun to introduce sweet West Indian tobacco to the colonial economy. After an abortive visit to her father, during which she accused him of loving a bunch of old swords, guns, and axes better than her, she married Rolfe in the Jamestown church in April 1614, witnessed by her uncle and two brothers. Powhatan sent the newly-weds two dressed deerskins and inquired warmly "how they lived, loved and liked."[44]

A year later she gave Powhatan a half-English grandson, and in 1616 sailed to England with her family and ten tribesmen to visit the royalty of her adopted empire. There she had a moody reunion with John Smith, whom she chastised for never sending her word of his health or whereabouts. As the young girl who had saved his neck more than once, at the risk of being a traitor to her own people, she rightly felt that he owed her that simple courtesy. With the bluff embarrassment of a bachelor soldier, Smith took his leave for the West Country and recommended the Indian princess to Queen Anne, "seeing this Kingdome may rightly have a Kingdome by her meanes."[45]

One of Pocahontas's native companions was Uttamatomakkin, a Powhatan councillor who had been sent to count the English population on a notched tally stick. "He was quickly wearie of that taske," Smith observed. The Indian was less impressed by his theology lessons from English divines and his audience with King James. "You gave Powhatan a white Dog," he complained to Smith, "but your King gave me nothing, and I am better than your white Dog.''[46] Another young native was taken under the wing of George Thorpe, a gentleman member of the Virginia Company. Thorpe's three-year relationship with the boy soon prompted him to adventure his purse and person in Virginia as the leading exponent of Indian conversion.

Pocahontas's capture, marriage, and premature death in March 1617, as she was sailing down the Thames on her way home, took its toll on her aging father, now more than seventy. He had been at war most of his adult life and now longed for peace. So he transferred the scepter to his younger brother Opechancanough and retired to an easy life of progresses around his empire, "taking his pleasure in good friendship" with the colonists, though at a respectful distance.[47] Having lost one daughter to the intruders, he declined to marry another to Sir Thomas Dale, who had a wife in England but sought to confirm the new peace by having the English symbolically become "one people" with the natives.[48] Powhatan did not live to see that alien dream fulfilled. He died in 1618, four years too early to witness, not the melding of two peoples, but the blazing resurgence of his imperial creation.

The Tawny Weed

Ironically, Powhatan's son-in-law contributed not a little to that fateful clash in 1622. Rolfe's successful experiments with tobacco milder than the bitter native variety gave the struggling colony an economic lease on life. The craze for "drinking" tobacco had already erupted in Europe, so dramatically that the puritanical King James felt compelled to issue an anonymous *Counterblaste to Tobacco* in 1604. He attributed the origin of smoking to "the barbarous and beastly maners of the wilde, godlesse, and slavish Indians" and thoroughly condemned it as "a custome lothsome to the eye, hateful to the Nose, harmefull to the braine, [and] dangerous to the Lungs."[49] The subjects of his American colony were not the least contrite, particularly when their hogsheads of cured leaf were bringing three shillings a pound on the London wharves. By 1617 "the market-place, and streets, and all other spare places were set with the crop, and the Colonie dispersed all about, planting Tobacco."[50] The colonists had to be reminded by authorities to plant enough grain crops to feed themselves, but many were deaf to such edicts. As more than 3,000 immigrants poured into the colony between 1619 and 1622, often with inadequate supplies, corn had to be traded from the Indians, once again, to fill the gap.

The boom mentality in Virginia put increasing pressure on the Powhatans for more land. After 1616 the company began to make land grants to its stockholders and to its servants at the end of their contracts, and the following year encouraged associations of private investors to sponsor settlers by granting large "hundreds" or "particular plantations" to them along the James and its tributaries. The rules governing these grants dictated that the colony would become dangerously distended, without adequate protection from concerted attack by land or sea. But in the relatively quiet years under Samuel Argall, Sir George Yeardley, and Sir Francis Wyatt, safety did not seem as important as the profits to be made from smoke.

Unfortunately, tobacco was a soil-depleting crop; three years were about as many as the sandy loams of the tidewater could give before their nutrients petered out. In the labor-expensive economy of Virginia, the best answer to worn-out fields was a move to new ground. And the best new grounds belonged to the Powhatans—their already-cleared village sites and fields.

There were several ways to acquire native land, all of which the English used at one time or another. One was to take it in "just wars," which the English deemed all their actions against the Indians. Another was to purchase it from a local werowance for trade goods mutually agreed upon. A third way was to claim lands depopulated by disease, famine, or migration. Fourth, when the English established economic hegemony on the James, the loss of wild game and the constriction of native croplands drove some local chiefs to mortgage their lands to the colony in exchange for English wheat or even seed corn. When they could not repay their debts, like other chiefs who could not pay their annual tribute, the English foreclosed and took the land. And finally, in 1621, for reasons not entirely clear, Opechancanough "gave the English leave to seate themselves any where on his Rivers where the Natives are not actually seated."[51] Through all these means, the colony acquired enough land before 1622 to grant forty-odd "particular plantations," some of which contained as many as eighty thousand acres.

The Cultural Offensive

Not content to squeeze the Powhatans out of their land, the colonists also sought to remake their culture to English specifications. The chief architect of this policy was George Thorpe, who came to Berkeley Plantation in 1620 as a member of the governor's council. Thorpe enjoyed a small legacy of good will and a larger one of ambitious plans. In 1616 the king had ordered his bishops to collect funds in their parishes for the education of American natives, and in two years some £1,500 was sent to the Virginia Company to administer. In the meantime private donors contributed hundreds of pounds to the same cause. In 1619 the company set aside ten thousand acres at Henrico and another thousand in Charles City for the generation of funds to build an Indian college and feeder school. Thorpe was appointed deputy over the hundred tenants sent by the company to work the college lands. Funds were also invested in an ironworks in hopes of subsidizing native students, and each major settlement in Virginia was ordered to educate a likely Indian lad toward admission to the college when it was built.[52]

But the colonial governors discovered that the Powhatans were extremely reluctant to part with their children, knowing they could be used as hostages for the good behavior of the tribe. Opechancanough was even more reluctant to put them in English hands after hearing Uttamatomakkin's disparaging report of "England, English people, and particularly his best friend Thomas Dale."[53] Three solutions to this personnel problem suggested themselves to Governor Yeardley. One was simply to "purchase" children from their parents with gifts of trade goods. Another was to capture students in raids on enemy tribes. In 1619 Jack-of-the-Feathers proposed that eight or ten English soldiers accompany a Powhatan war party above the falls to revenge the murder of some Powhatan women by a Siouan tribe. In addition to providing the English with moccasins and carrying their armor until it was needed, the Indians offered to "share all the booty of male and female children" and corn and to "divide the Conquered land into two equall parts." The governor's council embraced the offer because it was not a major investment of manpower and the captive chidren might in time "furnishe the intended Collidge." When the projected raid failed to materialize, Opechancanough agreed the following year to place whole families in the colonial settlements for education in English ways, provided the company would build them houses, lay out corn fields for their use, and provide them with a few head of cattle and some European clothing.[54]

For his part Thorpe promoted the idea of the Indian college and the conversion of his native neighbors with persistence and an excess of good will. When English mastiffs frightened the Indians, he caused some of the dogs to be killed in their presence, and would have gelded the rest to make them less fierce if he had had the chance. When any of his college

tenants did the Indians "the least displeasure," he punished
the workers "severely." He lavished gifts of clothes and household items upon the natives, thinking "nothing too deare [ex-
pensive] for them." For Opechancanough he built "a faire
house after the English fashion," complete with lock and key,
which the chief so admired that he would lock and unlock the
door "a hundred times a day." Thus "insinuating himselfe
into this Kings favour for his religious purpose," as John
Smith put it, "he conferred oft with him about Religion . . .
and this Pagan confessed to him [that] our God was better
then theirs, and seemed to be much pleased with that Discourse, and of his company."[55]

But Thorpe did not have a smooth road to evangelical success, nor was Opechancanough's conversion anything but apparent. For the Indians could not miss the sad fact that, as
Thorpe lamented, "there is scarce any man amongest us that
doth soe much as affoorde them a good thought in his hart
and most men with theire mouthes give them nothinge but
maledictions and bitter execrations." "If there bee wronge on
any side," he concluded, "it is on ours who are not soe charitable to them as Christians ought to bee."[56] Typical of these
un-Christian sentiments were those of the Reverend Jonas
Stockham, who in 1621 complained that the Indians "de-
voured" the gifts bestowed on them, "and so they would the
givers if they could," and returned nothing but "derision and
ridiculous answers" to the English attempts to convert them
with kindness. This man of the cloth, like many of his countrymen, was persuaded that "till their Priests and Ancients
have their throats cut, there is no hope to bring them to
conversion."[57]

The Powhatans' reluctance to be converted in any but su-
perficial ways stemmed from fierce cultural pride, which was
being fanned by Nemattanow's feathered pursuit of revitalization, and from their realization that Thorpe's educational

program was nothing but the company's old imperial goal in a new guise. As William Strachey, the colony secretary, expressed it in 1612, English policy toward the Indians was "by degrees [to] chaung their barbarous natures, make them ashamed the sooner of their savadge nakednes, informe them of the true god, and of the waie to their salvation, and fynally teach them obedience to the kings Majestie and to his Governours in those parts."[58] For the Indians, of course, this was tantamount to cultural suicide, a step they would not take lightly or prematurely. Indeed, they never took it but chose a much more radical solution for dealing with the suffocating presence of the Tassantasses.

The Empire Strikes Back

On March 22, 1622, according to a brilliant plan, the Powhatans rose in concert against the 1,240 colonists scattered up and down the James, killing 347 men, women, and children. To show their contempt for their victims, they fell upon the dead again, "defacing, dragging, and mangling the dead carkasses into many pieces, and carrying some parts away in derision." Among the fatalities was George Thorpe, their professed friend and protector.[59]

The key to the Powhatan success was complete surprise. They rose without warning as if at a predetermined signal, and they did not have far to go. They were sitting at breakfast, bending over trading counters, and standing with the colonists at work in the fields, enjoying their "daily familiarity," when they seized the nearest axe, knife, or hoe and struck deep into their unsuspecting foes. In the days preceding they had guided Englishmen safely through the woods, borrowed boats, and come unarmed to houses to trade game, fish, and furs. None of this was the least unusual, for the colo-

Theodor de Bry's rendering of the Powhatan uprising of March 22, 1622. Seizing tools and weapons from their unsuspecting hosts, the Indians slew 347 English men, women, and children in a concerted attack. Many more colonists died later of starvation, exposure, and disease. The buildings reflect contemporary German architecture in de Bry's Frankfurt-am-Main rather than American reality. As in the illustrations for Smith's works, the Indians tower over their hapless victims; in reality they may have been only slightly taller. From de Bry's *America Pars Decima*, Part XIII (1634).

nists' houses were "generally set open to the Savages, who were alwaies friendly entertained at the tables of the English, and commonly lodged in their bed-chambers."[60]

Why they struck when they did was no mystery to contemporaries. Edward Waterhouse, a Company spokesman, attributed the general cause of the uprising to "the dayly feare that possest them, that in time we by our growing continually upon them, would dispossesse them of this Country." As if to give weight to their reason, he went on to argue that one of the many hidden benefits to be gained from the bloody event was native real estate. "Now their cleared grounds in all their villages," he beamed, "(which are situate in the fruit-fullest places of the land) shall be inhabited by us, whereas heretofore the grubbing of woods was the greatest labour."[61]

But the timing of the event from a military standpoint was all wrong. Food supplies were low, corn had not even been planted, and the trees were still bare of protective foliage. Only an extraordinary event forced Opechancanough to launch his attack in March—the murder of Nemattanow. Two weeks before the "massacre," Jack-of-the-Feathers had killed a planter as he accompanied him to trade at Pamunkey. When he foolishly returned to the planter's house wearing the victim's cap, two young servants shot him. Before he expired, however, he asked the boys for two favors, which they could never guess were calculated to serve the Powhatan quest for spiritual power: "the one was, that they would not make it knowne hee was slaine with a bullet; the other, to bury him amongst the English." Understandably, he did not want his followers to discover that the magic ointment they wore was not immortal proof against English lead.[62]

To the edgy English, Opechancanough quickly sent word that the death of Nemattanow, "beinge but one man, should be noe occasione of the breach of the peace, and that the Skye should sooner falle then Peace be broken, one his parte."[63] But he had been seriously plotting the destruction of the colonists for at least a year. In the summer of 1621 he had tried to buy a quantity of poison from a tribe on the East-ern Shore for use on the settlers. Significantly, the assault was timed to coincide with a religious ceremony for "the taking upp of Powhatans bones." For some reason it was postponed—

until the sudden death of his chief war captain and spiritual catalyst.[64]

For nearly a month after the attack, the survivors reeled in stunned lethargy as the natives picked off stragglers and destroyed herds of cattle. While the settlers made their way to five or six fortified settlements, Governor Wyatt and his officers decided that total, unrelenting war was the only permanent solution to the natives' "perfidious treachery," a decision that was soon seconded by the London council. The goal was to wreak "a sharp revenge uppon the bloody miscreantes, even to . . . the rooting them out from being longer a people uppon the face of the Earth." Since the Indians were "swift as Roebucks," the only ways to beat them were "by force, by surprise, by famine in burning their Corne, by destroying and burning their Boats, Canoes, and Houses, by breaking their fishing Weares, by assailing them in their huntings, . . . by pursuing and chasing them with our horses, and blood-Hounds to draw after them, and Mastives to seaze them, . . . by driving them (when they flye) upon their enemies, who are round about them, and by animating and abetting their enemies against them."[65]

For the next several years the colonists stalked the Powhatans as they had once been stalked. They, too, sought to give their enemies a false sense of security by letting their corn ripen before pouncing and putting it and their villages to the sword. In one raid they cut down enough corn to feed four thousand people for a year. Likewise, they entertained Opechancanough's peace overtures only long enough to redeem English prisoners before setting on his settlements again. At a parley in May 1623, the English killed nearly two hundred natives by having them toast the peace with poisoned sack and another fifty by luring them into an ambush; the latter provided the colonists with their first scalps, whose collection and uses Powhatan had taught them several years before.[66]

Despite severe domestic problems, the colonists managed to

exact a fearsome price from the Powhatans for their audacity. At the end of the winter campaigns of 1622–23, the Indians themselves confessed that the English had slain more of them in one year than had been killed since the beginning of the colony. In a two-day battle in July 1624, sixty Englishmen cut down eight hundred Pamunkeys on their home ground. Apparently, the "old cast[-off] Armes" from the Tower of London that the colonists used, while "of no use for moderne Service," were perfectly "serviceable against that naked people."[67]

Of course, the war continued to claim colonial victims. The most important was the Virginia Company itself, which the king dissolved in May 1624 for its hapless handling of the colony and its dangerous neighbors. Henceforth Virginia was a royal colony, whose governor was appointed by the crown. From the Powhatans' perspective, it made little difference who governed the colony. Their major concern was to preserve their independence and the land base that made it possible. By 1632, however, it was clear that further resistance was impossible, so Opechancanough sued for peace. Many colonists still felt that "it is infinitely better to have no heathen among us, who at best were but as thornes in our sides, then to be at peace and league with them." But the attractions of new lands and quiet prosperity persuaded the English to accept the chief's capitulation, while still regarding him and his people as "irreconcilable enemies."[68] The Powhatans withdrew to the dark corners of the colony to lick their wounds, sharpen their resentment, and dream of a day when they might be free of the English.

The Empire in Eclipse

Such a day had come, they hoped, on April 18, 1644, when they rose again without warning, killing nearly five hundred colonists. But this time the English were too thick on the

ground to be seriously affected. With a reduced death rate
and royal supervision of immigration, the colony had grown
to perhaps ten thousand. The cause of the Powhatans' desperation was that English plantations were no longer confined
to the James but had spread up all the rivers that veined the
tidewater region, effectively pushing Opechancanough against
the western wall of his diminished empire. At the same time,
the colonists had shifted most of their trade around the Powhatans to the Potomac-Susquehanna region of the Chesapeake
and to the Occaneechis on the Roanoke River. When the
English civil war broke out, therefore, Opechancanough decided that, with factionalism in the colony and the unlikeli-
hood of aid from England, the colonists would be easy prey
to his warriors.

The war sputtered on for nearly two years, but the English
survivors felt confident enough to return to their plantations
within six months. Indeed, only planters on the Southside of
the James and high up the other rivers had been seriously
discommoded; the populous core of settlements on the James-
York peninsula had not been afflicted. When Governor William Berkeley captured Opechancanough in the late summer
of 1646, the once-powerful emperor was "now grown so de-
crepit, that he was not able to walk alone; but was carried
about by his Men" on a litter. "His Flesh was all macerated,
his Sinews slacken'd, and his Eye-lids became so heavy, that
he could not see, but as they were lifted up by his Servants."[69]

Berkeley brought his prisoner to Jamestown and clapped
him in jail, where crowds of curiosity-seekers came to peer at
him. Rising with difficulty on his cot, the Indian "call'd in
High Indignation for the Governour" and "scornfully told
him, That had it been his Fortune to take Sir William Berkeley Prisoner, he should not meanly have exposed him as a
Show to the People." Berkeley, indeed, had planned to take
Opechancanough to England to present King Charles with a
"Royal Captive." But within a fortnight of his capture, "one

of the Soldiers, resenting the Calamities the Colony had suffer'd by this Prince's Means, basely shot him thro' the back."[70]

By October, when a punitive treaty was imposed upon Opechancanough's malleable successor, the Powhatans were "so rowted, slayne and dispersed, that they are no longer a nation." The aggressive empire fashioned by Powhatan lay in ruins, completely supplanted by the imperial energy of the Tassantasses. The haunting prophecy of a Powhatan priest, that "bearded men should come & take away their Country," had at last come to pass.[71]

CHAPTER ELEVEN

Colonial America
Without the Indians

THE HISTORICAL PROFESSION CAN OFTEN BE AS HARD TO MOVE AS A
cemetery. At other times it rolls over for the latest and least fad.
Before the media maneuvers of the American Indian Movement
in the early 1970s, American historians and their textbooks paid
virtually no attention to the native role in American history. But
the disenchantment with the white, male "Establishment" growing out of the civil-rights movement and protests over U.S. involvement in Southeast Asia, and the simultaneous popularity of
"the New Social History," led many teachers and textbook writers
to add Indians to a growing syllabus of new subjects worthy of
attention. This venture in mostly compensatory history was often
flawed by quick-fix ideology and frustrated greatly by a lack of
ethnohistorical scholarship which focused at least in part on the
Euro-American side of the frontier. Too often good intentions
and political zeal stood in for viable history.

But the scholarly excesses of the time fomented a reaction by
a group of historians who also wanted to do justice to the Indian
story but knew that subtler methods were called for. Many of
these historians discovered the techniques and perspective of
ethnohistory and began to integrate the native Americans into
American history in a way that made anthropological as well as
historical sense. Their cumulative work eventually forced traditional historians to take seriously the native peoples of North
America.

Yet the work of persuasion is never done. In 1984, 1985, and 1986 the Newberry Library's D'Arcy McNickle Center for the History of the American Indian co-sponsored with the National Endowment for the Humanities a conference on "Indian History in American History," designed primarily for college teachers of survey courses and textbook authors and publishers. Held in Chicago, Washington, and Los Angeles, the forum eventually reached hundreds of educators and gave them information, ideas, and literature for application at home.

The following essay began as a plenary session paper at the first conference in Chicago in November 1984. In modified form and under another title, it was published in the Center's *Occasional Papers in Curriculum Series* the following year. In April 1985 I presented it again at the annual meeting of the Organization of American Historians in Minneapolis. The favorable reception it received prompted me to submit it to the *Journal of American History,* which, after further revisions, published it in March 1987. I am grateful to editor Dave Thelen for taking a chance on a non-traditional kind of "non-history" in order to jar readers out of their grooved thinking.

IT IS TAKING US PAINFULLY LONG TO REALIZE THAT THROUGH-out most of American history the Indians were "one of the principal *determinants* of historical events."[1] A growing number of scholars understand that fact, but the great majority of us still regard the native Americans—if we regard them at all— as exotic or pathetic footnotes to the main course of American history.

This is patently clear from American history textbooks. As Virgil Vogel, Alvin Josephy, and most recently Frederick Hoxie have shown in embarrassing detail, "Indians in textbooks either do nothing or they resist." In their colonial and nineteenth-century manifestations, they are either "obstacles to white settlement" or "victims of oppression." "As victims or obstacles, Indians have no textbook existence apart from their resistance." In short, the texts reflect our "deep-seated tendency to see whites and Indians as possessing two distinct species of historical experience" rather than a mutual history of continuous interaction and influence.[2]

Attempts to redress the balance have suffered from serious flaws. Some observers have exaggerated and oversimplified the Indian impact. We certainly ought to avoid the fatuity of the argument that "what is distinctive about America is Indian, through and through" or that Americans are simply Europeans with "Indian souls."[3] Historians have been more drawn to other, less sweeping, approaches. Robert Berkhofer described four well-meaning but unproductive remedial approaches to "minority" history, especially the history of American Indians. They are the "great man" or "heroes" approach (the "devious side of treaty-making"), the "who-is-more-civilized" approach ("barbarities committed by whites against Indians" contrasted with the "civilized" contributions of Indians), the "crushed personality" and "cultural theft" approach ("change only destroys Indian cultures, never adds to them"), and—by far the most important—the "contributions" approach ("long lists of the contributions Native Americans made to the general American way of life").[4] The first two approaches offer variations on the theme of Indian heroism and resistance. The third presents Indians as victims. None of the three gives much help in analyzing processes in which both Indians and whites played varying and evolving roles. At best they alert us to the moral dimensions of Indian-white history.

The contributions approach, although flawed, is useful. We inevitably employ it when we seek to define the Indian role in American history, rather than the white role in Indian history. Since most scholars who refer to Indian history are primarily interested in the evolution of the dominant Anglo-

American "core culture" and political nationhood, they will write in terms of Indian contributions. It is therefore essential to understand the pitfalls in the approach and to devise ways of avoiding them.

A relative disregard for chronology weakens the contributions approach. By focusing on the modern legacy of Indian culture, it usually ignores the specific timing of the various white adaptations and borrowings. Generic "Indian" contributions seem to have been made any time after 1492, it hardly matters when. Such cavalier chronology ought to offend historians, not only because it is imprecise but also because it prevents us from determining causation with any accuracy. If we do not know *which* Indian group lent the word, trait, or object and *when,* we will be unable to measure the impact of the adaptive changes in Anglo-American culture at the time they occurred and as they reverberated.

An even more serious flaw is an almost exclusive focus on native material culture (and names of native or American objects and places) that neglects how those items were used, perceived, and adapted by their white borrowers. That focus and the neglect of chronology restrict discussion to a narrow range of additions to contemporary American "life" (i.e., material culture) rather than opening it up to the cultural and social fullness of American *history*. What the approach sadly ignores are the changes wrought in Anglo-American culture, not by borrowing and adapting native cultural traits, words, and objects, but by reacting negatively and perhaps unconsciously to the native presence, threat, and challenge. Without consideration of these deeply formative *reactive* changes, we can have no true measure of the Indians' impact on American history.

In seventeenth- and eighteenth-century Anglo-America, the adaptive changes whites made in response to their contacts with Indians significantly shaped agriculture, transport, and economic life. The more elusive reactive changes significantly shaped the identity of a new people and the nation they founded.

One striking way to register the sheer *indispensability* of the Indians for understanding America's past is to imagine what early American history might have looked like in the utter *absence* of Indians in the New World. The emphasis should be on historical control, not the free flight of fancy. If we posited an Indian-less New World in 1492 and then tried to reconstruct the course of later history, we would end up in a speculative quagmire because each dependent variable could develop in many alternative ways, depending on the others. By the time we reached 1783 we might have a familiar historical product or, more likely, a virtually unrecognizable one. Whatever the outcome, its artificiality would make it heuristically useless. But by following the historical course of events in America and at selected points imaginatively removing the Indians from the picture, we reduce the artificiality of the exercise and the opportunity for conjectural mayhem. Such a controlled use of the counterfactual can invigorate the search for historical causation.

The following series of counterfactual reflections is offered as a heuristic exercise. (The footnotes are intended not as proof of the counterfactual statements but as suggested readings for those who wish to learn more about the Indian role in each event or process.) "Had the European colonists found an utterly unpopulated continent," we ask, "would colonial American life have differed in any major respect from its actual pattern?"[5]

To begin at the beginning, in the period of European discovery and exploration, we can say with confidence that if Christopher Columbus had not discovered the people whom he called *los Indios* (and they him), the history of Spanish America would have been extremely short and uneventful.

Since Columbus was looking for the Far East, not America or its native inhabitants, it would not have surprised him to find no Indians in the Caribbean—the new continent was surprise enough. But he would have been disappointed, not only because the islands of the Orient were known to be inhabited but also because there would have been little reason to explore and settle an unpopulated New World instead of pursuing his larger goal. He would have regarded America as simply a huge impediment to his plan to mount an old-fashioned crusade to liberate Jerusalem with profits derived from his shortcut to Cathay.[6]

If the Caribbean and Central and South America had been unpopulated, the placer mines of the islands and the deep mines of gold and silver on the mainland probably would not have been discovered; they certainly would not have been quickly exploited without Indian knowledge and labor. It is inconceivable that the Spanish would have stumbled on the silver deposits of Potosí or Zacatecas if the Incas and Aztecs had not set Spanish mouths to watering with their sumptuous gold jewelry and ornaments. Indeed, without the enormous wealth to be commandeered from the natives, it is likely that the Spanish would not have colonized New Spain at all except to establish a few supply bases from which to continue the search for the Southwest Passage.[7]

It is equally possible that without the immediate booty of Indian gold and silver, the Spanish would have dismissed Columbus after one voyage as a crack-brained Italian and redirected their economic energies eastward in the wake of the Portuguese, toward the certifiable wealth of Africa, India, and the East Indies. Eventually, sugar cane might have induced the Iberians to colonize their American discoveries, as it induced them to colonize the Cape Verde, Madeira, and Canary islands, but they would have to import black laborers. Without Indian labor and discovery, however, saltwater pearls and the bright red dye made from the cochineal beetle—the second largest export of the Spanish American empire in the colonial period—would not have contributed to Spain's bulging balance sheets, and to the impact of that wealth on the political and economic history of Europe in the sixteenth and early seventeenth centuries.[8]

Perhaps most important, without the millions of native Americans who inhabited New Spain, there would have been no Spanish conquest—no "Black Legend," no Cortés or Montezuma, no brown-robed friars baptizing thousands daily or ferreting out "idolatry" with whip and faggot, no legalized plunder under the encomienda system, no cruelty to those who extracted the mines' treasures and rebuilt Spanish cities on the rubble of their own, no mastiffs mangling runaways. And without the fabulous lure of Aztec gold and Inca silver carried to Seville in the annual bullion fleets, it is difficult to imagine Spain's European rivals racing to establish American colonies of their own as early as they did.[9]

Take the French, for example. As they did early in the sixteenth century, the cod teeming on the Grand Banks off Newfoundland would have drawn and supported a small seasonal population of fishermen. But without the Indians, the French would have colonized no farther. Giovanni da Verrazzano's 1524 reconnaissance of the Atlantic seaboard would have been an even bigger bust than it was, and Jacques Cartier would probably have made two voyages instead of three, the second only to explore the St. Lawrence River far enough to learn that China did not lie at the western end of Montreal Island. He would have reported to Francis I that "the land God gave to Cain" had no redeeming features, such as the greasy furs of Indian fishermen and the promise of gold and diamonds in the fabled Kingdom of the Saguenay, of which the Indians spoke with such apparent conviction.[10]

If by chance Samuel de Champlain had renewed the French search for the Northwest Passage in the seventeenth century, he would have lost his backers quickly without the lure of an established fur trade with the natives of Acadia and Canada, who hunted, processed, and transported the pelts in native canoes or on native snowshoes and toboggans. And without the "pagan" souls of the Indians as a goad and challenge, the French religious orders, male and female, would not have cast their lot with Champlain and the trading companies that governed and settled New France before 1663. In short, without the Indian fur trade, no seigneuries would have been granted along the St. Lawrence, no *habitants, engagés* (indentured servants) or marriageable "King's girls" shipped out to Canada. Quebec and Montreal would not have been founded even as crude *comptoirs,* and no Jesuit missionaries would have craved martyrdom at an Iroquois stake. No "French and Indian" wars would mar our textbooks with their ethnocentric denomination. North America would have belonged solely to settlements of English farmers, for without the Indians and their fur trade, the Swedish and the Dutch would have imitated the French by staying home or turning to the Far East for economic inspiration.[11]

Without the lure of American gold and the Elizabethan contest with Spain that it stimulated, the English, too, would probably have financed fewer ocean searches for the Northwest Passage. If no one thought that Indian chamber pots were made of gold, far fewer gentle-born investors and low-born sailors would have risked their lives and fortunes on the coasts of America. Unless the Spanish had reaped fabulous riches from the natives and then subjected them to cruel and unnatural bondage, Sir Walter Ralegh would not have sponsored his voyages of liberation to Guiana and Virginia. If the Spanish bullion fleets had not sailed regularly through the Straits of Florida, English privateers would not have preyed on the West Indies or captured the booty they used to launch permanent colonies in Ireland and North America. Arthur Barlowe's 1584 voyage to North Carolina would probably not have been followed up soon, if he had not discovered friendly natives able to secure a fledgling colony from Spanish incursions.[12]

Sooner or later, the English would have established colonies in America as a safety valve for the felt pressures of population growth and economic reorganization and as a sanctuary for religious dissenters. Once English settlement was under way, the absence of native villages, tribes, and war parties would have drastically altered the chronology of American history. In general, events would have been accelerated because the Indian presence acted as a major check on colonial development. Without a native barrier (which in the colonial period was much more daunting than the Appalachians), the most significant drag on colonial enterprise would have been the lack of Indian labor in a few minor industries, such as the domestic economy of southern New England (supplied by Indians captured in the Pequot and King Philip's wars) and the whale fisheries of Cape Cod, Long Island, and Nantucket. Indians were not crucial to wheat farming, lumbering, or rice and tobacco culture and would not have been missed by the English entrepreneurs engaged in them.[13]

Without Indians to contest the land, English colonists would have encountered opposition to their choice of prime locations for settlement only from English competitors. They would not have had to challenge Indian farmers for the fertile river valleys and coastal plains the natives had cultivated for centuries. Without potential Indian or European enemies, sites could be located for economic rather than military considerations, thus removing Jamestown, Plymouth, and St. Mary's City from the litany of American place-names. Boston, New York, Philadelphia, and Charleston would probably be where they are, either because Indian opposition did not much affect their founding or because they were situated for optimal access to inland markets and Atlantic shipping lanes.[14]

In an empty land, English leaders would also have had fewer strategic and ideological reasons for communal settlements of the classic New England type. Without the military and moral threat of Indian war parties, on the one hand, and the puzzling seduction of native life, on the other, English colonists would have had to be persuaded by other arguments to cast their lots together. One predictable result is that New England "Puritans" would have become unbridled "Yankees" even faster than they did. Other colonies would have spread quickly across the American map.[15] By 1776, Anglo-American farmers in large numbers would have spilled over the Appalachians, headed toward their "Manifest Destiny" in the West. Without Indians, Frenchmen, or Spaniards in the Mississippi Valley and beyond to stop them, only the technology of transportation, the supply of investment capital, and the organization of markets en route would have regulated the speed of their advance.

Another consequence of an Indian-less America would be that we could not speak with any accuracy of "the American frontier" because there would be no people on the other side; only where two peoples and cultures intersect do we have a bona fide frontier. The movement of one people into uninhabited land is merely exploration or settlement; it does not constitute a frontier situation.[16] In fact, without viable Indian societies, colonial America would have more nearly resembled Frederick Jackson Turner's famous frontier in which Indians are treated more as geographical features than as sociological teachers. In Turner's scenario, the European dandy fresh from his railroad car is "Americanized" less by contact with palpably attractive human societies than by the "wilderness" or Nature itself. Moreover, the distinctively American character traits that Turner attributed to life on the edge of westering "civilization" would have been exaggerated by the existence of truly limitless cheap land and much less control from the Old World and the Eastern Establishment.[17]

Not only would Turner's mythopoeic frontier really have existed in a non-Indian America, but three other common

misunderstandings of colonial history would have been realities. First, America would indeed have been a virgin land,
a barren wilderness, not home to perhaps four million native
people north of Mexico.[18] If those people had not existed, we
would not have to explain their catastrophic decline, by as
much as 90 percent, through warfare, injustice, forced migrations, and epidemics of imported diseases—the "widowing" of
the once-virgin land, as Francis Jennings has so aptly called it.[19]

Second, colonial history would be confined roughly to the
eastern and midwestern parts of the future United States
(which themselves would be different). Without Indians, we
could ignore French Canada and Louisiana, the Spanish
Southwest, the Russian Northwest (whose existence depended
on the Indian-staffed seal trade), and the borderless histories
of Indian-white contact that determined so much of the shape
and texture of colonial life.[20]

And third, we would not have to step up from the largely
black-and-white pageant of American history we are offered
in our textbooks and courses to a richer polychromatic treatment, if the Indians had no role in the past.[21] We would not
even have to pay lip service to the roll call of exclusively male
Indian leaders who have been squeezed into the corners of
our histories by Indian militance during the last twenty years.
Still less would we have to try to integrate into our texts an
understanding of the various native peoples who were here
first, remained against staggering odds, and are still here to
mold our collective past and future.

To get a sharper perspective on an Indian-free scenario of
colonial history, we should increase our focal magnification
and analyze briefly four distinguishable yet obviously related
aspects of colonial life—economics, religion, politics, and acculturation. The economy of Anglo-America without the Indians would have resembled in general outline the historical
economy, with several significant exceptions. Farming would
certainly have been the mainstay of colonial life, whether for

family subsistence or for capitalist marketing and accumulation.[22] But the initial task of establishing farms would have required far more grubbing and clearing without the meadows and park-like woods produced by seasonal Indian burning and especially without the cleared expanses of Indian corn fields and village sites. Many colonists found that they could acquire cleared Indian lands with a few fathoms of trading cloth, some unfenced cows, or a well-aimed barrel of buckshot.[23]

There would have been no maize or Indian corn, the staple crop grown throughout the colonial period to feed people and sometimes to fatten livestock for export. If Indians had not adapted wild Mexican corn to the colder, moister climates of North America and developed the agricultural techniques of hilling, fertilizing by annual burning, and co-planting with nitrogen-fixing beans to reduce soil depletion, the colonists would have lacked a secure livelihood, particularly in the early years before traditional European cereal crops had been adapted to the American climate and soils. Even if traditional crops could have been transplanted with ease, colonial productivity would not have benefitted from the efficiency and labor savings of native techniques, which were often taught by Indian prisoners (as at Jamestown) or by allies like Squanto at Plymouth.[24] So central was maize to the colonial economy that its absence might have acted as a severe brake on westward settlement, thereby somewhat counteracting the magnetic pull of free land.

The colonial economy would also have been affected by the lack of Indian trade, whose profits fueled the nascent economies of several colonies, including Massachusetts, Rhode Island, New York, Pennsylvania, Virginia, and South Carolina. Without fortunes made from furs, some of the "first families" of America—the Byrds, Penns, Logans, Winthrops, Schuylers—would not have begun to accumulate wealth so soon in the form of ships, slaves, rice, tobacco, or real estate.

Nor would the mature economies of a few major colonies have rested on the fur trade well into the eighteenth century. New York's and Pennsylvania's balance of payments with the mother country would have been badly skewed if furs supplied by Indians had not accounted for 30 to 50 percent of their annual exports between 1700 and 1750. A substantial portion of English exports to the colonies would not have been sent to colonial traders for Indian customers, whose desire for English cloth and appetite for West Indian rum were appreciated even though throughout the colonial period furs accounted for only .5 percent of England's colonial imports, far less than either tobacco or sugar.[25]

The lack of Indians and Indian property rights in America would have narrowed another classic American road to wealth. If the new land had been so close to inexhaustible and "dirt cheap," the range of legal and extralegal means to acquire relatively scarce land for hoarding and speculation would have been markedly reduced.[26] Within the unknown confines of the royal response to a huge, open continent, every man, great and small, would have been for himself. If the law condoned or fostered the selective aggrandizement of colonial elites, as it tended to do historically, unfavored farmers and entrepreneurs could simply move out of the government's effective jurisdiction or find leaders more willing to do their bidding. The proliferation of new colonies seeking economic and political independence from the felt tyranny of an Eastern Establishment would have been one certain result, as would a flattening of social hierarchy in all the mainland colonies.

Finally, in an America without Indians the history of black slavery would have been different. It is likely that, in the absence of Indians, the colonial demand for and use of African slaves would have begun earlier and accelerated faster. For although the historical natives were found to be poor workers and poorer slaves, the discovery took some time. Not only would the rapid westward spread of settlements have called for black labor, perhaps more of it indentured, but the rice and tobacco plantations of the Southeast probably would have been larger than they were historically, if scarce land and high prices had not restricted them. In a virgin-land economy, agricultural entrepreneurs who wanted to increase their acreage could easily buy out their smaller neighbors, who lacked no access to new lands in the west. Greater numbers of black laborers would have been needed because white indentured servants would have been extremely hard to get when so much land and opportunity beckoned. The slaves themselves would have been harder to keep to the task without surrounding tribes of Indians who could be taught to fear and hate the African strangers and to serve the English planters as slave catchers.[27] The number of maroon enclaves in the interior would have increased considerably.

While most colonists came to the New World to better their own material condition, not a few came to ameliorate the spiritual condition of the "godless" natives. Without the challenge of native "paganism" in America, the charters of most English colonies would have been frankly materialistic documents, with pride of motive going to the extension of His (or Her) Majesty's Eminent Domain. Thus American history would have lost much of its distinctively evangelical tone, though few of its millenarian, utopian strains. Without the long, frustrated history of Christian missions to the Indians, there would have been one less source of denominational competition in the eighteenth century. And we would lack a sensitive barometer of the cultural values that the European colonists sought to transplant in the New World.[28]

Without Indian targets and foils, even the New England colonists might not have retained their "Chosen People" conceit so long or so obdurately. On the other hand, without the steady native reminder of their evangelical mission in America, their early descent into ecclesiastical tribalism and spiri-

tual exclusiveness might have been swifter. The jeremiads of
New England would certainly have been less shrill in the absence of the Pequot War and King Philip's War, when the
hostile natives seemed to be "scourges" sent by God to punish
a sinful people. Without the military and psychological threat
of Indians within and without New England's borders, the
colonial fear of limitless and unpredictable social behavior
would have been reduced, thereby diminishing the harsh
treatment of religious deviants such as Roger Williams, Anne
Hutchinson, the Quakers, and the Salem witches.[29] Finally,
the French "Catholic menace" to the north would have been
no threat to English Protestant sensibilities without hundreds
of Indian converts, led by "deviously" effective Jesuit missionaries, ringing New England's borders. The French secular
clergy who would have ministered to the handful of fishermen and farmers in Canada would have had no interest in
converting Protestant "heretics" hundreds of miles away and
no extra manpower to attempt it.[30]

Colonial politics, too, would have had a different complexion in the absence of American natives. Even if the French
had settled the St. Lawrence Valley without a sustaining Indian fur trade, the proliferating English population and European power politics would have made short work of the tiny
Canadian population, now bereft of Indian allies and converts in the thousands. In all likelihood, we would write
about only one short intercolonial war, beginning much earlier than 1689. Perhaps the English privateers, David and
Jarvis Kirke, who captured New France in 1629, would not
have given it back to the French in 1632. Without the Catholic
Indian *reserves* (praying towns) of Lorette, Caughnawaga, and
St. François to serve as military buffers around French settlements, Canada would quickly have become English, at least
as far north as arable land and lumber-rich forests extended.[31]

Without a formidable French and Indian threat, early
Americans would not have developed—in conjunction with

their conceit as God's "Chosen People"—such a pronounced garrison mentality, picturing themselves as innocent and holy victims threatened by heavily armed satanic forces. If the English had not been virtually surrounded by Indian nations allied with the French and an arc of French trading forts and villages from Louisiana to Maine, the Anglo-American tendencies toward persecuted isolationism would have been greatly reduced.[32]

As the colonies matured, the absence of an Indian military threat would have lightened the taxpayers' burden for colonial defense, lessening the strains in the political relations between governors and representative assemblies. Indeed, the assemblies would not have risen to political parity with the royal administrators without the financial crises generated by war debts and defense needs. Intercolonial cooperation would have been even rarer than it was. Royal forces would not have arrived during the eighteenth century to bolster sagging colonial defenses and to pile up imperial debts that the colonies would be asked to help amortize.[33] Consequently, the colonies would have had few grievances against the mother country serious enough to ignite an American Revolution, at least not in 1776. On the other hand, without the concentration of Indian allies on the British side, the colonists might have achieved independence sooner than they did.[34]

Indeed, without the steady impress of Indian culture, the colonists would probably not have been ready for revolution in 1776, because they would not have been or felt sufficiently Americanized to stand before the world as an independent nation. The Indian presence precipitated the formation of an American identity.

Without Indian societies to form our colonial frontiers, Anglo-American culture would have been transformed only by internal developments, the evolving influence of the mother country, and the influence of the black and other ethnic groups who shared the New World with the English. Black culture probably would have done the most to change the shape and texture of colonial life, especially in the South. But English masters saw little reason to emulate their black slaves, to make *adaptive* changes in their own cultural practices or attitudes in order to accommodate perceived superiorities in black culture. English colonial culture changed in response to the imported Africans largely in *reaction* to their oppositional being, and pervasive and often virulent racism was the primary result. Other changes, of course, followed from the adoption of staple economies largely but not necessarily dependent on black labor.[35]

English reactions to the Indians, on the other hand, were far more mixed; the "savages" were noble as well as ignoble, depending on English needs and circumstances. Particularly on the frontier, colonists were not afraid or loath to borrow and adapt pieces of native culture if they found them advantageous or necessary for beating the American environment or besting the Indians in the contest for the continent.[36] Contrary to metropolitan colonial opinion, this cultural exchange did not turn the frontiersmen into Indians. Indian means were simply borrowed and adapted to English ends. The frontiersmen did not regard themselves as Indians nor did they appreciably alter their basic attitudes toward the native means they employed. But they also knew that their American encounters with the Indians made them very different from their English cousins at home.

While the colonists borrowed consciously and directly from Indian culture only on the frontier, English colonial culture as a whole received a substantial but indirect impress from the Indians by being forced to confront the novel otherness of native culture and to cope with its unpredictability, pride, and retaliatory violence. Having the Indians as adversaries sometimes and contraries at all times not only reinforced the continuity of vital English traits and institutions but also Americanized all levels of colonial society more fully than the material adaptations of the frontiersmen. The colonial experience of trying to solve a series of "Indian problems" did much to give the colonists an identity indissolubly linked to America and their apprenticeship in political and military cooperation. In large measure, it was the *reactive* changes that transformed colonial Englishmen into native Americans in feeling, allegiance, and identity, a transformation without which, John Adams said, the American Revolution would have been impossible.[37]

What identity-forming changes would *not* have taken place in colonial culture had the continent been devoid of Indians? The adaptive changes are the easiest to describe. Without native precedent, the names of twenty-eight states and myriad other place-names would carry a greater load of Anglophonic freight. The euphonious Shenandoah and Monongahela might well be known as the St. George and the Dudley rivers. We might still be searching for suitable names for the *moose, skunk,* and *raccoon,* the *muskellunge* and *quahog,* the *hickory* tree and marshy *muskeg*. It would be impossible, no doubt, to find *moccasins* in an L. L. Bean catalogue or canned *succotash* in the supermarket. We would never refer to our children playfully as *papooses* or to political bigshots as *mugwumps*. Southerners could not start their day with *hominy* grits.

Without Indian guides to the New World, the newly arrived English colonists could not have housed themselves in bark-covered wigwams and longhouses. Not only would their diet have depended largely on imported foods, but even their techniques for hunting American game and fowl and coping in the woods would have been meager. Without native medicines, many colonists would have perished and the *U.S. Pharmacopeia* would lack most of the 170 entries attributable to Indian discovery and use.[38] Without Indian snowshoes and toboggans, winter hunting and travel would have been sharply curtailed. Without the lightweight bark canoe, northern colonists would have penetrated the country on foot. English hunters probably would have careered around the woods in gaudy colors and torn English garments much longer, unaware that the unsmoked glint of their musket barrels frightened the game. And what would Virginia's patriotic rifle companies have worn in 1775 as an alternative to moccasins, leggings, fringed hunting shirts, scalping knives, and tomahawks?[39]

Without native opponents and instructors in the art of guerilla warfare, the colonists would have fought their American wars—primarily with the British—in traditional military style. In fact, without the constant need to suppress hostile natives and aggressive Europeans, they might have lost most of their martial spirit and prowess, making their victory in the now-postponed Revolution less than certain. Beating the British regulars at their own game without stratagems and equipment gained from the Indians would have been nearly impossible, particularly after the British gained experience in counterinsurgent warfare in Scotland and on the Continent.[40]

The absence of such adaptive changes would have done much to maintain the Anglicized tone and texture of colonial life; the absence of Indians would have preserved more fundamental cultural values that were altered historically. The generalized European fear of barbarism that colonial planners and leaders manifested would have dissipated without the Indian embodiment of a "heathenism" that seemed contagious to English frontiersmen or the danger of Englishmen converting to an Indian way of life in captivity or, worse still, voluntarily as "apostates" and "renegades." Without the seduction of an alternative lifestyle within easy reach, hundreds of colonists would not have become white Indians.[41]

More generally, the Anglo-Americans' definition of themselves would have lacked a crucial point of reference because the Indians would no longer symbolize the "savage" baseness that would dominate human nature if man did not "reduce" it to "civility" through government, religion, and the capi-

talist work ethic. Only imported Africans, not American natives, would then have shown "civilized men [what] they were
not and must not be."[42] Because the settlers were "especially
inclined to discover attributes in savages which they found
first but could not speak of in themselves," they defined themselves "less by the vitality of their affirmations than by the
violence of their abjurations."[43] All peoples define themselves
partly by contrast with other peoples, but the English colonists forged their particular American identity on an Indian
anvil more than on a (non-English) European or African one.

The Indians were so crucial to the formation of the Anglo-
American character because of the strong contrasts between
their culture and that of the intruders. which the English interpreted largely as native deficiencies. While English technology had reached the Age of Iron, Indian technology was
of the Stone Age, without wheels, clocks, compasses, cloth,
iron, glass, paper, or gunpowder. While the English partici-
pated in a capitalist economy of currency and credit, the natives bartered in kind from hand to hand. While the English
were governed by statutes, sheriffs, parliaments, and kings,
the Indians' suasive polities of chiefs and councils seemed to
be no government at all. While the English worshiped the
"true God" in churches with prayer books and Scripture, native shamans resembled "conjurers" who preyed on the "superstitious" natures of their dream-ridden, "devil-worshipping"
supplicants. While the English enjoyed the benefits of printing and alphabetic literacy, the Indians were locked in an
oral culture of impermanence and "hearsay." While the English sought to master nature as their religion taught them,
the natives saw themselves as part of nature, whose other
"spirits" deserved respect and thanks. While English men
worked in the fields and women in the house, Indian women
farmed and their menfolk "played" at hunting and fishing.
While English time shot straight ahead into a progressive
future, Indian time looped and circled upon itself, blurring

the boundaries between a hazy past, a spacious present, and an attenuated future. While the English lived in permanent towns and cities, the Indians' annual subsistence cycle of movement seemed aimlessly "nomadic." While the English waged wars of state for land, crowns, wealth, or faith, Indian warriors struck personally for revenge, honor, and captives. While English society was divided into "divinely sanctioned" strata of wealth, power, and prestige, Indian society fostered an "unnatural" sense of democratic individualism in the people. And while English ethnocentrism was based on a new religion, technology, social evolution, and ultimately race, the Indians' own strong sense of superiority, color-blind and religiously tolerant, could not be undermined except by inexplicable European disease.[44]

For the whole spectrum of colonial society, urban and rural, the Indians as cultural contraries were not so frustrating, alarming, or influential as the Indian enemy. As masters of an unconventional warfare of terror, they seared the collective memories, imaginations, and even subconscious of the colonists, leaving a deep but blurred intaglio of fear and envy, hatred and respect. Having the American natives as frequent and deadly adversaries—and even as allies—did more to "Americanize" the English colonists than any other human factor and had two contradictory results. When native warfare frustrated and humbled the English military machine, its successes cast into serious doubt the colonists' sense of superiority, especially when the only recourse seemed to be the hiring of mercenaries from other tribes.[45] At the same time, victorious Indians seemed so insufferably insolent—a projection of the Christians' original sin—that the colonists redoubled their efforts to claim divine grace and achieve spiritual and social regeneration through violence.[46] One of the pathetic ironies of early America is that in attempting to exterminate the wounding pride of their Indian enemies, the colonists inflated their own pride to sinful proportions.

The Indians' brand of guerilla warfare, which involved the "indiscriminate slaughter of all ranks, ages and sexes," torture, and captivity for adoption, gave rise to several colonial reactions. The first reaction was a well-founded increase in fear and paranoia. The second reaction was the development of a defensive garrison mentality, which in turn reinforced the colonists' sense of being a chosen if momentarily abandoned people. And the colonists' third response was a sense of being torn from their own "civilized" moorings and swept into the kind of "savage" conduct they deplored in their enemies, motivated by cold-blooded vengeance. Without Indian enemies, it is doubtful if the colonists would have slaughtered and tortured military prisoners, including women and children, taken scalps from friends and enemies to collect government bounties, encouraged the Spanish-style use of dogs, or made boot tops and tobacco pouches from the skin of fallen foes.[47] It is a certainty that non-Indian enemies would not have been the target of frequent if unrealized campaigns of genocide; it is difficult to imagine English settlers coining an aphorism to the effect that "the only good Dutchman is a dead one."

It is both fitting and ironic that the symbol chosen by Revolutionary cartoonists to represent the American colonies was the Indian, whose love of liberty and fierce independence had done so much to Americanize the shape and content of English colonial culture.[48] It is fitting because the Indians by their long and determined opposition helped to meld thirteen disparate colonies into one (albeit fragile) nation, different from England largely by virtue of having shared that common history of conflict on and over Indian soil. It is ironic because after nearly two centuries of trying to take the Indians' lives and lands, the colonists appropriated not only the native identity but the very characteristics that thwarted the colonists' arrogations.

The Scholar's Obligations
to Native Peoples

LIKE POLITICIANS, HISTORIANS HAVE CONSTITUENTS WHO NEED their services and fair representation. The historian's human subjects, no less than other citizens, have certain inalienable rights, the most important of which is to have the truth, the whole truth, and nothing but the truth told about them. The analogy weakens somewhat when we consider that historians elect themselves, and their constituents are usually dead, like some of the voters in Chicago's famous Democratic wards. But for the historian, constituents' rights do not end at the grave; they really begin there because the dead are no longer able to speak for themselves or to ensure that what is said and written about them squares with their vision of the truth. The historian's first and most important duty, therefore, is to ascertain the full and complicated truth about his subjects and to present it as clearly, forcefully, and impartially as he can.

But "the truth" has many faces, or rather one face that appears different according to the vantage point and eyesight of the observer. To further complicate matters, the ethnohistorian of North America quickly discovers that his Indian constituents left numerous descendants who care passionately about the treatment their ancestors receive in "the white man's" history books. In combination these two circumstances—the protean quality of historical truth and the pressure exerted by ethnic heirs—pose special problems for the ethnohistorian and raise vital questions about the scholar's obligations to native peoples.

In May 1985 I discussed these questions on a panel at the Mohawk town of Kahnawake (formerly Caughnawaga) in Quebec province. Francis Jennings and I obviously represented non-Indian scholars of Indian history because the other two panelists were identifiably Indians. Brian Deer was the town's knowledgeable historian and archivist; John Mohawk was an outspoken activist, former editor of *Akwesasne Notes* (a major Indian newspaper), and lecturer in American Studies at the State University of New York in Buffalo. The discussion was held in the Kahnawake Survival School, a spacious new facility where native children are taught Mohawk language, history, and traditional arts and crafts. The audience consisted of two different groups: native townspeople of all ages and a couple of hundred participants in the Fifth North American Fur Trade Conference, being held across the river at McGill University in Montreal. After a tasty Iroquois meal served by the traditional clan mothers, the panel began to sort out the issue of scholarly obligations from both sides of the longhouse.

Francis Jennings began by suggesting that one of the most important things a non-Indian scholar could do for Indian people today is to "attempt to write an accurate history" of Indian-white relations, "a history of real human beings" with all their warts and wonderfulness, rather than a farce about cardboard stereotypes. The task of historians, he said, is not to please their readers but to educate and enlighten them. All forms of censorship, whether by Indian politicians or government agencies, publishers or lawyers, should be firmly resisted. He rejected as insidious the fallacy that a tribe holds exclusive proprietary rights to its history, with full control over access to information and ultimate disposition of, even proceeds from, the final product. As for taking seriously the "Indian" side of the story, he noted that all native traditions are *tribal* traditions, not generically Indian, and that one tribe's tradition often contradicts that of another. Traditions have to be evaluated and used as carefully as any other historical source.

Perhaps because we share the elusive though indispensable goal of impartial scholarship, I found nothing to disagree with in Jennings's argument. So I continued in the following vein:

Although tribal censorship should not be allowed and native traditions are often difficult to use, native people today, particularly older traditionalists, can assist historians in two important ways. First, they can demonstrate and explain the uses and meanings of traditional ceremonies, dances, observances, artifacts, customs, and words to the best of their knowledge and ability. The historian, however, will have to discern for himself just how old these legacies are and whether they have changed appreciably from the time-period he is studying. But by moving "upstream" from present informants to past documents, he can often discover the surprising longevity of traditional thought and behavior.

Second, and perhaps more universally useful, present-day Indians, traditional or highly acculturated, can suggest important questions for historical enquiry that non-Indians might never raise because of ethnic, temporal, professional, or other brands of myopia. It is crucial to collect the viewpoints of many different native people, representing different ages, genders, statuses, and political and religious persuasions, just as it is in the study of any other group. And it is vital to remember that their views of the distant past—of the colonial period, for example—are likely to be uninformed and warped by the intervening centuries, for the simple reason that history has to be re-learned by every generation and is not a

genetic inheritance. Although native people can seldom provide *answers,* they are uniquely qualified to raise *questions*
that the historian may wish to pursue in the ethnohistorical
record. In the end, only this record—written and archaeological, oral and artistic—can give us reliable answers about the
past, native or European. "Experts" of any stripe who have
not carefully studied that record, who have not put in their
time in the field, the museum, and the library, simply lack
credibility.

The obligations of scholars who write books and articles
about the distant Indian past are fairly uncomplicated. While
the reconstruction of the truth will always be a challenge, the
descendants of many Eastern Woodland groups that inhabited
colonial North America either do not exist at all (because the
group was extinguished by disease, warfare, or factionalism),
possess few or no cultural continuities with their ancestors
(because of acute acculturation, intermarriage, or failing
memory), or have no desire or ability to influence the historians of their ancestral culture. But even ethnohistorians of
colonial America often find themselves involved with contemporary Indian groups, directly or indirectly.

Advising television producers and film-makers on ethnohistorical subjects can sometimes bring the historian into competition or conflict with the Indian advisers. Here the general
rules that apply to the more traditional medium of print
should prevail: bow to the superior knowledge of native experts when it can be validated, tolerate no censorship, and
pursue the truth as you see it as vigorously as possible. The
historian's more frequent and more serious challenge is to
prevent the visual artists from taking undue liberties with the
complexity of the truth (some is necessary and desirable, given
the nature of the medium and its time constraints) and from
perpetuating visual stereotypes that are as damaging as intellectual ones. The historical consultant's frustrations, vividly
portrayed in Alan Alda's film *Sweet Liberty,* usually rise

between the reading of the script and the actual filming, cutting, and editing. In my experience, public television offers the fewest frustrations to scholarly consultants by translating the complexity of the native past with reasonable fullness and faithfulness. The commercial networks and studios put less confidence in their audiences and therefore in their scholarly advisers.

The design of museums of Indian history and culture can also confront the scholar with political and intellectual challenges. Not long ago I helped the Rochester [N.Y.] Museum and Science Center design and write the label copy for its new exhibit on the history of Seneca-white relations. In designing the exhibit, which covers one floor of a large new wing of the museum, the museum staff worked closely with political and religious leaders from nearby Seneca communities. Cooperation and mutual understanding were everywhere evident. When the museum submitted outlines of historical sequences and artifactual accompaniments to the Seneca experts for comment, the only major objection was to the public display of sacred False Face masks, those actually consecrated and used in the religious ceremonies of the False Face Society. Since it was necessary to display False Faces in order to explain the vital role of religion in Iroquois society, staff members returned to the Indian communities and explained their dilemma. In the spirit of compromise, the Senecas sanctioned

A typical "broken nose" or "crooked mouth" False Face mask from the Grand River Reserve in southern Ontario. Carved from a live basswood tree to retain the tree's "spirit" or soul, the masks are worn by members of the False Face Society in ceremonies of the traditional Iroquois "Longhouse" or Handsome Lake religion. Masks used in these ceremonies are consecrated and regularly maintained by offerings of tobacco smoke and cornmeal mush. Others are carved from pine for nonreligious purposes. This mask can be seen in the Milwaukee Public Museum, by whose courtesy it is reproduced here.

the use of unconsecrated masks that had been carved for commercial sale by Seneca craftsmen.

The only other issue of moment also involved native religious sensibilities. One preliminary label for some artifacts mentioned "offerings to the dead," what archaeologists more commonly call "grave goods." These were objects placed in graves in the belief that the souls of those objects would accompany the soul of the deceased in its long journey to the Land of the Dead, somewhere in the Southwest. All over North America, native descendants today are understandably concerned when the graves of their ancestors are disturbed by archaeologists and other non-Indian scholars and especially that grave offerings are removed and placed in secular contexts in public museums.[1] Fortunately, many Indians realize that, despite the sordid history of grave-robbing and pot-hunting by amateurs and profiteers, professional archaeology is indispensable to our mutual understanding of native life and history, particularly before the advent of Europeans and their more conventional written records. When fully informed about the goals and methods of archaeology, and especially when involved in the selection and actual excavation of sites, Indian people are usually willing to cooperate with scholars in re-creating the lifeways of their ancestors.

Today, however, few native groups are willing to allow their ancestors' bones to be stored permanently in museums after study or to be displayed in public exhibits. The common practice now, following the 1973 precedent of William Simmons at a Narragansett site in Rhode Island, is, after proper study of the bones, to reinter them in a religious ceremony conducted by the nearest tribal descendants of the dead.[2] The artifacts from the graves normally remain in university or government museums, where they can be compared with similar items from other sites, cultures, and periods. But some artifacts go to tribal museums, which increasingly are staffed by professionally trained native curators who can ensure their proper conservation, interpretation, and display.

The sharpest dilemma for scholars of Indian history arises from legal disputes over Indian land claims, in which each side relies on expert witnesses to substantiate the evidential side of its case. Ideally, each side is entitled to the best counsel it can get because justice is supposed to be blind. But should an ethnohistorian serve as an expert witness for a non-Indian litigant who is seeking either to take land or traditional rights from Indians or to prevent Indians from reclaiming traditional land lost through legal or extra-legal confiscation or sale? An even stickier question is, should he serve either side in a case involving two factions of the same tribe or two tribes?

No easy answers can be found to either question, especially if we believe in the abstract equity of the judicial system. My own philosophy, arrived at after extensive participation in the Mashpee (Cape Cod) land case in 1977 and an invitation (declined) to work in another in New York State, is admittedly a moral compromise. First, I would never work for a party whose position was not clearly borne out by the historical record as I read it. (Legal precedents and definitions are the lawyers' concerns.) Second, I would never testify against an Indian tribe on behalf of non-Indians, no matter how strong the latter's historical case. The European and American judicial systems have too often been instrumental in unfairly depriving native peoples of their lands and liberties, and I do not wish to perpetuate such misuses of justice. Finally, for purely prudential reasons, I would choose not to testify in a case involving two Indian litigants. Such cases are always no-win situations for the non-Indian scholar and should be settled without his intervention. But every historian must decide for himself whether or when to become engaged in Indian court cases.

Several other issues speak directly to the scholar's obligations to native peoples, but they all revolve around the central issue of audience: for whom does the ethnohistorian
write? The question is important because a firm answer to it
allows us to decide other issues that preoccupy scholars of Indian history, at least from time to time. For example, how
should we refer to and describe our native subjects? Without
quotation marks to indicate their pejorative historicity, "savage," "nomadic," and "vengeful" would rightly offend contemporary natives. "Red" is anachronistic before the late
eighteenth century and always inaccurate. And what about
"Indian" (Columbus's geographical misnomer) vs. "Native
American" (the preferred language of federal grant and college applications)? Reservation and rural Indians prefer the
former; politically savvy urban-dwellers affect the latter.[3]

Another issue related to audience is, how do we handle potentially or actually sensitive subjects pertaining to native
people? Do we skirt or ignore them or do we confront them
head on, confident that our readers possess the reason and
good will to decide each issue on its historical merits? In my
experience, ethnohistorians spend a good deal of time debunking tenacious stereotypes and myths, which are entertained as fervently by Indian people as by other Americans.
Since the Red Power movement of the late 1960s, for example, it has been widely held that the Indians did not practice
scalping until they were taught the bloody technique by invading Europeans in the seventeenth century through the use
of scalp bounties. Another myth, which floated up once again
at Kahnawake and is very much before us during the bicen-
tennial, is that the United States Constitution was closely pat-
terned upon the League of the Iroquois. Each myth contains
just enough truth to be plausible, but both are logically and
historically fallacious.[4] Should the scholar risk the displeasure
of the disabused by constantly and forcefully saying so?

The answers to all these questions depend partly on the

audience he envisions for his historical writing. Although the declared Indian population of the United States is well over a million, few historians aim their work solely at native audiences. One powerful reason why they should not is that America's so-called "Indian problem" is largely a non-Indian problem, the result of misinformation and prejudice on the part of non-Indians. It is not that Indians have no need for opportunities to learn about "their own" histories; they have an educational need for them as strong as do any other people who are not born with total cultural recall. But descendants of the European invaders and more recent immigrants are in greater need of being reminded that the Indians deserve chronological and moral priority in our consideration of America's multi-ethnic past.

Accordingly, this book, like all my writing, is directed toward an "ideal reader," someone (in Margaret Atwood's description) "intelligent, capable of feeling, possessed of a moral sense, a lover of language, and very demanding."[5] Ethnicity is of little concern. I will have fulfilled my primary obligation to native peoples, living and dead, if I can obtain for them a full and fair hearing from historians, from authors of textbooks as well as monographic specialists.[6] If the readers of those historians thereby gain a deeper understanding of Indian history and culture, North American society stands a better chance of treating new generations of native people with true justice and human respect.

Notes

PREFACE

1. *The European and the Indian: Essays in the Ethnohistory of Colonial North America* (New York: Oxford University Press, 1981).
2. James Axtell, "A North American Perspective for Colonial History," *The History Teacher*, 12 (1979), 549–62.
3. *The Invasion Within: The Contest of Cultures in Colonial North America* (New York: Oxford University Press, 1985).

FOREWORD

1. Samuel Eliot Morison, *The Oxford History of the American People* (New York, 1965), 23.
2. Garsilaso de la Vega, el Inca, *Royal Commentaries of the Incas*, trans. Harold V. Livermore, 2 vols. (Austin, 1966), 1:9.
3. D. W. Meinig, *The Shaping of America: A Geographical Perspective on 500 Years of History, 1: Atlantic America, 1492–1800* (New Haven, 1986), 3.

CHAPTER ONE

1. *Ethnohistory*, 4 (1957), 47–61.
2. James Morton Smith, ed., *Seventeenth-Century America: Essays in*

Colonial History (Chapel Hill, 1959), 15–32. The essay was presented at a symposium in April 1957.

3. *Ibid.*, 31–32.

4. Wilcomb E. Washburn, ed., *The Indian and the White Man*, Documents in American Civilization (Garden City, N.Y., 1964), chs. 1, 8; *idem*, "Relations between Europeans and Amerindians during the Seventeenth and Eighteenth Centuries: The Epistemological Problem," paper delivered at the International Colloquium on Colonial History, University of Ottawa, Nov. 27–28, 1969; *idem*, "James Adair's 'Noble Savages,' " in Lawrence H. Leder, ed., *The Colonial Legacy III: Historians of Nature and Man's Nature* (New York, 1973), 91–120; *idem*, "The Clash of Morality in the American Forest," in Fredi Chiappelli, ed., *First Images of America: The Impact of the New World on the Old*, 2 vols. (Berkeley and Los Angeles, 1976), 1:335–50.

5. Washburn, "Relations between Europeans and Amerindians," 2; *idem*, "The Clash of Morality," in Chiappelli, ed., *First Images of America*, 1:336; *idem*, "Adair's 'Noble Savages,' " in Leder, ed., *Colonial Legacy*, 91.

6. Cornelius Jaenen, "Amerindian Views of French Culture in the Seventeenth Century," *Canadian Historical Review*, 55 (1974), 261–91; James P. Ronda, " 'We Are Well as We Are': An Indian Critique of Seventeenth-Century Christian Missions," *William and Mary Quarterly*, 3d ser. 34 (1977), 66–82.

7. *WMQ*, 3d ser. 26 (1969), 267–86.

8. *Ibid.*, 269, 272, 283–85.

9. *Ibid.*, 270.

10. Bernard W. Sheehan, *Seeds of Extinction: Jeffersonian Philanthropy and the American Indian* (Chapel Hill, 1973); *idem*, "The American Indian as Victim," *The Alternative: An American Spectator*, 8:4 (Jan. 1975), 5–8; *idem*, *Savagism and Civility: Indians and Englishmen in Colonial Virginia* (Cambridge, 1980).

11. Alasdair MacIntyre, "What Morality Is Not," *Against the Self-Images of the Age* (New York, 1971), ch. 12.

12. Adrian Oldfield, "Moral Judgments in History," *History and Theory*, 20 (1981), 260–77 at 273.

13. Sheehan, "The Indian as Victim," *The Alternative*, 8:4 (Jan. 1975), 7.

14. *Ibid.*; Sheehan, *Savagism and Civility*, ix, 34, 95; *idem*, *Seeds of Extinction*, 12.

15. David Hackett Fischer, *Historians' Fallacies: Toward a Logic of Historical Thought* (New York, 1970), 42 n.4. All learning or gain-

ing of knowledge is subjective ("conditioned by personal character-istics of mind"—Webster) unless it is reflexive. But *subjective* is a correlative term; no knowledge can be subjective unless some knowl-edge is objective. See also J. H. Hexter, *The History Primer* (New York, 1971), 61–62, 96.

16. Cushing Strout, *The Pragmatic Revolt in American History: Carl Becker and Charles Beard* (New York, 1958), 84.
17. Hexter, *History Primer*, 62.
18. 2 vols. (Montreal, 1976).
19. *Ethnohistory*, 22 (1975), 51–56.
20. Oldfield, "Moral Judgments in History," *History and Theory*, 20 (1981), 274.
21. Trigger, "Brecht and Ethnohistory," *Ethnohistory*, 22 (1975), 54.
22. Washburn, "Relations between Europeans and Amerindians," 19.
23. John Higham, "Beyond Consensus: The Historian as Moral Critic," *American Historical Review*, 67 (1962), 609–25 at 620, 625; Gordon Leff, *History and Social Theory* (University, Alabama, 1969), ch. 5; Ann Low-Beer, "Moral Judgments in History and History Teach-ing," in W. H. Burton and D. Thompson, eds., *Studies in the Na-ture and Teaching of History* (New York, 1967), 137–58 at 141, 143.
24. Hexter, *History Primer*, 217; Higham, "Beyond Consensus," *AHR*, 67 (1962), 620; "W. J. Eccles: detective, lawyer, and judge," inter-view by Robert Armstrong, *McGill News*, 61:2 (Fall 1980), 9; Gar-rett Mattingly, *The Armada* (Boston, 1959), 375; Arthur Child, "Moral Judgment in History," *Ethics*, 61 (1951), 297–308 at 302.
25. Roy Harvey Pearce, "From the History of Ideas to Ethnohistory," *Journal of Ethnic Studies*, 2 (1974), 86–92; Francis Jennings, *The Invasion of America: Indians, Colonialism, and the Cant of Con-quest* (Chapel Hill, 1975), x; Lord Bolingbroke, *Letters on the Study and Use of History* (new ed., London, 1779), 14 (letter 2); Edmund Burke quoted in Lord Acton, *Essays on Freedom and Power*, ed. Gertrude Himmelfarb (New York, 1955), 52; Leff, *His-tory and Social Theory*, 109; Oldfield, "Moral Judgments in His-tory," *History and Theory*, 20 (1981), 276.
26. Pearce, "From the History of Ideas," *J. of Ethnic Studies*, 2 (1974), 86–92; Charles Frankel, "Explanation and Interpretation in History," in Patrick Gardiner, ed., *Theories of History* (Glencoe, Ill., 1959), 424; Higham, "Beyond Consensus," *AHR*, 67 (1962), 625; Hexter, *History Primer*, 216; Peter Winch, "Understanding a Primitive So-ciety," in D. Z. Phillips, ed., *Religion and Understanding* (New York, 1967), 9–42 at 30, 37.
27. Hexter, *History Primer*, 216–17; Low-Beer, "Moral Judgments in

History," in Burton and Thompson, eds., *Studies in the Nature and Teaching of History*, 149–58; Oldfield, "Moral Judgments in History," *History and Theory*, 20 (1981), 274–77.

28. Higham, "Beyond Consensus," *AHR*, 67 (1962), 624; Oldfield, "Moral Judgments in History," *History and Theory*, 20 (1981), 260; Child, "Moral Judgment in History," *Ethics*, 61 (1951), 297–302; Leff, *History and Social Theory*, 114.

29. Robert Redfield, *The Primitive World and Its Transformations* (Chicago, 1953), 164; W. B. Gallie, *Philosophy and the Historical Understanding* (London, 1964), 203–204.

30. Gordon Wright, "History as a Moral Science," *AHR*, 81 (1976), 9; Leff, *History and Social Theory*, 113; Oldfield, "Moral Judgments in History," *History and Theory*, 20 (1981), 260–77 *passim;* Low-Beer, "Moral Judgments in History," in Burton and Thompson, eds., *Studies in the Nature and Teaching of History*, 144–48.

31. Oldfield, "Moral Judgments in History," *History and Theory*, 20 (1981), 271.

32. Washburn, "Relations between Europeans and Amerindians," 12–13. For an excellent application of this technique, see W. J. Eccles, *Frontenac, The Courtier Governor* (Toronto, 1959), 182–83, which treats Denonville's enslavement of Iroquois warriors for the king's galleys. For another attempt, see James Axtell, *The European and the Indian: Essays in the Ethnohistory of Colonial North America* (New York, 1981), ch. 8.

33. Norton paperback, 1976.

34. Jennings, *Invasion of America*, vii, ix–x.

35. *Ibid.*, 185.

36. Richard Drinnon in *The Indian Historian*, 9:4 (Fall 1976), 24–26; Nancy O. Lurie, "Laundered Colonial Linen," *Reviews in American History*, 4 (1976), 365–71; William C. Sturtevant in *WMQ*, 3d ser. 34 (1977), 312–14; James P. Ronda in *AHR*, 82 (1977), 168–69; Neal Salisbury in *New England Quarterly*, 49 (1976), 158–61.

37. Dena Dincauze in *American Anthropologist*, 79 (1977), 150–51; Bernard W. Sheehan in *Journal of American History*, 63 (1976), 378–79; Alden T. Vaughan in *Western Historical Quarterly*, 7 (1976), 421–22.

38. *AHR*, 82 (1977), 169.

39. Leff, *History and Social Theory*, 111; Low-Beer, "Moral Judgments in History," in Burton and Thompson, eds., *Studies in the Nature and Teaching of History*, 144–48; Bayle quoted in Edward P. Hamilton, ed. and trans., *Adventure in the Wilderness: The American*

Journals of Louis Antoine de Bougainville, 1756–1760 (Norman, 1964), 237.

40. Guy Frégault, *Canada: The War of the Conquest,* trans. Margaret M. Cameron (Toronto, 1969; orig. pub. Montreal, 1955), 318; Paul Horgan, *Approaches to Writing* (New York, 1973), 167.

41. James Axtell, "The Ethnohistory of Early America: A Review Essay," *WMQ,* 3d ser. 35 (1978), 110–44; Wilbur R. Jacobs, "Native American History: How It Illuminates Our Past," *AHR,* 80 (1975), 595–609; Wilcomb Washburn, "The Writing of American Indian History: A Status Report," *Pacific Historical Review,* 40 (1971), 261–81.

42. Hayden White, *Tropics of Discourse: Essays in Cultural Criticism* (Baltimore, 1978), 66–67; *idem, Metahistory: The Historical Imagination in Nineteenth-Century Europe* (Baltimore, 1973), 5–11, 29–31. I am grateful to Bob Berkhofer for pointing me to White's notion of "emplotment."

43. Hans Meyerhoff, ed., *The Philosophy of History in Our Time* (Garden City, N.Y., 1959), 188–215; Sidney Hook, ed., *Philosophy and History* (New York, 1963), chs. 3, 4, 5, 17; Arthur C. Danto, *Analytical Philosophy of History* (Cambridge, 1965), ch. 6; William H. Dray, ed., *Philosophical Analysis and History* (New York, 1966), 75–94; Fischer, *Historians' Fallacies,* 41–43; Hexter, *History Primer,* 61–62, 96; Frank Cunningham, *Objectivity in Social Science* (Toronto, 1973); Peter Gay, *Style in History* (New York, 1974), 194–217; Maurice Mandelbaum, *The Anatomy of Historical Knowledge* (Baltimore, 1977), chs. 6–7; R. F. Atkinson, *Knowledge and Explanation in History: An Introduction to the Philosophy of History* (Ithaca, 1978), ch. 3.

CHAPTER TWO

1. James Axtell, "A Moral History of Indian-White Relations Revisited," *The History Teacher,* 16 (1983), 169–90.

2. Francis Jennings, *The Invasion of America: Indians, Colonialism, and the Cant of Conquest* (Chapel Hill, 1975), 43, 49n., 73–74, 114.

3. Neal Salisbury, *Manitou and Providence: Indians, Europeans, and the Making of New England, 1500–1643* (New York, 1982), 181, 195, 200; review of Salisbury by Alden Vaughan, *New England Quarterly,* 56 (1983), 129–32 at 131.

4. Jennings, *Invasion of America,* ix–x.

5. Alden T. Vaughan, *New England Frontier: Puritans and Indians, 1620–1675* (Boston, 1965), 323. In fairness, Vaughan has considerably modified this statement in his revised edition (New York, 1979).
6. James Axtell and William C. Sturtevant, "The Unkindest Cut, or Who Invented Scalping?" *William and Mary Quarterly,* 3d ser. 37 (1980), 451–72 at 470.
7. Francis L. K. Hsu, "Rethinking the Concept 'Primitive,'" *Current Anthropology,* 5 (1964), 169–78.
8. Thomas Hobbes, *Leviathan,* ed. Michael Oakeshott (Oxford, 1946), 69.
9. Alden T. Vaughan, "From White Man to Redskin: Changing Anglo-American Perceptions of the American Indian," *American Historical Review,* 87 (1982), 917–53.
10. Jacqueline Peterson and Jennifer S. H. Brown, eds., *The New Peoples: Being and Becoming Métis in North America* (Winnipeg, 1985), 4–6.
11. Francis Jennings, *The Ambiguous Iroquois Empire* (New York, 1984), 58–60.

CHAPTER THREE

1. *The Invasion Within: The Contest of Cultures in Colonial North America* (New York, 1985) is the first volume of a proposed trilogy on cultural interaction in colonial North America. The study of religious conversion in Africa is perhaps the most sophisticated. See, for example, J. D. Y. Peel, "Syncretism and Religious Change," *Comparative Studies in Society and History,* 10 (1968), 121–41; H. W. Mobley, *The Ghanaian's Image of the Missionary* (*Leiden, 1970*); Robin Horton, "African Conversion," *Africa,* 41 (1971), 85–108; T. O. Ranger and I. N. Kimambo, eds., *The Historical Study of African Religions* (Berkeley and Los Angeles, 1972); Humphrey J. Fisher, "Conversion Reconsidered," *Africa,* 43 (1973), 27–40; T. O. Beidelman, "Social Theory and the Study of Christian Missions in Africa," *Africa,* 44 (1974), 235–49; Beidelman, *Colonial Evangelism: A Socio-Historical Study of an Eastern African Mission at Grassroots* (Bloomington, 1982).
2. Typical of this genre of numerological assessment is Léon Pouliot, S.J., *Étude sur les Relations des Jésuites de la Nouvelle-France (1632–1672)* (Montreal and Paris, 1940), pt. 2, ch. 6. See also James P. Ronda and James Axtell, *Indian Missions: A Critical Bibliography* (Bloomington, 1978), 1–7, 48–50.
3. Francis Jennings, "Goals and Functions of Puritan Missions to the

Indians," *Ethnohistory*, 18 (1971), 197–212; Neal Salisbury, "Red Puritans: The 'Praying Indians' of Massachusetts and John Eliot," *William and Mary Quarterly*, 3d ser. 31 (1974), 27–54; Salisbury, "Prospero in New England: The Puritan Missionary as Colonist," *Papers of the Sixth Algonquian Conference, 1974*, ed. William Cowan, National Museum of Man, Mercury Series, Canadian Ethnology Service Paper 23 (Ottawa, 1975), 253–73; James Axtell, "The European Failure to Convert the Indians: An Autopsy," *ibid.*, 274–90; Kenneth M. Morrison, " 'That Art of Coyning Christians:' John Eliot and the Praying Indians of Massachusetts," *Ethnohistory*, 21 (1974), 77–92.

4. William Kellaway, *The New England Company, 1649–1776: Missionary Society to the American Indians* (London, 1961); Alden T. Vaughan, *New England Frontier: Puritans and Indians, 1620–1675* (Boston, 1965; rev. ed. New York, 1979), chs. 9–11; Ola Elizabeth Winslow, *John Eliot: 'Apostle to the Indians'* (Boston, 1968).

5. Francis Jennings, *The Invasion of America: Indians, Colonialism, and the Cant of Conquest* (Chapel Hill, 1975), 251 n. 67, a table drawn from Daniel Gookin, "Historical Collections of the Indians of New England" [1674], *Collections of the Massachusetts Historical Society*, 1st ser. 1 (1792), 141–226. Gookin gave no figure for the number of baptized in Natick; I have estimated about 80 persons on the basis of a 2 : 1 ratio between baptized and full communicants in two other "old" towns.

6. John G. Palfrey, the late-nineteenth-century historian of New England, estimated that in 1670 80% of New England's adults were not full church members, a figure that has been generally accepted by more recent scholars such as Perry Miller, Samuel Eliot Morison, and Edmund Morgan. Morgan, *The Puritan Family: Religion and Domestic Relations in Seventeenth-Century New England* (rev. ed. New York, 1966), 171 n.32. See also Kenneth A. Lockridge, "The History of a Puritan Church, 1637–1736," *New England Quarterly*, 40 (1967), 399–424; Robert G. Pope, *The Half-Way Covenant: Church Membership in Puritan New England* (Princeton, 1969); Gerald F. Moran, "Religious Renewal, Puritan Tribalism and the Family in Seventeenth-Century Milford, Connecticut," *William and Mary Quarterly*, 3d ser. 36 (1979), 236–54; Christine Alice Young, *From 'Good Order' to Glorious Revolution: Salem, Massachusetts, 1628–1689* (Ann Arbor, 1980), 98, 105–38, 240–41.

7. Frederick L. Weis, "The New England Company of 1649 and Its Missionary Enterprises," *Publications of the Colonial Society of Massachusetts*, 38 (1947–51 [1959]), 134–218.

8. Anthony F. C. Wallace, *Religion: An Anthropological View* (New York, 1966), 30.

9. Anthony F. C. Wallace, *The Death and Rebirth of the Seneca* (New York, 1970).

10. For an analysis of this concept, see James Axtell, *The European and the Indian: Essays in the Ethnohistory of Colonial North America* (New York, 1981), ch. 3.

11. Christopher Hill, *Society and Puritanism in Pre-Revolutionary England* (New York, 1964); George Lee Haskins, *Law and Authority in Early Massachusetts* (New York, 1960), ch. 9; Michael Walzer, *The Revolution of the Saints; A Study in the Origins of Radical Politics* (Cambridge, Mass., 1965).

12. Robert F. Berkhofer, Jr., "Protestants, Pagans, and Sequences among the North American Indians, 1760–1860," *Ethnohistory*, 10 (1963), 201–16.

13. James Axtell, "The White Indians of Colonial America," *William and Mary Quarterly*, 3d ser. 32 (1975), 55–88.

CHAPTER FOUR

1. Samuel Hopkins, *Historical Memoirs Relating to the Housatonic Indians* [Boston, 1753], reprinted in *The Magazine of History with Notes and Queries*, Extra No. 17 (New York, 1911), 164–65.

2. Sarah Cabot Sedgwick and Christina Sedgwick Marquand, *Stockbridge, 1739–1939: A Chronicle* (Great Barrington, Mass., 1939), 23, 51, 69; Daniel R. Mandell, Change and Continuity in a Native American Community: Eighteenth Century Stockbridge (M.A. thesis, Dept. of History, U. of Virginia, 1982), 33–34.

3. Hopkins, *Historical Memoirs*, 39, 46.

4. *Ibid.*, 28, 65–66.

5. *Ibid.*, 81–82.

6. *Ibid.*, 73–76.

7. *Ibid.*, 94–95, 106–11, 148.

8. *Ibid.*, 117–34, 144–47, 154.

9. *Ibid.*, 145, 154–55; Emma Lewis Coleman, *New England Captives Carried to Canada between 1677 and 1760 during the French and Indian Wars,* 2 vols. (Portland, Maine, 1925), 2:97–99, 113.

10. Edmund S. Morgan, *The Gentle Puritan: A Life of Ezra Stiles, 1727–1795* (New Haven, 1962), ch. 5 at 87.

11. *Journals of the House of Representatives of Massachusetts, 1749–*

1750 (Boston, 1951), 225–26; Massachusetts Archives, State House, Boston, 32:30–32; Sereno E. Dwight, *The Works of President [Jonathan] Edwards with a Memoir of His Life,* 10 vols. (New York, 1830), 1:452.

12. William Kellaway, *The New England Company, 1649–1776* (London, 1961), 274–75.

13. John L. Sibley and Clifford K. Shipton, *Biographical Sketches of Those Who Attended Harvard College* (Cambridge, Mass., 1873–), 7:62–63.

14. Mass. Archives, 32:300, 367–68; Dwight, *Works of President Edwards,* 1:480, 491, 494, 527.

15. Mass. Archives, 32:206–12, 248–49, 370; Dwight, *Works of President Edwards,* 1:486.

16. Mass. Archives, 32:299, 303, 305, 366; Dwight, *Works of President Edwards,* 1:470, 490–91; *Colls. Mass. His. Soc.,* 1st ser. 10 (1809), 142–53 at 148.

17. Jonathan Edwards to Joshua Paine, Feb. 24, 1752, Yale Univ. Lib., Andover-Newton Edwards Collection (transcript), folder 1752B; *Sibley's Harvard Graduates,* 12:392–411.

18. Dwight, *Works of President Edwards,* 1:303–304, 490–91, 504–505; *Sibley's Harvard Graduates,* 7:62–63, 13:399; Sedgwick and Marquand, *Stockbridge,* 66–67.

19. *Colls. Mass. His. Soc.,* 1st ser. 4 (1795), 54–56; Dwight, *Works of President Edwards,* 1:527; Mass. Archives, 32:476–77, 508.

CHAPTER FIVE

1. Clayton Colman Hall, ed., *Narratives of Early Maryland, 1633–1684* (New York, 1910), 39–41, 71; Saint Ignatius of Loyola, *The Constitutions of the Society of Jesus,* ed. and trans. George E. Ganss (St. Louis, 1970), 275.

2. Hall, *Narratives,* 41, 72. On Fleet, see J. Frederick Fausz, "Profits, Pelts, and Power: The 'Americanization' of English Culture in the Chesapeake, 1620–1652," *The Maryland Historian,* 15 (Jan. 1984); Fausz, "Present at the 'Creation': The Chesapeake World That Greeted the Maryland Colonists," *Maryland Historical Magazine,* 79 (1984), 7–20.

3. Hall, *Narratives,* 42, 72–74.

4. Hall, *Narratives,* 40, 42, 44, 74, 88.

5. Hall, *Narratives,* 119–20, 122–23.

6. Hall, *Narratives*, 124–25; James H. Merrell, "Cultural Continuity among the Piscataway Indians of Colonial Maryland," *William and Mary Quarterly*, 3d ser. 36 (1979), 548–70 at 555–56.
7. Hall, *Narratives*, 125–27.
8. Hall, *Narratives*, 127–28.
9. Hall, *Narratives*, 131–32; Thomas Hughes, *History of the Society of Jesus in North America, Colonial and Federal*, 4 vols. (London, 1907–17), Text, vol. 1, 481.
10. Hall, *Narratives*, 131, 132; Hughes, *History of the Society of Jesus*, Text, 1:481–82.
11. Hughes, *History of the Society of Jesus*, Text, 1:482, 492; Vatican Archives of the Sacred Congregation of the Propaganda Fide, Calendar of Manuscripts Pertaining to North America by Luca Codignola, Public Archives of Canada microfiche (Ottawa, 1984), Series S.O.C.G., 402 (1641): 112r-v, 116r-v (I am extremely grateful to Professor Codignola for advance copies of his calendar items relating to Maryland); Hall, *Narratives*, 132.
12. Hall, *Narratives*, 136–37.
13. Hall, *Narratives*, 137; Hughes, *History of the Society of Jesus*, Text, 1:471–72, 547, 550.
14. Hall, *Narratives*, 135–36. On the rigor of Jesuit standards for baptism, see Hall, *Narratives*, 127, 128, 129, 131, 132.
15. Hall, *Narratives*, 138–39.
16. Hughes, *History of the Society of Jesus*, Text, 1:473, 475, 559–60; Documents, vol. 1, pt. 1, 31; Archives of the Propaganda Fide, Calendar, Series Acta, 85 (1715):82r–83r.
17. Hughes, *History of the Society of Jesus*, Text, 1:551–53; Raphael Semmes, *Captains and Mariners of Early Maryland* (Baltimore, 1937), 440–41, 794 n.27.
18. Hughes, *History of the Society of Jesus*, Text, 1:562–64; Archives of the Propaganda Fide, Calendar, Series FV, S.O.C.G., 12 (1653–1663):71r–72v.
19. Léon Pouliot, *Étude sur les Relations des Jésuites de la Nouvelle-France (1632–1672)* (Montreal and Paris, 1940), 308 n.1.
20. A.M.D.G. [Arthur Melançon], *Liste des Missionnaires-Jésuites, Nouvelle-France et Louisiane, 1611–1800* (Montreal, 1929), 75–76 and *passim;* Hughes, *History of the Society of Jesus*, Text, 1:162, 564; Caroline M. Hibbard, "Early Stuart Catholicism: Revisions and Re-Revisions," *Journal of Modern History*, 52 (1980), 1–34.
21. Semmes, *Captains and Mariners of Early Maryland*, ch. 4; Hughes, *History of the Society of Jesus*, Text, 1:482.
22. Guy Frégault, *Le XVIIIe Siècle Canadien: Études* (Montreal, 1968),

104–11; Richard Colebrook Harris, *The Seigneurial System in Early Canada: A Geographical Study* (Madison, 1968), 42–44; Pouliot, *Étude sur les Relations*, 194–99, 264–66. On the Jesuit fur trade, see Bruce G. Trigger, "The Jesuits and the Fur Trade," *Ethnohistory*, 12 (1965), 30–53; Cornelius J. Jaenen, "The Catholic Clergy and the Fur Trade, 1585–1685," Canadian Historical Association, *Historical Papers 1970*, 60–80; Lucien Campeau, "Le Commerce des clercs en Nouvelle-France," *Revue de l'Université d'Ottawa/University of Ottawa Quarterly*, 47 (1977), 27–35.

23. Merrell, "Cultural Continuity among the Piscataway," *WMQ*, 3d ser. 36 (1979), 548–70.

24. Reuben Gold Thwaites, ed., *The Jesuit Relations and Allied Documents*, 73 vols. (Cleveland, 1896–1901), 3:140–55, 11:138–41, 14:77, 39:142–45.

25. Larzer Ziff, ed., *John Cotton on the Churches of New England* (Cambridge, Mass., 1968), 276.

26. James Axtell, *The Invasion Within: The Contest of Cultures in Colonial North America* (New York, 1985), chs. 5–6. Other treatments of the Maryland mission are B. U. Campbell, "Early Missions among the Indians in Maryland," *Maryland Historical Magazine*, 1 (1906), 293–316; Edwin Warfield Beitzell, *The Jesuit Missions of St. Mary's County, Maryland* (Privately printed, 1959), ch. 1; Edward D. Neill, *The Founders of Maryland* (Albany, N.Y., 1876), 87–107; Semmes, *Captains and Mariners of Early Maryland*, ch. 17; William P. Treacy, *Old Catholic Maryland and Its Early Jesuit Missionaries* (Swedesboro, N.J., 1889?), chs. 1–3.

CHAPTER SIX

1. James Axtell, *The Invasion Within: The Contest of Cultures in Colonial North America* (New York, 1985), chs. 4–6.

2. *Ibid.*, chap. 11; quotation is from Daniel Gookin, *Historical Collections of the Indians in New England . . .* (1674), ed. Jeffrey H. Fiske (Towtaid, N.J., 1970), 87.

3. David Beers Quinn, ed., *The Roanoke Voyages, 1584–1590*, Hakluyt Society Publications, 2d ser. 104–5 (London, 1955), 375–77 (continuous pagination).

4. Roger Williams, *A Key into the Language of America: or, An Help to the Language of the Natives in That Part of America, Called New-England* (London, 1643), 118.

5. Gabriel Sagard-Théodat, *Historie du Canada et voyages que les*

frères mineurs Recollects y ont faicts pour la conversion des infideles . . . (Paris, 1636), trans. H. H. Langton, MS 7, 285, University of Toronto Library (pagination follows that of the book).

6. *Ibid.*, 638.

7. Reuben Gold Thwaites, ed., *The Jesuit Relations and Allied Documents*, 73 vols. (Cleveland, 1896–1901), 16:43–45 (1639), hereafter cited as *JR*.

8. *JR* 9:207.

9. *JR* 11:195.

10. *JR* 20:31–33.

11. *JR* 39:59.

12. Jack Goody and Ian Watt, "The Consequences of Literacy," in Goody, ed., *Literacy in Traditional Societies* (Cambridge, 1968), 27–68; Walter J. Ong, *The Presence of the Word: Some Prolegomena for Cultural and Religious History* (New Haven, 1967), and *Orality and Literacy: The Technologizing of the Word* (New York, 1982); Marshall McLuhan, *The Gutenberg Galaxy: The Making of Typographic Man* (Toronto, 1962); Harvey J. Graff, *The Legacies of Literacy: Continuities and Contradictions in Western Culture and Society* (Bloomington, 1987).

13. Axtell, *The Invasion Within*, 17–19.

14. Jack Goody, "Restricted Literacy in Northern Ghana," in Goody, ed., *Literacy in Traditional Societies*, 201.

15. *JR* 12:183–85.

16. *JR* 9:195 (1636).

17. Alexander Long, "A Small Postscript of the ways and maners of the Indians called Charikees" (1725), ed. David H. Corkran, *Southern Indian Studies*, 21 (1969), 18.

18. Goody, "Restricted Literacy in Ghana," in Goody, ed., *Literacy in Traditional Society*, 206, 230, 239.

19. *JR* 11:153, 209.

20. *JR* 30:63 (1646), 39:149 (1653), 45:51 (1657), 67:187 (1697). As late as the 1740s, Father Pierre Potier was making the same argument for the superiority of Christian doctrine over Huron "stories" (Alexander Fraser, ed., "Huron Manuscripts from Rev. Pierre Potier's Collection," *Fifteenth Report of the Bureau of Archives for the Province of Ontario, 1918–1919* [Toronto, 1920], 609–22).

21. *JR* 15:121.

22. Axtell, *The Invasion Within*, 276–77.

23. Henry W. Bowden and James P. Ronda, eds., *John Eliot's Indian Dialogues: A Study in Cultural Interaction* (Westport, Conn., 1980), 71, 139, 140–41.

24. Evarts B. Greene and Virginia D. Harrington, *American Population before the Federal Census of 1790* (New York, 1932), 11, 13; Kenneth A. Lockridge, *Literacy in Colonial New England: An Enquiry into the Social Context of Literacy in the Early Modern West* (New York, 1974), 19, 39–41.
25. Axtell, *The Invasion Within*, 99–102.
26. William Kellaway, *The New England Company, 1649–1776: Missionary Society to the American Indians* (London, 1961), ch. 6.

CHAPTER SEVEN

1. Francis Jennings, *The Invasion of America: Indians, Colonialism, and the Cant of Conquest* (Chapel Hill, 1975), ch. 14, published previously as "Goals and Functions of Puritan Missions to the Indians," *Ethnohistory*, 18 (1971), 197–212.
2. Neal Salisbury, "Red Puritans: The 'Praying Indians' of Massachusetts Bay and John Eliot," *William and Mary Quarterly*, 3d ser. 31 (1974), 27–54.
3. David Blanchard, ". . . To the Other Side of the Sky: Catholicism at Kahnawake, 1667–1700," *Anthropologica*, 24 (1982), 77–102.
4. Cornelius J. Jaenen, *Friend and Foe: Aspects of French-Amerindian Cultural Contact in the Sixteenth and Seventeenth Centuries* (Toronto, 1976), ch. 2.
5. Allen W. Trelease, *Indian Affairs in Colonial New York: The Seventeenth Century* (Ithaca, 1960), 172.
6. Bruce G. Trigger, *Natives and Newcomers: Canada's 'Heroic Age' Reconsidered* (Kingston and Montreal, 1985), 294–96 (my emphasis).
7. See, for example, Roger Williams, *Christenings make not Christians* (London, 1645), in *Complete Writings*, 7 vols. (New York, 1963), 7:36; *Collections of the Rhode-Island Historical Society* 4 (1838), 138; John Wolfe Lydekker, *The Faithful Mohawks* (Cambridge, 1938), 36.
8. Father François Du Creux, *The History of Canada or New France* [Paris, 1664], trans. Percy J. Robinson, ed. James B. Conacher, 2 vols. (Toronto: Champlain Society, 1951–52), 1:19.
9. Father Christian Le Clercq, *First Establishment of the Faith in New France* [Paris, 1691], trans. John Gilmary Shea, 2 vols. (New York, 1881), 1:255. See also *Rapport de l'Archiviste de la Province de Québec* (1939–40), 216 (1671).
10. Baron de Lahontan, *New Voyages to North-America* [The Hague, 1703], ed. Reuben Gold Thwaites, 2 vols. (Chicago, 1905), 1:146, 329, 2:413–14, 438.

11. Reuben Gold Thwaites, ed., *The Jesuit Relations and Allied Documents*, 73 vols. (Cleveland, 1896–1901), 1:161–65, 3:147 (hereafter cited as *JR*); Le Clercq, *First Establishment of the Faith*, 1:142.

12. Léon Pouliot, *Étude sur les Relations des Jésuites de la Nouvelle-France (1632–1672)* (Montreal and Paris, 1940), ch. 6.

13. James Axtell, *The Invasion Within: The Contest of Cultures in Colonial North America* (New York, 1985), 262.

14. *JR* 58:81.

15. *JR* 55:297. See also Axtell, *The Invasion Within*, 281, 284, 333.

16. Rev. Samuel Hopkins, *Historical Memoirs Relating to the Housatonic Indians* (Boston, 1753), reprinted in *The Magazine of History with Notes and Queries*, Extra No. 17 (New York, 1911), 138.

17. Le Clercq, *First Establishment of the Faith*, 1:221.

18. François Gendron, *Quelques Particularitez du pays des Hurons en la Nouvelle France* (Paris, 1660), reprinted by John Gilmary Shea (Albany, N.Y., 1868), 25.

19. *JR* 25:113.

20. See above p. 261n.5.

21. *JR* 39:143.

22. *JR* 28:83–85.

23. Axtell, *The Invasion Within*, chs. 4, 7.

24. *JR* 25:247. See also Axtell, *The Invasion Within*, 123–24.

25. *JR* 9:73.

26. Axtell, *The Invasion Within*, chs. 5–6.

27. *JR* 39:143.

28. Axtell, *The Invasion Within*, ch. 9, esp. 238–39.

29. *Ibid.*, 232–34.

30. David Kobrin, "The Expansion of the Visible Church in New England: 1629–1650," *Church History*, 36 (1967), 189–209.

31. Axtell, *The Invasion Within*, 240.

32. *Ibid.*, 225, 227.

33. *Ibid.*, 125–27.

34. *Ibid.*, 117; James P. Ronda, "Generations of Faith: The Christian Indians of Martha's Vineyard," *William and Mary Quarterly*, 3d ser. 38 (1981), 369–94.

35. Axtell, *The Invasion Within*, 110–13.

36. See J. D. Y. Peel, "Syncretism and Religious Change," *Comparative Studies in Society and History*, 10 (1968), 121–41.

37. *Ibid.*, 124, 129; Robin Horton, "African Conversion," *Africa*, 41 (1971), 85–108.

38. James Axtell, ed., *The Indian Peoples of Eastern America: A Docu-*

mentary History of the Sexes (New York, 1981), ch. 2; George A. Pettitt, *Primitive Education in North America,* U. of Calif. Pubs. in Amer. Archaeology and Ethnology 43:1 (Berkeley and Los Angeles, 1946), 6–14.

CHAPTER EIGHT

1. James Axtell, "Bronze Men and Golden Ages: The Intellectual History of Indian-White Relations in Colonial America," *Journal of Interdisciplinary History,* 12 (1982), 663–75.
2. David Hackett Fischer, *Historians' Fallacies: Toward a Logic of Historical Thought* (New York, 1970), 195–200. Fischer calls it the "idealist fallacy."
3. James Axtell, *The Invasion Within: The Contest of Cultures in Colonial North America* (New York, 1985), 24, 27, 55–56; Olive Patricia Dickason, *The Myth of the Savage and the Beginnings of French Colonialism in the Americas* (Edmonton, 1984), ch. 10; above ch. 9, pp. 148–52.
4. Edmund Berkeley and Dorothy Smith Berkeley, eds., *The Reverend John Clayton: . . . His Scientific Writings and Other Related Papers* (Charlottesville, 1965), 39, Clayton to Dr. Nehemiah Grew, 1687.
5. William S. Simmons, *Spirit of the New England Tribes: Indian History and Folklore, 1620–1984* (Hanover, N.H., 1986), 66–67, 71.
6. Reuben Gold Thwaites, ed., *The Jesuit Relations and Allied Documents,* 73 vols. (Cleveland, 1896–1901), 5:119–21 (hereafter cited as *JR*); Father Gabriel Sagard, *The Long Journey to the Country of the Hurons* [Paris, 1632], ed. George M. Wrong, trans. H. H. Langton (Toronto: Champlain Society, 1939), 79.
7. Father Chrestien Le Clercq, *New Relation of Gaspesia* [Paris, 1691], ed. and trans. William F. Ganong (Toronto: Champlain Society, 1910), 109.
8. Ella Elizabeth Clark, ed., *Indian Legends of Canada* (Toronto, 1960), 150–51. This story was told by a member of the Bear clan in 1855.
9. John Heckewelder, *History, Manners, and Customs of the Indian Nations Who Once Inhabited Pennsylvania and the Neighbouring States* [1818], ed. William G. Reichel (Philadelphia, 1876), 71–75. Heckewelder received this story from an intelligent Delaware man at the end of the eighteenth century.

10. David Beers Quinn, ed., *The Roanoke Voyages, 1584–1590*, Hakluyt Society Publications, 2d ser. 104–5 (London, 1955), 111–12 (continuous pagination).

11. Lawrence G. Wroth, *The Voyages of Giovanni da Verrazzano* (New Haven, 1970), 135.

12. Emma Helen Blair, ed. and trans., *The Indian Tribes of the Upper Mississippi Valley and Region of the Great Lakes*, 2 vols. (Cleveland, 1911), 1:309.

13. H. P. Biggar, ed., *The Voyages of Jacques Cartier*, Publications of the Public Archives of Canada 11 (Ottawa, 1924), 56, 62, 162–63.

14. *Ibid.*, 165; Louis Phelps Kellogg, ed., *Early Narratives of the Northwest, 1634–1699*, Original Narratives of Early American History (New York, 1917), 129, 155–56.

15. Walter James Hoffman, "The Menomini Indians," Bureau of American Ethnology, *14th Annual Report* (Washington, D.C., 1896), pt. 1: 214–16 at 215.

16. Quinn, *Roanoke Voyages*, 378–79.

17. Wroth, *Voyages of Verrazzano*, 137.

18. Blair, *Indian Tribes of the Upper Mississippi*, 1:308–9; Kellogg, *Early Narratives of the Northwest*, 45–46.

19. Quinn, *Roanoke Voyages*, 375–76.

20. *Father Louis Hennepin's Description of Louisiana* [Paris, 1683], trans. Marion E. Cross (Minneapolis, 1938), 82, 96, 98, 105, 108–9, 130.

21. William Wood, *New England's Prospect* [London, 1634], ed. Alden T. Vaughan (Amherst, Mass., 1977), 96.

22. Roger Williams, *A Key into the Language of America* (London, 1643), 59; Bruce G. Trigger, *The Children of Aataentsic: A History of the Huron People to 1660*, 2 vols. (Montreal, 1976), 307, 360, 617–18 (continuous pagination); Gordon M. Day, *The Mots loups of Father Mathevet*, National Museum of Man, Publications in Ethnology 9 (Ottawa, 1975), 353 n.424; Arthur Woodward, "The 'Long Knives,'" *Indian Notes* [Heye Foundation], 5:1 (Jan. 1928), 64–79; Gabriel Sagard-Théodat, *Histoire du Canada* (Paris, 1636), 465; Axtell, *The Invasion Within*, 109.

23. Noah T. Clarke, "The Wampum Belt Collection of the New York State Museum," 24th Report of the Director of the Division of Sciences and the State Museum, *New York State Museum Bulletin*, 288 (Albany, N.Y., 1931), 85–121 at 90, 109.

24. *Ibid.*, 108, 109; Tehanetorens, *Wampum Belts* (Onchiota, N.Y.: Six Nations Indian Museum, n.d.), 61, 62, 66.

25. Rochester Museum and Science Center, Rochester, N.Y., collections

from the Steele, Dann, and Boughton Hill sites; "Excavations on Boughton Hill," 16th Report of the Director . . . 1919, *N.Y.S. Mus. Bull.*, 227–28 (Albany, N.Y., 1921), 11–13 and plates.

26. Richard M. Dorson, "Comic Indian Anecdotes," *Southern Folklore Quarterly*, 10 (1946), 113–28 at 113.

27. *Ibid.*, 121.

28. *Ibid.*, 123.

29. Susan Myra Kingsbury, ed., *The Records of the Virginia Company of London*, 4 vols. (Washington, D.C., 1906–35), 3:556.

30. Dorson, "Comic Indian Anecdotes," 124.

31. Donald M. Frame, trans., *The Complete Works of Montaigne* (Stanford, 1948), 159.

32. Sagard, *Histoire du Canada*, 241–42, 275–76, 291; Marc Lescarbot, *The History of New France* [Paris, 1609], trans. W. L. Grant, intro. H. P. Biggar, 3 vols. (Toronto: Champlain Society, 1907–14), 3:22.

33. Samuel Purchas, *Hakluytus Posthumus, or Purchas His Pilgrimes*, 20 vols. (Glasgow, 1905–07), 19:118–19.

34. Williams, *Key into the Language*, 59–60.

35. *JR* 1:173–77; Le Clercq, *New Relation of Gaspesia*, 106.

36. Wood, *New England's Prospect*, 85.

37. The Letters and Papers of Cadwallader Colden, 8, *Collections of the New-York Historical Society*, 67 (New York, 1937), 279, Rev. Henry Barclay to Colden, Dec. 7, 1741.

38. Le Clercq, *New Relation of Gaspesia*, 103–4.

39. John Lawson, *A New Voyage to Carolina* [London, 1709], ed. Hugh Talmage Lefler (Chapel Hill, 1967), 206; Frame, *Complete Works of Montaigne*, 152.

CHAPTER NINE

1. Nicolas Denys, *The Description and Natural History of the Coasts of North America (Acadia)* [Paris, 1672], ed. and trans. William F. Ganong (Toronto: Champlain Society, 1908), 257.

2. David Beers Quinn, *England and the Discovery of America, 1481–1620* (New York, 1974), ch. 1.

3. David B. Quinn, ed., *New American World: A Documentary History of North America to 1612*, 5 vols. (New York, 1979), 1:171.

4. Laurier Turgeon, "Pour redécouvrir notre 16e siècle: les pêches à Terre-Neuve d'après les archives notariales de Bordeaux," *Revue d'histoire de l'Amérique française*, 39 (1986), 523–49 at 528; Monique Bois, "Tabellionage de Rouen: Meubles—1ere et 2eme séries:

selection de documents concernant l'histoire du Canada," Public Archives of Canada, Manuscript Report (Sept. 1984), 7, 10.

5. René Bélanger, *Les Basques dan l'estuaire du Saint-Laurent, 1535–1635* (Montreal, 1971); Selma Barkham, "The Spanish Province of Terra Nova," *Canadian Archivist,* 2 (1974), 73–83; Barkham, "Guipuzcoan Shipping in 1571 with Particular Reference to the Decline of the Transatlantic Fishing Industry," in William A. Douglass, Richard W. Etulain, and William H. Jacobsen, Jr., eds., *Anglo-American Contributions to Basque Studies: Essays in Honor of Jon Bilbao* (Reno, 1977), 73–81; Barkham, "The Basques: filling a gap in our history between Jacques Cartier and Champlain," *Canadian Geographical Journal,* 96 (1978), 8–19; Barkham, "A Note on the Strait of Belle Isle during the Period of Basque Contact with Indians and Inuit," *Études/Inuit/Studies,* 4 (1980), 51–58; Barkham, "The Documentary Evidence for Basque Whaling Ships in the Strait of Belle Isle," in G. M. Story, ed., *Early European Settlement and Exploitation in Atlantic Canada: Selected Papers* (St. John's, Newf., 1982), 53–95; Barkham, "The Basque Whaling Establishments in Labrador, 1536–1632: A Summary," *Arctic,* 37 (1984), 515–19; "16th-Century Basque Whalers in America," *National Geographic,* 168 (July 1985), 40–71; Laurier Turgeon, "Pêcheurs basques et indiens des côtes du Saint-Laurent au XVIᵉ siècle: Perspectives de recherches," *Études canadiennes/Canadian Studies,* 13 (1982), 9–14.

6. H. P. Biggar, ed., *A Collection of Documents Relating to Jacques Cartier and the Sieur de Roberval,* Pubs. of the Public Archives of Canada 14 (Ottawa, 1930), 453–54, 462.

7. Turgeon, "Pour redécouvrir notre 16ᵉ siècle," *RHAF,* 39 (1986), 534–35, 537–39.

8. Quinn, *New American World,* 4:46, 60–61; Quinn, *England and the Discovery of America,* 316–21.

9. David B. Quinn, *North America from Earliest Discovery to First Settlements: The Norse Voyages to 1612* (New York, 1977).

10. Salvador de Madariaga, *Christopher Columbus* (London, 1949), 216–17, 288, 296, 310; Bartolomé de Las Casas, *History of the Indies,* ed. and trans. Andrée Collard (New York, 1971), 37, 56; Olive Patricia Dickason, *The Myth of the Savage and the Beginnings of French Colonialism in the Americas* (Edmonton, 1984), 205–6.

11. Quinn, *New American World,* 1:148–51.

12. Quinn, *New American World,* 1:273–75.

13. Quinn, *New American World,* 1:110, 157, 283.

14. David B. Quinn, *Sources for the Ethnography of Northeastern*

North America to 1611, National Museum of Man, Mercury Series, Canadian Ethnology Service Paper 76 (Ottawa, 1981), 35; Quinn, "La Femme et l'enfant inuit de Nuremberg, 1566," *Recherches amérindiennes au Québec,* 11 (1981), 311–13.

15. Neal Cheshire, Tony Waldron, Alison Quinn, and David Quinn, "Frobisher's Eskimos in England," *Archivaria,* 10 (1980), 23–50; Quinn, *New American World,* 4:216–18.

16. H. P. Biggar, *The Voyages of Jacques Cartier,* Pubs. of the Public Archives of Canada 11 (Ottawa, 1924), 66–67, 224–27; Quinn, *Sources,* 24–25; Dickason, *Myth of the Savage,* 210–11.

17. *The Journal of Christopher Columbus,* trans. Cecil Jane (New York, 1960), 40; Biggar, *Voyages of Cartier,* 267; Quinn, *New American World,* 1:217–18, 2:195, 559–60.

18. Erik Wahlgren, *The Vikings and America* (London, 1986), chs. 7–9; Quinn, *North America,* 10–11, 14; John Witthoft, "Archaeology as a Key to the Colonial Fur Trade," *Minnesota History,* 40 (1966), 204–5; Denys, *Description of Acadia,* 445.

19. Quinn, *New American World,* 1:151. Quinn's translations of Damião de Góis in *New American World,* 1:152 ("they wound *as if* they were overlaid with steel") and *Sources,* 11 ("tipped with steel") seem to be contradictory.

20. Quinn, *New American World,* 1:287; Biggar, *Voyages of Cartier,* 49.

21. Quinn, *New American World,* 1:284, 285. It is somewhat difficult, though not impossible, to reconcile this kind of pragmatic behavior with the later Delaware legend of the first meeting with Dutch ships in the Hudson. According to John Heckewelder, the Moravian missionary to the Delawares in the eighteenth century, the surprised Indians took Hudson's ship for "a remarkably large house in which the Mannitto (the Great or Supreme Being) himself was present" and its captain, dressed in "a red coat all glittering with gold lace," for the selfsame Mannitto. Since the crew of Verrazzano's longboat and ship never disembarked at New York because of a sudden squall, the natives may have retained no strong memory of their arrival nearly a century before Hudson. Verrazzano did say that he arrived to "loud cries of wonderment" (Rev. John Heckewelder, *History, Manners, and Customs of the Indian Nations Who Once Inhabited Pennsylvania and the Neighbouring States,* ed. Rev. William C. Reichel [Philadelphia, 1876], 71–75).

22. James Axtell, *The Invasion Within: The Contest of Cultures in Colonial North America* (New York, 1985), ch. 1; George R. Hamell, "Trading in Metaphors: The Magic of Beads," in Charles F. Hayes

III, ed., *Proceedings of the 1982 Glass Trade Bead Conference*, Rochester Museum & Science Center, Research Records 16 (Rochester, N.Y., 1983), 17–20.

23. Biggar, *Voyages of Cartier*, 42; Quinn, *New American World*, 4: 209–10. Beothuks were to behave the same way toward the English colonists of Newfoundland early in the next century. See Gillian T. Cell, ed., *Newfoundland Discovered: English Attempts at Colonisation, 1610–1630*, Hakluyt Society Publications, 2d ser. 160 (London, 1982), 71, 76, 85–86; also Quinn, *New American World*, 4:153, 156, 163.

24. Quinn, *New American World*, 1:287.

25. Quinn, *New American World*, 4:235, 240, 242; Biggar, *Voyages of Cartier*, 53, 56, 62, 143.

26. Quinn, *New American World*, 3:190, 4:29, 235; David B. Quinn and Alison M. Quinn, eds., *The English New England Voyages, 1602–1608*, Hakluyt Soc. Pubs., 2d ser. 161 (London, 1983), 157, 220.

27. Biggar, *Voyages of Cartier*, 53, 60–62, 64–67.

28. Biggar, *Voyages of Cartier*, 151–53, 162–66.

29. David Beers Quinn, ed., *The Voyages and Colonising Enterprises of Sir Humphrey Gilbert*, Hakluyt Soc. Pubs., 2d ser. 83–84 (London, 1940), 297 (continuous pagination).

30. Biggar, *Voyages of Cartier*, 187.

31. Quinn, *New American World*, 3:78–79.

32. James A. Tuck, *Onondaga Iroquois Prehistory* (Syracuse, 1971), 44, 70, 118, 135, 146; William A. Ritchie and Robert E. Funk, *Aboriginal Settlement Patterns in the Northeast*, New York State Museum and Science Service, Memoir 20 (Albany, 1973), 269, 290, 329.

33. Axtell, *The Invasion Within*, 30.

34. Robert Delort, "Les fourrures en France au XVIe et au début du XVIIe siècle," paper delivered at the 5th North American Fur Trade Conference, Montreal, May 31, 1985.

35. Quinn, *New American World*, 1:217–18, 3:142, 4:307.

36. Quinn, *Sources*, 28; Roger Schlesinger and Arthur P. Stabler, ed. and trans., *André Thevet's North America: A Sixteenth-Century View* (Kingston and Montreal, 1986), 11, 12, 13.

37. Marc Lescarbot, *The History of New France* [Paris, 1609], ed. and trans. W. L. Grant, intro. H. P. Biggar, 3 vols. (Toronto: Champlain Society, 1907–14), 3:7; Father Gabriel Sagard, *The Long Journey to the Country of the Hurons* [Paris, 1632], ed. George M. Wrong, trans. H. H. Langton (Toronto: Champlain Society, 1939), 222; Quinn, *New American World*, 4:46, 61. See also Cell, *Newfoundland*

Discovered, 88; Denys, *Description of Acadia,* 384; and Reuben Gold Thwaites, ed., *The Jesuit Relations and Allied Documents,* 73 vols. (Cleveland, 1896–1901), 69:127 (hereafter cited as *JR*).

38. Biggar, *Cartier and Roberval,* 78; Quinn, *Voyages of Gilbert,* 464; Quinn, *New American World,* 3:78, 142, 214, 4:307.

39. Denys, *Description of Acadia,* 441; *JR* 6:297–99; Roger Williams, *A Key into the Language of America* (London, 1643), 166.

40. James Axtell, *The European and the Indian: Essays in the Ethnohistory of Colonial North America* (New York, 1981), 370 n.28.

41. *Journal of Columbus,* 24; Quinn, *New American World,* 1:285.

42. Biggar, *Voyages of Cartier,* 80–81, 243; Quinn, *New American World,* 2:366, 4:214, 248; Ralph Pastore, "Beothuk Acquisition and Use of European Goods," paper delivered at 1983 meeting of Canadian Archaeological Association, Halifax, N.S.; Pastore, "Fishermen, Furriers, and Beothuks: The Economy of Extinction," *Man in the Northeast,* 33 (Spring 1987), 47–62.

43. Quinn, *Sources,* 41; Quinn, *New American World,* 2:290 (scraper), 3:206, 4:29 (Morris bells); Jeffrey P. Brain, "Artifacts of the Adelantado," *Conference on Historic Site Archeology Papers* 8 (1975), 129–38; Hale G. Smith, *The European and the Indian: European-Indian Contacts in Georgia and Florida,* Florida Anthropological Society Publications 4 (Gainesville, 1956), 30–31, 38 (sleigh bells).

44. Quinn, *New American World,* 2:290; Smith, *European and Indian,* frontispiece, 32.

45. Quinn, *New American World,* 2:368, 482; Smith, *European and Indian,* 17, 23, 32, 35 (silver beads); Charles Pearson, "Evidence of Early Spanish Contact on the Georgia Coast," *Historical Archaeology,* 11 (1977), 74–83 (copper coins).

46. Quinn, *New American World,* 1:102, 162, 3:83; Biggar, *Voyages of Cartier,* 80–81. "Points" were thread laces made wholly by needle; "dozens" were coarse wool kerseys (*OED*).

47. Quinn, *New American World,* 1:285; William Bradford, *Of Plymouth Plantation, 1620–1647,* ed. Samuel Eliot Morison (New York, 1952), 202, 220.

48. Quinn, *New American World,* 1:193–96, 218, 2:288–89, 334, 341, 345; Chester B. DePratter and Marvin T. Smith, "Sixteenth Century European Trade in the Southeastern United States: Evidence from the Juan Pardo Expeditions (1566–1568)," in Henry F. Dobyns, ed., *Spanish Colonial Frontier Research,* Spanish Borderlands Research 1 (Albuquerque: Center for Anthropological Studies, 1980), 71–72.

49. Carolyn Gilman, *Where Two Worlds Meet: The Great Lakes Fur*

Trade (St. Paul: Minnesota Historical Society, 1982) illustrates the intersecting commercial journeys of a European axe and an Indian fur.

50. Quinn, *New American World*, 2:331 (tablets), 482 (card), 4:236 (paper), 250 (cards). The spoon handle is in the material assemblage from the Adams site, a Seneca village occupied c. 1555–1575 (Rochester Museum & Science Center, Rochester, N.Y.).

51. Quinn, *New American World*, 4:224.

52. Smith, *European and Indian*, 33, 37 (pipes); Quinn, *New American World*, 4:120, 5:123.

53. Biggar, *Voyages of Cartier*, 223; Quinn, *New American World*, 1: 338.

54. Quinn, *New American World*, 2:306, 353; DePratter and Smith, "Sixteenth Century European Trade," in Dobyns, *Spanish Colonial Frontier Research*, 73.

55. Quinn, *North America*, ch. 9; Quinn, *New American World*, 2:97–188.

56. Sagard, *Long Journey to the Hurons*, 86–87; Bruce G. Trigger, *Natives and Newcomers: Canada's 'Heroic Age' Reconsidered* (Kingston and Montreal, 1985), 150.

57. James F. Pendergast, The Introduction of European Goods on the Atlantic Coast and the Iroquoian Protohistoric Era (MS, 1985); "Marine Shell in Iroquoia: Some of Its Significance" (MS, 1987). Thanks to the author for both of these important reports.

58. Bruce J. Bourque and Ruth Holmes Whitehead, "Tarrentines and the Introduction of European Trade Goods in the Gulf of Maine," *Ethnohistory*, 32 (1985), 327–41; Quinn, *New American World*, 3: 214; Quinn, *Voyages of Gilbert*, 464.

59. Quinn, *New American World*, 2:298 (French), 4:241 (Davis); Quinn, *Sources*, 41 (Florida); Quinn, *English New England Voyages*, 303.

60. Quinn, *New American World*, 1:285, 4:240, 246.

61. Quinn, *New American World*, 4:241; Biggar, *Voyages of Cartier*, 241–46.

62. Quinn, *New American World*, 1:207, 4:211, 220.

63. Quinn, *New American World*, 4:211, 214, 240, 243.

64. Quinn, *New American World*, 2:349, 4:62 (gun), 212, 307.

65. Christian F. Feest, "Powhatan: A Study in Political Organization," *Wiener Völkerkundliche Mitteilungen*, 13 (1966), 69–83; Elisabeth Tooker, "The League of the Iroquois: Its History, Politics, and Ritual," in William C. Sturtevant, gen. ed., *Handbook of North American Indians*, 15: *Northeast*, ed. Bruce G. Trigger (Washington, D.C.: Smithsonian Institution, 1978), 418–22; Trigger, *The*

Children of Aataentsic: A History of the Huron People to 1660, 2 vols. (Montreal, 1976), 1:156–63.

CHAPTER TEN

1. Christian F. Feest, "Powhatan: A Study in Political Organization," *Wiener Völkerkundliche Mitteilungen,* 13 (1966), 69–83; Feest, "Virginia Algonquians," in William C. Sturtevant, gen. ed., *Handbook of North American Indians,* 15: *Northeast,* ed. Bruce G. Trigger (Washington, D.C.: Smithsonian Institution, 1978), 271–81.
2. William Strachey, *The Historie of Travell into Virginia Britania (1612),* ed. Louis B. Wright and Virginia Freund, Hakluyt Society Publications, 2d ser. 103 (London, 1953), 59.
3. Philip L. Barbour, ed., *The Jamestown Voyages Under the First Charter, 1606–1609,* Hakluyt Soc. Pubs., 2d ser. 136–37 (Cambridge, 1969), 426 (continuous pagination).
4. Clifford M. Lewis and Albert J. Loomie, *The Spanish Jesuit Mission in Virginia, 1570–1572* (Chapel Hill, 1953).
5. See above, chapter 9.
6. Strachey, *Historie,* 34.
7. Barbour, *Jamestown Voyages,* 191.
8. *Ibid.,* 371.
9. Strachey, *Historie,* 56, 62, 63, 68, 87, 92; Barbour, *Jamestown Voyages,* 370–71.
10. Barbour, *Jamestown Voyages,* 43.
11. *Ibid.,* 51–52.
12. *Ibid.,* 382–83, 397–99, 418–20.
13. *Ibid.,* 80–95, 141, 170–72.
14. *Ibid.,* 88.
15. *Ibid.,* 141.
16. *Ibid.,* 139–40.
17. *Ibid.,* 91.
18. *Ibid.,* 216.
19. *Ibid.,* 141.
20. *Ibid.,* 448.
21. *Ibid.,* 426; George Percy, " 'A Trewe Relacyon': Virginia from 1609 to 1612," *Tyler's Quarterly Historical and Genealogical Magazine,* 3 (1922), 265.
22. Percy, "Trewe Relacyon," 265.
23. Barbour, *Jamestown Voyages,* 154, 163, 191, 193, 199, 274.
24. *Ibid.,* 154.

25. *Ibid.*, 393–94.
26. Carville V. Earle, "Environment, Disease, and Mortality in Early Virginia," in Thad W. Tate and David L. Ammerman, eds., *The Chesapeake in the Seventeenth Century: Essays on Anglo-American Society* (Chapel Hill, 1979), 96–125; Karen Ordahl Kupperman, "Apathy and Death in Early Jamestown," *Journal of American History*, 66 (1979), 24–40.
27. Barbour, *Jamestown Voyages*, 191–92.
28. *Ibid.*, 194–95.
29. *Ibid.*, 414–15. This may be the famous "Powhatan's mantle" that now resides in the Ashmolean Museum in Oxford, England.
30. *Ibid.*, 354, 411.
31. *Ibid.*, 202, 395, 423, 458.
32. Percy, "Trewe Relacyon," 263, 266.
33. Barbour, *Jamestown Voyages*, 426.
34. *Ibid.*, 432–34.
35. *Ibid.*, 428.
36. *Ibid.*, 461; Capt. John Smith, *Works, 1608–1631*, ed. Edward Arber (Birmingham, Eng., 1884), 498–99; Percy, "Trewe Relacyon," 266–67; *A Voyage to Virginia in 1609*, ed. Louis B. Wright (Charlottesville, 1964), 99.
37. Samuel M. Bemiss, ed., *The Three Charters of the Virginia Company of London* (Williamsburg, 1957), 55–69.
38. Percy, "Trewe Relacyon," 270, 273.
39. *Ibid.*, 271–73.
40. *Ibid.*, 276–77.
41. *Ibid.*, 280; Smith, *Works*, 509–11.
42. Strachey, *Historie*, 85–86.
43. Percy, "Trewe Relacyon," 279–80. See J. Frederick Fausz, "George Thorpe, Nemattanew, and the Powhatan Uprising of 1622," *Virginia Cavalcade*, 28 (1979), 110–17, and "Opechancanough: Indian Resistance Leader," in David G. Sweet and Gary B. Nash, eds., *Struggle and Survival in Colonial America* (Berkeley and Los Angeles, 1981), 21–37.
44. Smith, *Works*, 511–14, 518; Ralph Hamor, *A True Discourse of the Present State of Virginia* [London, 1615], ed. A. L. Rowse (Richmond, 1957), 10–11; Samuel Purchas, *Hakluytus Posthumus, or Purchas His Pilgrimes*, 20 vols. (Glasgow, 1905–07), 19:104–6, 117–18.
45. Smith, *Works*, 530–33. On Pocahontas's treasonable behavior, see Barbour, *Jamestown Voyages*, 459; Smith, *Works*, 455, 531.
46. Smith, *Works*, 533–34; Purchas, *Pilgrimes*, 19:118–19.

47. Susan Myra Kingsbury, ed., *The Records of the Virginia Company of London*, 4 vols. (Washington, D.C., 1906–35), 3:92.

48. Smith, *Works*, 518–19; Hamor, *True Discourse*, 40–42.

49. [James I,] *A Counter-Blaste to Tobacco* [London, 1604] (Emmaus, Pa., 1954), 36.

50. Smith, *Works*, 535.

51. Purchas, *Pilgrimes*, 19:153.

52. Fausz, "George Thorpe"; Alden T. Vaughan, " 'Expulsion of the Salvages': English Policy and the Virginia Massacre of 1622," *William and Mary Quarterly*, 3d ser. 35 (1978), 57–84 at 68–71; Eric Gethyn-Jones, *George Thorpe and the Berkeley Company: A Gloucestershire Enterprise in Virginia* (Gloucester, Eng., 1982); James Axtell, *The Invasion Within: The Contest of Cultures in Colonial North America* (New York, 1985), 179–82.

53. Kingsbury, *Va. Co. Recs.*, 3:73.

54. *Ibid.*, 3:128–29, 228.

55. Smith, *Works*, 574–75; Kingsbury, *Va. Co. Recs.*, 3:552.

56. Kingsbury, *Va. Co. Recs.*, 3:446.

57. Smith, *Works*, 564; Bemiss, *Three Charters*, 57–58; Strachey, *Historie*, 90; Kingsbury, *Va. Co. Recs.*, 3:557.

58. Strachey, *Historie*, 91.

59. Smith, *Works*, 574; Kingsbury, *Va. Co. Recs.*, 3:551.

60. Kingsbury, *Va. Co. Recs.*, 3:550–51, 554–55; Purchas, *Pilgrimes*, 19: 159, 162–64; Smith, *Works*, 563, 573.

61. Kingsbury, *Va. Co. Recs.*, 3:556–57.

62. Smith, *Works*, 572, 587; J. Frederick Fausz and Jon Kukla, eds., "A Letter of Advice to the Governor of Virginia, 1624," *WMQ*, 3d ser. 34 (1977), 117.

63. Kingsbury, *Va. Co. Recs.*, 3:550, 4:11.

64. *Ibid.*, 3:556, 4:10; Smith, *Works*, 578.

65. Kingsbury, *Va. Co. Recs.*, 3:557–58, 672, 683, 4:71.

66. *Ibid.*, 4:71, 75, 221–22; Barbour, *Jamestown Voyages*, 372.

67. Kingsbury, *Va. Co. Recs.*, 3:665, 4:10, 507–8; W. L. Grant and James Munro, eds., *Acts of the Privy Council of England, Colonial Series, 1613–1680*, 1:pt. 1 (Hereford, Eng., 1908), 54.

68. Gov. Francis Wyatt to [earl of Southampton?], 1624, *WMQ*, 2d ser. 6 (1926), 118; Kingsbury, *Va. Co. Recs.*, 3:683; H. R. McIlwaine, ed., *Minutes of the Council and General Court of Virginia* (Richmond, 1924), 484. See William S. Powell, "Aftermath of the Massacre: The First Indian War, 1622–1632," *Virginia Magazine of History and Biography*, 66 (1958), 44–75, and Michael J. Puglisi, "Revitalization

or Extirpation: Anglo-Powhatan Relations, 1622–1644" (M.A. thesis, Dept. of History, College of William and Mary, 1982).

69. Robert Beverley, *The History and Present State of Virginia* [London, 1705], ed. Louis B. Wright (Chapel Hill, 1947), 60–62.

70. *Ibid.*, 62.

71. Leo F. Stock, ed., *Proceedings and Debates of the British Parliaments Respecting North America,* 5 vols. (Washington, D.C., 1924), 1:182; Edmund Berkeley and Dorothy Smith Berkeley, eds., *The Reverend John Clayton: . . . His Scientific Writings and Other Related Papers* (Charlottesville, 1965), 39.

CHAPTER ELEVEN

1. Bernard De Voto, "Preface," in Joseph Kinsey Howard, *Strange Empire: A Narrative of the Northwest* (New York, 1952), 8–9 (italics mine).

2. Virgil J. Vogel, *The Indian in American History* (Chicago, 1968); Alvin M. Josephy, Jr., "Indians in History," *Atlantic,* 225 (June 1970), 67–72; Frederick E. Hoxie, *The Indians Versus the Textbooks: Is There Any Way Out?* (Chicago, 1984), 22–24. A briefer, unfootnoted version of Hoxie's study appeared in *Perspectives: AHA Newsletter,* 23 (April 1985), 18–22.

3. Felix S. Cohen, "Americanizing the White Man," *American Scholar,* 21 (Spring 1952), 177–91, esp. 178; C. G. Jung, *Contributions to Analytical Psychology,* trans. H. G. Barnes and Cary F. Barnes (New York, 1928), 136–40.

4. Robert F. Berkhofer, Jr., "Native Americans and United States History," in *The Reinterpretation of American History and Culture,* ed. William H. Cartwright and Richard L. Watson (Washington, D.C., 1973), 37–52, esp. 41–45.

5. Wilbur Zelinsky, *The Cultural Geography of the United States* (Englewood Cliffs, N.J., 1973), 15, 17, came to a negative conclusion after a cursory look at the question.

6. Samuel Eliot Morison, *Admiral of the Ocean Sea: A Life of Christopher Columbus,* 2 vols. (Boston, 1942); *The Life of the Admiral Christopher Columbus by His Son Ferdinand,* trans. Benjamin Keen (New Brunswick, N.J., 1959); Tzvetan Todorov, *The Conquest of America: The Question of the Other,* trans. Richard Howard (New York, 1984), 10–11; Pauline Moffitt Watts, "Prophecy and Discovery: On the Spiritual Origins of Christopher Columbus's 'Enterprise of the Indies,' " *American Historical Review,* 90 (Feb. 1985), 73–102.

7. Carl Ortwin Sauer, *The Early Spanish Main* (Berkeley and Los Angeles, 1966); Jeffrey A. Cole, *The Potosí Mita, 1573–1700: Compulsory Indian Labor in the Andes* (Stanford, 1985); Peter Bakewell, *Miners of the Red Mountain: Indian Labor in Potosí, 1545–1650* (Albuquerque, 1985); Peter Bakewell, *Silver Mining and Society in Colonial Mexico: Zacatecas, 1546–1700* (New York, 1971).

8. C. R. Boxer, *The Portuguese Seaborne Empire, 1415–1825* (London, 1969); G. V. Scammell, *The World Encompassed: The First European Maritime Empires, c. 800–1650* (Berkeley and Los Angeles, 1981), 225–300; Frédéric Mauro, *La Portugal et l'Atlantique au XVIIe siècle (1570–1670)* (Paris, 1960); James Lockhart and Stuart B. Schwartz, *Early Latin America: A History of Colonial Spanish America and Brazil* (Cambridge, 1983), 61–121, 202–304; Ralph Davis, *The Rise of the Atlantic Economies* (Ithaca, 1973), 37–72; J. H. Elliott, *Imperial Spain, 1469–1716* (New York, 1964); J. H. Elliott, *The Old World and the New, 1492–1650* (Cambridge, 1972), 54–78.

9. Todorov, *Conquest of America;* Charles Gibson, ed., *The Black Legend: Anti-Spanish Attitudes in the Old World and the New* (New York, 1971); Benjamin Keen, "The Black Legend Revisited: Assumptions and Realities," *Hispanic American Historical Review,* 49 (Nov. 1969), 703–19; Lewis Hanke, "A Modest Proposal for a Moratorium on Grand Generalizations: Some Thoughts on the Black Legend," *ibid.,* 51 (Feb. 1971), 112–27; Benjamin Keen, "The White Legend Revisited: A Reply to Professor Hanke's 'Modest Proposal,'" *ibid.* (May 1971), 336–55; Nathan Wachtel, *The Vision of the Vanquished: The Spanish Conquest of Peru through Indian Eyes, 1530–1570,* trans. Ben and Siân Reynolds (New York, 1977); Miguel Léon-Portilla, *The Broken Spears: The Aztec Account of the Conquest of Mexico,* trans. Angel Maria Garibay K. and Lysander Kemp (Boston, 1962); Charles Gibson, *The Aztecs under Spanish Rule: A History of the Indians of the Valley of Mexico, 1519–1810* (Stanford, 1964); John Grier Varner and Jeannette Johnson Varner, *Dogs of the Conquest* (Norman, 1983); William L. Sherman, *Forced Native Labor in Sixteenth-Century Central America* (Lincoln, Neb., 1979); Robert Ricard, *The Spiritual Conquest of Mexico: An Essay on the Apostolate and the Evangelizing Methods of the Mendicant Orders in New Spain, 1523–1572,* trans. Lesley Byrd Simpson (Berkeley and Los Angeles, 1966); Huguette Chaunu and Pierre Chaunu, *Seville et l'Atlantique (1504–1650),* 8 vols. (Paris, 1955–59).

10. Marcel Trudel, *Histoire de la Nouvelle-France,* 4 vols. (Montreal, 1963–83); Marcel Trudel, *The Beginnings of New France, 1524–1663* (Toronto, 1973), 1–70; Samuel Eliot Morison, *The European*

Discovery of America: The Northern Voyages, A.D. *500–1600* (New York, 1971), 252–325, 339–463.

11. Trudel, *Histoire de la Nouvelle-France*, 2; Trudel, *Beginnings of New France*, 71–280; Morris Bishop, *Champlain: The Life of Fortitude* (New York, 1948); W. J. Eccles, *The Canadian Frontier, 1534–1760* (Albuquerque, 1983); W. J. Eccles, "A Belated Review of Harold Adams Innis, *The Fur Trade in Canada*," *Canadian Historical Review*, 60 (Dec. 1979), 419–41; W. J. Eccles, "The Fur Trade and Eighteenth-Century Imperialism," *William and Mary Quarterly*, 40 (July 1983), 341–62; W. J. Eccles, "Sovereignty-Association, 1500–1783," *Canadian Historical Review*, 65 (Dec. 1984), 475–510; Cornelius J. Jaenen, *Friend and Foe: Aspects of French-Amerindian Cultural Contact in the Sixteenth and Seventeenth Centuries* (Toronto, 1976); Cornelius J. Jaenen, *The French Relationship with the Native Peoples of New France and Acadia* (Ottawa, 1984); James Axtell, *The Invasion Within: The Contest of Cultures in Colonial North America* (New York, 1985), 23–127; Bruce G. Trigger, *Natives and Newcomers: Canada's 'Heroic Age' Reconsidered* (Kingston and Montreal, 1985).

12. David Beers Quinn, *England and the Discovery of America, 1481–1620* (New York, 1974); David Beers Quinn, *Set Fair for Roanoke: Voyages and Colonies, 1584–1606* (Chapel Hill, 1985); Kenneth R. Andrews, *The Spanish Caribbean: Trade and Plunder, 1530–1630* (New Haven, 1978); Kenneth R. Andrews, *Trade, Plunder, and Settlement: Maritime Enterprise and the Genesis of the British Empire, 1480–1630* (Cambridge, 1984).

13. Alden T. Vaughan, *New England Frontier: Puritans and Indians, 1620–1675* (New York, 1979), 148, 150–51; Douglas Edward Leach, *Flintlock and Tomahawk: New England in King Philip's War* (New York, 1958), 125, 148, 171, 178, 197, 217, 224–28, 231; Daniel Vickers, "The First Whalemen of Nantucket," *William and Mary Quarterly*, 40 (Oct. 1983), 560–83; John A. Sainsbury, "Indian Labor in Early Rhode Island," *New England Quarterly*, 48 (Sept. 1975), 378–93; Almon Wheeler Lauber, *Indian Slavery in Colonial Times within the Present Limits of the United States* (New York, 1913).

14. Kingsley Davis, "Colonial Expansion and Urban Diffusion in the Americas," *International Journal of Comparative Sociology*, 1 (March 1960), 43–66; Carville V. Earle, "The First English Towns of North America," *Geographical Review*, 67 (Jan. 1977), 34–50; James O'Mara, "Town Founding in Seventeenth-Century North America: Jamestown in Virginia," *Journal of Historical Geography*, 8 (Jan.

1982), 1–11; Douglas R. McManis, *Colonial New England: A Historical Geography* (New York, 1975), 24–40; John W. Reps, *Town Planning in Frontier America* (Princeton, 1969).

15. William Haller, Jr., *The Puritan Frontier: Town Planting in New England Colonial Development, 1630–1660* (New York, 1951); Darrett B. Rutman, *Winthrop's Boston: A Portrait of a Puritan Town, 1630–1649* (Chapel Hill, 1965), 135–201, 241–79; Richard L. Bushman, *From Puritan to Yankee: Character and the Social Order in Connecticut, 1690–1765* (Cambridge, Mass., 1967); Joseph S. Wood, "The Origin of the New England Village" (Ph.D. diss., Pennsylvania State University, 1978); T. H. Breen, *Puritans and Adventurers: Change and Persistence in Early America* (New York, 1980), 68–80; Peter N. Carroll, *Puritanism and the Wilderness: The Intellectual Significance of the New England Frontier, 1629–1700* (New York, 1969).

16. Jack D. Forbes, "Frontiers in American History and the Role of the Frontier Historian," *Ethnohistory*, 15 (Summer 1968), 203–35; Robert F. Berkhofer, Jr., "Space, Time, Culture and the New Frontier," *Agricultural History*, 38 (Jan. 1964), 21–30; Robin F. Wells, "Frontier Systems as a Sociocultural Type," *Papers in Anthropology*, 14 (Spring 1973), 6–15; James Axtell, "The Ethnohistory of Early America: A Review Essay," *William and Mary Quarterly*, 35 (Jan. 1978), 110–44; Howard Lamar and Leonard Thompson, *The Frontier in History: North America and Southern Africa Compared* (New Haven, 1981), 3–13, 43–75.

17. Frederick Jackson Turner, "The Significance of the Frontier in American History," in *The Frontier in American History* (New York, 1920), 1–38.

18. William M. Denevan, ed., *The Native Population of the Americas in 1492* (Madison, 1976), 291. The latest estimate of eighteen million by Henry F. Dobyns is doubtful because of serious flaws in methodology. See Henry F. Dobyns, *Their Number Become Thinned: Native American Population Dynamics in Eastern North America* (Knoxville, 1983), 42.

19. Francis Jennings, *The Invasion of America: Indians, Colonialism, and the Cant of Conquest* (Chapel Hill, 1975), 15–31.

20. James Axtell, "A North American Perspective for Colonial History," *History Teacher*, 12 (Aug. 1979), 549–62.

21. Gary B. Nash, *Red, White, and Black: The Peoples of Early America* (2d ed., Englewood Cliffs, N.J., 1982); Dwight W. Hoover, *The Red and the Black* (Chicago, 1976); Wesley Frank Craven, *White,*

Red, and Black: The Seventeenth-Century Virginian (Charlottes-ville, 1971); Charles Hudson, ed., *Red, White, and Black: Symposium on Indians in the Old South* (Athens, Ga., 1971).

22. James Henretta, "Families and Farms: *Mentalité* in Pre-Industrial America," *William and Mary Quarterly*, 35 (Jan. 1978), 3–32; R. Cole Harris, "The Simplification of Europe Overseas," *Annals of the Association of American Geographers*, 67 (Dec. 1977), 469–83; James T. Lemon, "Early Americans and Their Social Environment," *Journal of Historical Geography*, 6 (April 1980), 115–31; James T. Lemon, "Early Americans and Their Social Environment: Further Thoughts and Elaboration," paper delivered at the University of Wisconsin, Feb. 1981 (in my possession).

23. William Cronon, *Changes in the Land: Indians, Colonists, and the Ecology of New England* (New York, 1983), 19–53; Timothy H. Silver, "A New Face on the Countryside: Indians and Colonists in the Southeastern Forest" (Ph.D. diss., College of William and Mary, 1985); Francis Jennings, "Virgin Land and Savage People," *American Quarterly*, 23 (Oct. 1971), 519–41; Marshall Harris, *Origins of the Land Tenure System in the United States* (Ames, Iowa, 1953), 155–78; Robert R. Gradie III, "New England Indians and Colonizing Pigs," *Papers of the Fifteenth Algonquian Conference*, ed. William Cowan (Ottawa, 1984), 147–69.

24. James Axtell, *The European and the Indian: Essays in the Ethnohistory of Colonial North America* (New York, 1981), 292–95; Paul Weatherwax, *Indian Corn in Old America* (New York, 1954); Camille Wells, "The Cultivation of Indian Corn in the Colonial Chesapeake" (Seminar paper, Dept. of History, College of William and Mary, 1981).

25. John J. McCusker and Russell R. Menard, *The Economy of British America, 1607–1789* (Chapel Hill, 1985), 94, 173–75; Bernard Bailyn, *The New England Merchants in the Seventeenth Century* (Cambridge, Mass., 1955), 23–32, 49–60; Francis Jennings, "The Indian Trade of the Susquehanna Valley," *Proceedings of the American Philosophical Society*, 110 (Dec. 1966), 406–24; Thomas Elliott Norton, *The Fur Trade in Colonial New York, 1686–1776* (Madison, 1974); Mary Theobald, "The Indian Trade in Colonial Virginia, 1584–1725" (M.A. thesis, Dept. of History, College of William and Mary, 1980); Philip M. Brown, "Early Indian Trade in the Development of South Carolina: Politics, Economics, and Social Mobility during the Proprietary Period, 1670–1719," *South Carolina Historical Magazine*, 76 (July 1975), 118–28; Stephen H. Cutcliffe, "Colonial Indian Policy as a Measure of Rising Imperialism: New York and

Pennsylvania, 1700–1755," *Western Pennsylvania Historical Magazine*, 64 (July 1981), 237–68; Murray Lawson, *Fur: A Study in English Mercantilism, 1700–1775* (Toronto, 1940), 70, 72.

26. Harris, *Origins of the Land Tenure System*, 155–78; Imre Sutton, *Indian Land Tenure* (New York, 1975), 40–44.

27. Lauber, *Indian Slavery in Colonial Times;* William Robert Snell, "Indian Slavery in Colonial South Carolina, 1671–1795" (Ph.D. diss., U. of Alabama, 1972); Amy Ellen Friedlander, "Indian Slavery in Proprietary South Carolina" (M.A. thesis, Dept. of History, Emory University, 1975); Winthrop D. Jordan, *White over Black: American Attitudes toward the Negro, 1550–1812* (Chapel Hill, 1968), 89–92; Kenneth W. Porter, *The Negro on the American Frontier* (New York, 1971); William S. Willis, "Divide and Rule: Red, White, and Black in the Southeast," *Journal of Negro History,* 48 (July 1963), 157–76.

28. Axtell, *The Invasion Within*, 131–286; Axtell, *The European and the Indian*, 304–7.

29. Edmund S. Morgan, *The Puritan Family: Religion and Domestic Relations in Seventeenth-Century New England* (New York, 1966), 161–86; Carroll, *Puritanism and the Wilderness*, 131–79, 199–222; Richard Slotkin, *Regeneration through Violence: The Mythology of the American Frontier, 1600–1860* (Middletown, Conn., 1973), 3–179; Richard Slotkin, "Massacre," *Berkshire Review*, 14 (1979), 112–32; Richard Slotkin and James K. Folsom, eds., *So Dreadful a Judgment: Puritan Responses to King Philip's War, 1676–1677* (Middletown, Conn., 1978), 3–39; Larzer Ziff, *Puritanism in America: New Culture in a New World* (New York, 1973); Kai T. Erikson, *Wayward Puritans: A Study in the Sociology of Deviance* (New York, 1966), 65–159.

30. Sister Mary Augustina (Ray), *American Opinion of Roman Catholicism in the Eighteenth Century* (New York, 1936); J. M. Bumsted, " 'Carried to Canada!': Perceptions of the French in British Colonial Captivity Narratives, 1690–1760," *American Review of Canadian Studies,* 13 (Spring 1983), 79–96; Axtell, *The Invasion Within,* 287–301.

31. Lawrence Henry Gipson, *The British Empire before the American Revolution*, 15 vols. (Caldwell, Idaho–New York, 1936–70), 5:20–21, 39–41, 75–84, 98–110; Axtell, *The Invasion Within*, 247–59, 276–77; I. K. Steele, *Guerrillas and Grenadiers: The Struggle for Canada, 1689–1760* (Toronto, 1969), 2–6, 19–20, 66–68. Obviously, English naval and military ineptitude also played a role in securing New France to the French.

32. William Thomas Morgan, "English Fear of 'Encirclement' in the Seventeenth Century," *Canadian Historical Review*, 10 (March 1929), 4–22; Emmett Francis O'Neil, "English Fear of French Encirclement in North America, 1680–1763" (Ph.D. diss., U. of Michigan, 1941); Lois Mulkearn, "The English Eye the French in North America," *Pennsylvania History*, 21 (Oct. 1954), 316–37.

33. Breen, *Puritans and Adventurers*, 81–105; Stanley McCrory Pargellis, *Lord Loudon in North America* (New Haven, 1933); Alan Rogers, *Empire and Liberty: American Resistance to British Authority, 1755–1763* (Berkeley and Los Angeles, 1974); John M. Murrin, "The French and Indian War, the American Revolution, and the Counterfactual Hypothesis: Reflections on Lawrence Henry Gipson and John Shy," *Reviews in American History*, 1 (Sept. 1973), 307–18; Peter Marshall, "Colonial Protest and Imperial Retrenchment: Indian Policy, 1764–1768," *Journal of American Studies*, 5 (April 1971), 1–17; Jack P. Greene, "A Posture of Hostility: A Reconsideration of Some Aspects of the Origin of the American Revolution," *Proceedings of the American Antiquarian Society*, 87 (April 1977), 27–68; Jack P. Greene, "The Seven Years' War and the American Revolution: The Causal Relationship Reconsidered," *Journal of Imperial and Commonwealth History*, 8 (Jan. 1980), 85–105.

34. Jack M. Sosin, "The Use of Indians in the War of the American Revolution: A Reassessment of Responsibility," *Canadian Historical Review*, 46 (June 1965), 101–21; S. F. Wise, "The American Revolution and Indian History," in *Character and Circumstance: Essays in Honour of Donald Grant Creighton*, ed. John S. Moir (Toronto, 1970), 182–200; Barbara Graymont, *The Iroquois in the American Revolution* (Syracuse, 1972); James H. O'Donnell III, *Southern Indians in the American Revolution* (Knoxville, 1973); Francis Jennings, "The Indians' Revolution," in *The American Revolution: Explorations in the History of American Radicalism*, ed. Alfred F. Young (DeKalb, 1976), 319–48.

35. Jordan, *White over Black*; Nash, *Red, White, and Black*, 141–97, 273–98; Ira Berlin, "Time, Space, and the Evolution of Afro-American Society in British Mainland North America," *American Historical Review*, 85 (Feb. 1980), 44–78; Allan Kulikoff, *Tobacco and Slaves: The Development of Southern Culture in the Chesapeake Colonies, 1680–1800* (Chapel Hill, 1987); Philip Morgan, *Slave Counterpoint: Black Culture in the Eighteenth-Century Chesapeake and Low Country* (Chapel Hill, 1988); Philip Morgan, "Black Life

in Eighteenth-Century Charleston," *Perspectives in American History*, 1 (1984), 187–232.

36. Much of what follows is drawn from my essay on "The Indian Impact on English Colonial Culture" in *The European and the Indian*, 272–315.

37. Charles Francis Adams, ed., *The Works of John Adams*, 10 vols. (Boston, 1850–56), 10:282–83, 288, 313.

38. Virgil J. Vogel, *American Indian Medicine* (Norman, 1970), 267.

39. Rhys Isaac, "Dramatizing the Ideology of the Revolution: Popular Mobilization in Virginia, 1774 to 1776," *William and Mary Quarterly*, 33 (July 1976), 379–82.

40. Louis Morton, "The End of Formalized Warfare," *American Heritage*, 6 (Aug. 1955), 12–19, 95; John K. Mahon, "Anglo-American Methods of Indian Warfare, 1676–1794," *Mississippi Valley Historical Review*, 45 (Sept. 1958), 254–75; Douglas Edward Leach, *Arms for Empire: A Military History of the British Colonies in North America, 1607–1763* (New York, 1973); Peter E. Russell, "Redcoats in the Wilderness: British Officers and Irregular Warfare in Europe and America, 1740 to 1760," *William and Mary Quarterly*, 35 (Oct. 1978), 629–52.

41. Axtell, *The European and the Indian*, 168–206.

42. Roy Harvey Pearce, *Savagism and Civilization: A Study of the Indian and the American Mind* (Baltimore, 1965), 5.

43. Jordan, *White over Black*, 40; Michael Zuckerman, "The Fabrication of Identity in Early America," *William and Mary Quarterly*, 34 (April 1977), 183–214, esp. 204.

44. Edmund S. Morgan, "The American Indian: Incorrigible Individualist," *The Mirror of the Indian* (Providence, 1958); H. C. Porter, *The Inconstant Savage: England and the North American Indian, 1500–1660* (London, 1979); Bernard Sheehan, *Savagism and Civility: Indians and Englishmen in Colonial Virginia* (New York, 1980); Karen Ordahl Kupperman, *Settling with the Indians: The Meeting of English and Indian Culture in America, 1580–1640* (Totowa, N.J., 1980); Jennings, *Invasion of America*, 3–174; Pearce, *Savagism and Civilization;* Axtell, *The Invasion Within*, 131–78.

45. Richard P. Johnson, "The Search for a Usable Indian: An Aspect of the Defense of Colonial New England," *Journal of American History*, 64 (Dec. 1977), 623–51.

46. Slotkin, *Regeneration through Violence;* Slotkin, "Massacre"; Robert Shulman, "Parkman's Indians and American Violence," *Massachusetts Review*, 12 (Spring 1971), 221–39.

47. Axtell, *The European and the Indian*, 141–50, 207–41, 311–14; Mark A. Mastromarino, " 'Cry Havoc and Let Loose the Dogs of War': Canines and the Colonial American Military Experience" (M.A. thesis, Dept. of History, College of William and Mary, 1984); Mastromarino, "Teaching Old Dogs New Tricks: The English Mastiff and the Anglo-American Experience," *The Historian*, 49 (1986), 10–25.

48. E. McClung Fleming, "The American Image as Indian Princess, 1765–1783," *Winterthur Portfolio*, 2 (1965), 65–81; Hugh Honour, *The New Golden Land: European Images of America from the Discoveries to the Present Time* (New York, 1975), 138–60.

AFTERWORD

1. See, for example, John Darnton, "Iroquois Meet About Unearthing of Bones by 18 Students Upstate," *New York Times*, Aug. 6, 1972, p. 48; Ben O. Bridgers and Duane H. King, "Rest in Peace: A Cherokee Dilemma," *Americans Before Columbus* [National Indian Youth Council], Special Edition on Indian Religious Freedom, n.d. [c. 1982], p. 13; R. Westwood Winfree, "Archaeology and the Law: Can 'Red Power' Block Archaeological Excavation of Indian Burials? Can Illicit Grave Looting Be Stopped?," *Quarterly Bulletin of the Archaeological Society of Virginia*, 27 (1973), 158–61; Steve Moore, "Federal Indian Burial Policy—Historical Anachronism or Contemporary Reality?" *Native American Rights Fund Legal Review*, 12:2 (Spring 1987), 1–7.

2. William Scranton Simmons, *Cautantowwit's House: An Indian Burial Ground on the Island of Conanicut in Narragansett Bay* (Providence, 1970); Lenny Glyn, "Reburial in Rhode Island," *Parade (Boston Sunday Globe)*, June 24, 1973, pp. 16–19.

3. Canadian social scientists are fond of "Amerindian" or "Amerind" to distinguish the indigenous variety from West or East Indian immigrants; in writing about early North America it seems hardly necessary and is awkward jargon.

4. James Axtell and William C. Sturtevant, "The Unkindest Cut, or Who Invented Scalping?," *William and Mary Quarterly*, 3d ser. 37 (1980), 451–72; James Axtell, *The European and the Indian: Essays in the Ethnohistory of Colonial North America* (New York, 1981), chs. 2, 8; "Iroquois Constitution: A Forerunner to Colonists [*sic*] Democratic Principles," *New York Times*, June 28, 1987; Elisabeth S. Tooker, "The U.S. Constitution and the Iroquois League,"

NOTES TO PAGES 252–53

Ethnohistory (forthcoming); Nancy Dieter Egloff, " 'Six Nations of Ignorant Savages': Benjamin Franklin and the Iroquois League of Nations" (M.A. thesis, Dept. of History, College of William and Mary, 1987).

5. Margaret Atwood, *Second Words: Selected Critical Prose* (Boston, 1984), 346.

6. James Axtell, "Europeans, Indians, and the Age of Discovery in American History Textbooks," *American Historical Review*, 92 (1987), 621–32.

Index

DATE DUE

MAR 16 '98		
JUN 9 '98		
AUG 6 '98		
AP 5 05		
	WITHDRAWN	

GAYLORD | | | PRINTED IN U.S.A.